# The World of Pope's Satires

PETER DIXON

# THE WORLD
# OF
# POPE'S SATIRES

An Introduction to the *Epistles*
and *Imitations of Horace*

Methuen & Co Ltd

TO
MARGARET

# Contents

# Plates

# Preface

This study of Pope's poetry is based on research for a Master's degree in the University of London. I count myself particularly fortunate in that my research was supervised by Dr Joyce Tompkins; under her wise and tolerant guidance my ideas about Pope first began to take shape. When the book was nearing completion Professor Norman Callan generously gave me detailed advice and assistance, and my colleague Patricia Thomson kindly read through the typescript and made valuable suggestions. My indebtedness to the editors of the Twickenham Pope will be evident throughout. I am grateful to the many students who have helped to clarify my views: to classicists in Adelaide and Belfast who explained the intricacies of Horace; to Miss Jennifer Howlett for her patience and accuracy in reducing my very rough drafts into typewritten order; and to Miss Valerie Campling for preparing much of the final version.

In Chapters Two and Six I have drawn upon material already published in *English Studies*; its editor, Professor R. W. Zandvoort, has very kindly allowed me to use this material again. I also wish to thank the Trustees of the British Museum for permission to reproduce the three plates accompanying the text; the Clarendon Press for permission to quote from George Sherburn's edition of Pope's *Correspondence*, and from Professor Donald Bond's edition of the *Spectator*; the Loeb Classical Library, Harvard University Press, and William Heinemann Ltd for permission to quote from the following volumes in the Loeb series: Horace, *Satires, Epistles and Ars Poetica*, trans. H. R. Fairclough; Quintilian, *Institutio Oratoria*, trans. H. S. Butler; Aristotle, *Ethics*, trans. H. Rackham, and *Art of Rhetoric*, trans. J. H. Freese; Lucan, *The Civil War*, trans. J. D. Duff. My wife has given constant help and encouragement, and has shown immense forbearance; for all this I am deeply grateful.

Queen Mary College                               P.D.
London

# A Note on Texts and Titles

All quotations from Pope's poems, including the Homer translations, follow the text of the Twickenham Edition, prepared under the general editorship of John Butt (10 vols., 1939–67). Unless otherwise stated, *The Dunciad* is cited from the four-book ('B') version of 1743. It was Pope's practice (usually on first publication, occasionally in a later edition) to accompany his Imitations of Horace and Donne with the full texts of their originals; these texts are reproduced in the Twickenham Edition, vol. IV, and are used here.

Shakespeare is quoted from Pope's own edition (6 vols., 1725), with line references supplied from the Globe edition. The text used for quotations from Dryden's poems is that of the edition by James Kinsley, 4 vols., Oxford, 1958; and for the *Spectator* that of Donald F. Bond (5 vols., Oxford, 1965). Prose translations of classical authors are taken from the relevant volumes of the Loeb Classical Library.

In his 1751 edition of Pope's *Works* William Warburton gave conveniently distinctive sub-titles to four of the *Imitations of Horace*. To make identification of these poems easier I have used his sub-titles as full titles, so that *Epistle I i* is here referred to as the *Epistle to Bolingbroke*, and *Epistle I vi* as the *Epistle to Murray; Satire II i* and *Satire II ii* become, respectively, *To Fortescue* and *To Bethel*. In all other cases the titles given here are those of the Twickenham Edition.

The following short titles have been used throughout:

COWLEY *Essays*     *The English Writings of Abraham Cowley*, ed. A. R. Waller, vol. II ('Essays, Plays and Sundry Verses'). Cambridge, 1906.

| | |
|---|---|
| DRYDEN *Essays* | John Dryden, *Of Dramatic Poesy and other Critical Essays*, ed. George Watson. 2 vols. 1962. |
| MACK *Essential Articles* | *Essential Articles for the Study of Alexander Pope*, ed. Maynard Mack. Hamden, Connecticut, and London, 1964. |
| POPE *Correspondence* | *The Correspondence of Alexander Pope*, ed. George Sherburn. 5 vols. Oxford, 1956. |
| POPE *Works* | *The Works of Alexander Pope*, ed. William Warburton. 9 vols. 1751. |
| PRIOR *Works* | *The Literary Works of Matthew Prior*, ed. H. Bunker Wright and Monroe K. Spears. 2 vols. Oxford, 1959. |
| SPENCE | Joseph Spence, *Observations, Anecdotes, and Characters of Books and Men*, ed. James M. Osborn. 2 vols. Oxford, 1966. |
| SWIFT *Poems* | *The Poems of Jonathan Swift*, ed. Harold Williams. 2nd ed. 3 vols. Oxford, 1958. |
| SWIFT *Prose Works* | *The Prose Works of Jonathan Swift*, ed. Herbert Davis *et al.* 14 vols. Oxford, 1939—. |

Material originally printed throughout in italic (as, for example, the Horatian sources of Pope's Imitations) is here reproduced in Roman type. Obvious misprints in quotations have been silently corrected, and unusual abbreviations in passages quoted from eighteenth-century diaries have been expanded. Words supplied by the happy conjectures of editors have here been assimilated, without benefit of square brackets, into the quoted text.

# CHAPTER ONE

# 'Alexander Pope of Twickenham'

On more than one occasion Swift expressed regret over the topicality of Pope's satire. He pointed out that the day-to-day affairs of London, however sensational, would quickly be forgotten; even at the time of writing, a witty allusion to some metropolitan rogue or fool might well be simply mystifying to a reader twenty miles from the capital. In another way Pope's eagerness to name contemporary names could defeat the avowed purpose of his satire. Instead of extinguishing the dunces of the age he might succeed only in conferring on them the immortality of great art. 'Take care the bad poets do not outwit you,' Swift warned him, 'as they have served the good ones in every Age, whom they have provoked to transmit their Names to posterity. Maevius is as well known as Virgil, and Gildon will be as well known as you if his name gets into your Verses.'[1] Swift's fears were prophetic. One reason for the eclipsing of Pope's reputation in the nineteenth century was that he was felt to have been ignobly enmeshed in the mundane and the trivial. Francis Jeffrey reproved the writers of the early eighteenth century because 'they never pass beyond "the visible diurnal sphere", or deal in any thing that can either lift us above our vulgar nature, or ennoble its reality'.[2] And, to take Swift's second point, Pope has certainly endowed the dunces

---

[1] Letter to Pope, 26 November 1725, *Correspondence*, vol. II, p. 343. (Maevius, one of a group of poetasters who attacked Horace and Virgil, is ridiculed in Virgil's third Eclogue.) For Swift's other reservations about Pope's topicality see *Correspondence*, vol. II, p. 504, and vol. III, p. 343.
[2] Review of Sir Walter Scott's edition of Swift, *Edinburgh Review*, vol. XXVII (1816), p. 3.

with a dubious kind of immortality. The details of obscure lives and works have been patiently exhumed by editors and commentators in order to elucidate the names preserved in the amber of *The Dunciad*, the *Epistles*, and the *Imitations of Horace*.

If the reader of Pope cannot avoid learning something of the career of Charles Gildon, that is partly because Pope himself, as his own first editor, supplied plentiful (and not unprejudiced) information about the names and events to which his poems allude. The immediate ethical occasion of the *Epistle to Bathurst*, for example, is provided by the misdemeanours of Peter Walter and Francis Chartres, of South Sea Company directors and the fraudulent governors of the Charitable Corporation; Pope's copious annotations on the lives and works of these malefactors serve both to justify his satirical attacks and to anchor in reality the absurd obsessions of the avaricious and the prodigal. The truth about men's behaviour may be quite as bizarre as satirical fiction paints it. Yet the *Epistle to Bathurst* also exists to honour the Man of Ross, whose philanthropy, transcending the local and temporary, assumes in Pope's lines a Christ-like significance:

> Behold the Market-place with poor o'erspread!
> The MAN of ROSS divides the weekly bread:
> Behold yon Alms-house, neat, but void of state,
> Where Age and Want sit smiling at the gate:
> Him portion'd maids, apprentic'd orphans blest,
> The young who labour, and the old who rest.
>
> (263–8)

This portrait goes some way towards meeting Jeffrey's objection, for the charity of the Man of Ross ennobles our real human nature. Yet it does so only because Pope reminds us of reality by describing charitable acts which belong to the recent past, to a recognizable world of 'portions' and apprenticeships. The exemplary force of such good works depends upon our acknowledging that they are both divinely sanctioned and humanly practicable. Lest we try to shrug off their implications for our own conduct, and deny their practicability, Pope's own footnote insists upon the historical identity of this anonymous patriarch, and upon the actuality of his deeds: 'The person here celebrated, who with a small Estate actually per-

[ 2 ]

formed all these good works, and whose true name was almost lost . . . was called Mr John Kyrle. He died in the year 1724, aged 90, and lies interr'd in the chancel of the church of Ross in Herefordshire.'

In the poems of the early 1730s Pope speaks both for and against his age. The 'visible diurnal sphere' at once provokes him to satire and provides him with patterns of those very qualities, aesthetic, social, and moral, which the objects of his satire signally lack. If he condemns Cloe and Timon and Peter Walter, he writes with an opposite but equal warmth on behalf of Martha Blount, Lord Burlington, and John Kyrle. Hence the note of authority in his poetry, its characteristic air of confidence; true standards and values are demonstrably being upheld by a select circle which includes the poet and his friends. Hence, too, the infrequency with which Pope makes any sustained use of what Henry James called 'operative irony', the irony which 'implies and projects the possible other case, the case rich and edifying where the actuality is pretentious and vain'.[1] The ironic *Epistle to Augustus* is unique among Pope's works precisely because the man it addresses is unique. Comparisons with an inadequate monarch have to be fetched from afar, and the 'possible other case' is here implied and projected by means of Horace's unironical Epistle to Augustus, the poem which Pope has so brilliantly inverted. Rome's Augustus Caesar, a man of culture, a patron of the arts, confronts the stolid indifference and meagre materialism of England's George Augustus. Normally, however, Pope does not need to have recourse to a *possible* other case. To expose the false magnificence of Timon's villa and gardens he can point to vastly superior, but no less real, achievements – the buildings of Lord Burlington and the plantations of Lord Bathurst. In the same way Martha Blount's good-humoured equanimity, eulogized at the end of the *Epistle to a Lady*, rebukes the silliness and excesses of the women whose portraits form the body of that poem. It is the satirist's part to cherish and honour those of his contemporaries whose virtuous examples can be truly said to be rich and edifying.

---

[1] Preface to *The Lesson of the Master*.

Pope's predilection for the verse-epistle is as understandable as it is unmistakable.[1] Apart from George II, the recipients of his verse-letters are embodiments of those values which the poet seeks to uphold. Lord Burlington's designs and buildings display the sensible elegance of true taste. Dr Arbuthnot is the poet's true friend, the antithesis of the false flatterers and hostile detractors who plague the successful satirist. And just as at the end of a letter the writer, however far he may have strayed, properly reminds himself of the person he is addressing, so Pope concludes his *Epistles* by declaring the virtues of his 'correspondents':

> You too proceed! make falling Arts your care,
> Erect new wonders, and the old repair,
> Jones and Palladio to themselves restore,
> And be whate'er Vitruvius was before:
> Till Kings call forth th'Idea's of your mind,
> Proud to accomplish what such hands design'd. . . .
>
> (*To Burlington* 191 ff.)

This peroration does more than assert Burlington's place in an architectural tradition which goes back, through Inigo Jones and Palladio, to the fountain-head of classicism. It affirms also the dignity of genuine artistic endeavour, a dignity founded on the architect's sense of responsibility towards the tradition ('make falling Arts your care'), and towards his age. The contrast with Timon's selfish irresponsibility is absolute. Moreover, this sense of responsibility is shared by the poet; Pope's lines have a Roman grandeur that fits the high public occasion, and they appropriately invoke a literary tradition strictly comparable to the architectural one.[2]

The *Epistle to Burlington*, which closes on this Virgilian note, begins with an urbanity that is very evidently Horatian:

---

[1] It is perhaps worth noting that of the six most important and substantial *Imitations of Horace* four are Epistles.

[2] Mr F. W. Bateson notes some specific Latinisms in these closing lines ('You too proceed'; 'worthier of the God'), and observes that the passage is 'full of echoes' of Dryden's version of *AEneid* VI: Twickenham Edition, vol. III (ii), pp. 155–6. Dryden, like Palladio and Jones, is the mediator of classical styles and values.

[4]

'Tis strange, the Miser should his Cares employ,
To gain those Riches he can ne'er enjoy:
Is it less strange, the Prodigal should waste
His wealth, to purchase what he ne'er can taste?

This opening, easy and informal, has the accent of sociability, and its writer persuades us that he is a truly polite man, a man who may raise his eyebrows in amused surprise but will rarely raise his voice. The miser and the prodigal, foolish men, are beyond the social pale; they are damned, but damned politely. Because the speaker's wit is never flippant, because he appears thoughtful, sensible, and intelligent, there is no discontinuity between the relaxed and intimate opening of the poem and its more formal close. The easy modulations of this *Epistle* show that Pope has already taken to heart the advice from Horace which stands as epigraph to the 'Epistles to Several Persons' in the 1740 edition of his *Works*:

> Est brevitate opus, ut currat sententia, neu se
> Impediat verbis lassas onerantibus aures;
> Et sermone opus est, modo tristi, sæpe jocoso,
> Defendente vicem modo Rhetoris atque Poetæ;
> Interdum Urbani, parcentis viribus, atque
> Extenuantis eas consultò.[1]

Horace is asking for more than merely stylistic variety; all variations must be determined by the role which the writer adopts in compliance with the total strategy of his poem. Pope's principal roles or manners are those defined by Horace: the one public, the poet as spokesman; the other private, the poet as the urbane friend and conversationalist. At the beginning of the *Epistle to Burlington* Pope is the witty writer who keeps his strength in reserve; at its conclusion he is the Orator and Poet.

Any lively and extended conversation between intimate friends will be characterized by the same modulations of tone and changes of tempo that we can hear in Pope's *Epistles*. There may also enter a

---

[1] Satire I x 9–14: 'You need terseness, that the thought may run on, and not become entangled in verbiage that weighs upon wearied ears. You also need a style, now grave now gay, in keeping with the role, now of orator or poet, at times of the wit, who holds his strength in check and husbands it with wisdom.'

measure of impersonation, expressing itself in vocal drollery and mimicry, or in the striking of an attitude of, for example, mock-modesty or mock-pride. During the early eighteenth century, in particular, the preoccupation with 'raillery' would appear to have fostered such quasi-dramatic elements in conversation.[1] Similarly, in those areas of Pope's satire where an urbane and witty manner predominates, the poet may assume a temporary pose of credulous naïvety, bland unconcern, or self-depreciation. In ordinary conversation we recognize at once the discrepancy between the attitude briefly and lightheartedly taken up, and the known personality of the speaker in front of our eyes; we enjoy the impersonation because we can see through it. So, when the author of *To Fortescue* (*Satire II i*) – a poet who counts *The Dunciad* and the *Epistle to Bathurst* among his works – describes himself as 'Tim'rous by Nature, of the Rich in awe' (line 7), we are not for a moment deceived into believing that he literally means what he says. The words 'of the Rich in awe' reveal nothing of Pope's actual personality; their satirical function is to hint darkly at the sinister uses to which wealth may be put. The comic force of the line arises from our instant recognition that Pope is playing a part. We relish the dexterity with which he plays it, and with which he makes it a stalking-horse for satire; and we are encouraged to see it as a lightly assumed part because in the opening lines of the poem Pope has so skilfully set a conversational scene (the poet in informal consultation with his legal adviser), the kind of scene in which this amusing and transparent dissimulation is at home.

The wit resides in the transparency, in our seeing, quite unmistakably, the courageous and outspoken satirist through the timorous words. In short, the opening lines of *To Fortescue* would seem to depend rather upon techniques of conversational raillery than upon the satirical device of the *persona*. It is true that the concept of the *persona*, a fictional character through whom a satirist can speak but with whom he is not to be equated, has recently been applied with great profit to the study of Swift. The author of *Gulliver's Travels* carefully conceals himself. With deceptive cir-

---

[1] See pp. 23ff. below.

cumstantiality the title-page of the first edition reads: *Travels into Several Remote Nations of the World. . . . By Lemuel Gulliver, First a Surgeon, and then a Captain of Several ships.* To strip away this subterfuge, to identify Gulliver with his creator, is to neutralize Swift's comic spirit and to destroy his meaning. But Swift's way is not Pope's, as the full title of *To Fortescue* makes abundantly plain: *The First Satire of the Second Book of Horace, Imitated in a Dialogue between Alexander Pope of Twickenham in Com. Midd. Esq; on the one Part, and his Learned Council on the other.* With its legal formulas and parade of particularities this has its own kind of playfulness; but it is those very particularities, announcing a real poet in a real place, that so clearly distinguish Alexander Pope from a fictitious Captain of several ships. Pope's name usually stood proudly in the forefront of his satires. When, in such cases as *The Dunciad* and his version of Donne's fourth Satire, he chose anonymity, his motives seem to have been dictated either by literary politics or by a cautious prudence that is somewhat at odds with the image of the plain-speaking satirist. He is never, I think, moved by the desire to create within the poem the image of a purely fictional speaker who stands apart from his author and through whom the satire can, in all apparent simplicity, be uttered.

There is, of course, another presence in *To Fortescue* besides that of Pope, the presence of Horace. But Pope is not so much speaking *through* Horace as joining his English voice to that of the Roman poet. For to imitate Horace successfully is, as Pope himself admitted, to gain immediate reinforcement for one's satirical position: 'The Occasion of publishing these *Imitations* was the Clamour raised on some of my *Epistles*. An Answer from *Horace* was both more full, and of more Dignity, than any I cou'd have made in my own person.'[1] Contemporary aberrations of taste and behaviour are condemned out of two mouths, while Horace's acknowledged moderation and good sense endorse Pope's words. Indeed, the whole edifice of Pope's satire is ingeniously strengthened and secured by its ties with the

---

1 'Advertisement' prefixed to the *Imitations of Horace* in the *Works* of 1735: Twickenham Edition, vol. IV, p. 3.

past, with satire English and Roman, recent and remote. At the opening of *The Dunciad* a brief echo of Dryden has the same function as the pervasive allusion to Horace in the *Imitations*:

> Say from what cause, in vain decry'd and curst,
> Still Dunce the second reigns like Dunce the first?
>
> (*Dunciad* [A] I 5–6)

The borrowing from Dryden's epistle 'To my Dear Friend Mr Congreve' ('For *Tom* the Second reigns like *Tom* the first') does far more than sharpen a jibe at the recently-crowned George II. Pope is referring us to a particular salvo in Dryden's battle with the dunces of his day, and inviting us to see his own work as a continuation of that struggle. The prestige of the greatest poet of the last age adds weight to Pope's denunciation of the new crop of Smithfield Muses, even while the hopeless nature of the struggle ('in vain decry'd and curst') anticipates the felt approach of Universal Darkness at the conclusion of *The Dunciad*. Among Dryden's English predecessors Pope drew particularly on the support of Elizabethan satirists in order to strengthen his attack on the vices and follies of the Court. He 'versified' and new-dressed two of Donne's satires, and towards the end of his life was contemplating a similar treatment for some of the satires of Donne's contemporary, Joseph Hall. Pope's vivid awareness of the satirical tradition, a tradition of which he was both heir and custodian, is neatly indicated by the title which he first gave to his version of Donne's fourth Satire: *The Impertinent*. This had been John Oldham's title for his closer imitation of the same poem on which Donne's is loosely based, Horace's ninth Satire of the first Book. More largely, Pope's sense of tradition is attested by the complex tone of even the strictly Horatian poems, in which we hear the accents of Boileau, Persius, and Juvenal blending with those of Horace.

Pope is not merely allusively familiar with his predecessors; he has assimilated their various and distinctive excellences. His poetic range encompasses the vigour of Dryden's couplets, the serious wit of Donne, Horace's 'delicacy' and winning grace, and the indignation of Juvenal. His poetic personality is likewise compounded of the proper satiric virtues. At the climax of *To Fortescue* Pope boldly transforms Horace's description of his predecessor Lucilius into a statement of his own character:

> What? arm'd for *Virtue* when I point the Pen,
> Brand the bold Front of shameless, guilty Men,
> Dash the proud Gamester in his gilded Car,
> Bare the mean Heart that lurks beneath a Star. . . .
> Hear this, and tremble! you, who 'scape the Laws.
> Yes, while I live, no rich or noble knave
> Shall walk the World, in credit, to his grave.
> TO VIRTUE ONLY and HER FRIENDS, A FRIEND,
> The World beside may murmur, or commend.
>
> (105 ff.)

Pope, like Lucilius, and like Donne, appears in his poems as courageously and passionately outspoken. A friend to truth and virtue, he is therefore a friend to all honest men. He knows the ways of the world, the kingdoms of greed and corruption, yet stands rigidly aloof. Above all, and this is Pope's own particular contribution to the composite image of the satirist, he is independent, a man of uncompromisable integrity whose disinterestedness is guaranteed by his financial independence of social and political patrons.

Much more emphatically than the conclusion of the *Epistle to Burlington*, and with a moral fervour that refutes Francis Jeffrey's charge, the climax of *To Fortescue* reveals Pope in the public role defined by Horace, the grave responsible role of the poet and orator. Horace's coupling of 'Rhetor' and 'Poeta' reminds us of the specially close relationship between the aims and methods of satirical poetry and oratory. Rhetorical theory has always insisted that the speaker's character constitutes an indispensable element in his persuasiveness. According to Aristotle, 'the orator persuades by moral character when his speech is delivered in such a manner as to render him worthy of confidence; for we feel confidence in a greater degree and more readily in persons of worth . . .'; since Pope, unlike Swift, chooses to speak with what purports to be his own voice, the moral character behind the voice assumes a very considerable, if not quite an ultimate, authority for the judgments which the satire seeks to enforce.

[ 9 ]

Aristotle further argues that 'this confidence must be due to the speech itself, not to any preconceived idea of the speaker's character'.[1] It follows that the speech must be planned so as to display those aspects of character appropriate to the occasion, and to show them to advantage. This, in turn, will involve the suppression of irrelevant aspects of the orator's real personality, and the highlighting, even idealization, of others. It may also be expedient for the speaker to strike some specially persuasive pose. Quintilian remarks that 'we shall derive some silent support from representing that we are weak, unprepared, and no match for the powerful talents arrayed against us'; and, still more ingeniously, that 'our opponent's advocate will sometimes provide us with material for our *exordium*: we may speak of him in honorific terms, pretending to fear his eloquence and influence with a view to rendering them suspect to the judge.'[2] Considered as oratory, the opening of *To Fortescue* economically gains 'silent support' for Pope by representing him as 'Tim'rous by Nature'; it proceeds, in a phrase which has no counterpart in Horace, to disparage the poet's enemies by rendering their power and influence suspect: 'of the Rich in awe'. We can regard this passage both as an oratorical device, since the poem is addressed to the general public, and as a piece of raillery, since Pope is ostensibly talking to a single friend. From either point of view the passage is seen to be essentially and transparently a pose, a pretence that can be dropped as the poem goes on its way. Neither the orator nor the formal verse satirist will risk acting a part for too long; to do so is to invite uncertainty and incomprehension among one's hearers. Only under the most exceptional circumstances, as when addressing the ruling monarch, would either of them wish to sacrifice the persuasive force of his moral character for the deviousness of a created *persona*, a stratagem that ultimately derives, as we may usefully remind ourselves, from the conventions of Roman acting.

The mists of critical confusion generated by Lemuel Gulliver bear witness to the difficulties and misunderstandings which beset a satirist who chooses the technique of the *persona*. On the other hand,

---

[1] *Rhetoric* I ii 4.    [2] *Institutio Oratoria* IV i 8 and 11.

the oratorical satirist who disdains to wear a mask finds that his very disdain exposes him to a different but no less dangerous threat. For the orator and the satirist must represent themselves as worthily virtuous, as absolute for truth and justice:

> Not Fortune's Worshipper, nor Fashion's Fool,
> Not Lucre's Madman, nor Ambition's Tool,
> Not proud, nor servile, be one Poet's praise
> That, if he pleas'd, he pleas'd by manly ways;
> That Flatt'ry, ev'n to Kings, he held a shame,
> And thought a Lye in Verse or Prose the same.
>
> (*To Arbuthnot* 334-9)

What is only too easy, as Pope's unsympathetic editors and critics have demonstrated, is to cut this infallible satirist down to human size, by pointing to gaps between Pope's public professions and the petty dishonesties, the 'genteel equivocations', of his private life.[1] Even Mark Pattison, who deplored the zealous editorial excesses of Whitwell Elwin, was constrained to admit that 'a satirist, of all men, should have his own hands clean. . . . When Pope is inclined to spread his plumes and hint at his own virtues, let it be remembered that he cheated his friends Swift and Lord Oxford out of the originals of his own letters.'[2] It is tempting to reply that biographical considerations are irrelevant to Pope's art, except that Pope himself would have thought otherwise. Holding as he did the Renaissance doctrine that to be a good poet one must also be a good man,[3] Pope constantly sought to live up to the necessarily exaggerated claims which he made for himself by virtue of his satirical office, and the impossibly exalted standards he set. Mere prudence would have demanded as much, for any flagrant discrepancy between the conduct of the orator or satirist and his public utterance will spoil his image and weaken,

---

[1] 'I have not told a lye (which we both abhominate) but equivocated pretty genteely': Pope to Teresa Blount, 7 August 1716, *Correspondence*, vol. I, p. 350.

[2] 'Pope and his Editors,' in *Essays*, ed. Henry Nettleship (Oxford, 1889), vol. II, pp. 383-4. Ironically, the sly means which Pope stooped to in order to get his letters printed were directed to the end of confirming, through his published correspondence, the worthy satiric character manifested in the poems.

[3] See his letter to Caryll of January 1733, *Correspondence*, vol. III, p. 340.

if not entirely nullify, the force of his pleadings. Aristotle wisely advises the orator against relying on his audience's prepossession in favour of his moral character; but a speaker (or poet) cannot prevent his audience from allowing its unfavourable knowledge to undermine the character he is endeavouring to establish. So the spokesman for virtue, though he can never be impeccably virtuous, must speak with genuine authority: 'For he, who would have all men trust his judgment as to what is expedient and honourable, should both possess and be regarded as possessing genuine wisdom and excellence of character.'[1]

Certainly, as to his independence, the quality on which Pope most prided himself, there can be no reason for qualifying Dr Johnson's words: 'Pope never set genius to sale: he never flattered those whom he did not love, or praised those whom he did not esteem.'[2] The poems of the 1730s are deeply concerned with this quality. In *To Bethel* Pope presents himself as enjoying the material independence of the country gentleman together with the emotional independence and stability of the Christian Stoic. The *Epistle to Dr Arbuthnot* reveals a poet who, though he cannot achieve physical seclusion from pestering scribblers, is morally and artistically remote from them. Finally, at the end of the first *Epilogue to the Satires* Pope declares himself in a proud minority of one, confronting the total corruption of his country:

> All, all look up, with reverential Awe,
> On Crimes that scape, or triumph o'er the Law:
> While Truth, Worth, Wisdom, daily they decry –
> "Nothing is Sacred now but Villany."
>
> Yet may this Verse (if such a Verse remain)
> Show there was one who held it in disdain.

This emphasis on independence, and the increasing concern with moral centrality, entail a shift in Pope's attitude towards Horace. The high moral note of the public orator is not characteristically Horace's

---

[1] Quintilian, *Institutio Oratoria* III viii 12.
[2] 'Life of Pope', *Lives of the English Poets*, ed. G. Birkbeck Hill (Oxford, 1905), vol. III, p. 205.

note, and his sly indirectness may come to seem a failure of moral nerve. William Warburton shrewdly pointed to the fundamental difference between the 'tempers' of the two poets: 'What Horace would only smile at, Mr Pope would treat with the grave severity of Persius: And what Mr Pope would strike with the caustic lightening of Juvenal, Horace would content himself in turning into ridicule.'[1] Throughout his *Imitations* Pope is continually pressing Horace towards greater moral outspokenness, and at last, in the *Epilogue to the Satires*, the passionate satirical manner owes more to Juvenal than to Horace, and more to Pope himself than to all his predecessors.

The figure of 'Pope', as Pope himself presents it, is a complex one. It embodies many aspects of the real Pope, and at the same time speaks with the voices of earlier satirists. It has the distinctive features of the Christian Stoic, and of the retired and rural 'happy man'. Its demeanour is normally that of the polite man of breeding, the witty friend, though as the satires succeed one another their author is seen to grow in moral stature, and increasingly the sturdy independent tones of the serious and plain-spoken moralist break through. This figure, whether it appears as commentator or protagonist, focuses a range of values drawn from literary tradition, from whatever seemed best in eighteenth-century life, and from Pope's own, somewhat idealized, personality. In considering Pope's work it is impossible to avoid considering some at least of the contemporary manifestations of 'lordly Luxury' and 'City Gain',[2] for what he satirized can be seen to have shaped, indeed to have predetermined, the way in which he satirized it. But what makes his poems rewarding, and far more than merely topical, is the richness, the weight, the amplitude of what he forcefully brings to bear on the life of his age.

---

[1] Warburton's preliminary note on the *Imitations of Horace*, in *Works*, vol. IV, p. 51.
[2] *Epistle to Bathurst* 148.

CHAPTER TWO

# 'Talking upon Paper'

In 1738 Father John Constable published anonymously a lively treatise entitled *The Conversation of Gentlemen*, in which he observed that 'Writing is a sort of Conversing. There is consequently a proportionable Accuracy to be observed in both.'[1] This declaration carries weight; Constable was also the author of a study of contemporary prose, *Reflections upon Accuracy of Style* (1731), and therefore an expert witness of the liaison between writing and conversing in the early eighteenth century. His emphasis on 'Accuracy', and his deliberate use of the word 'consequently', draw attention to the fact that the relationship mutually affected both parties. In the first place, men were encouraged to talk like books. 'Never enter upon any Discourse, unless the form and image of what you are to speak to, be well imprinted in your mind; that so your Discourse may prove a full and perfect Birth, and not an abortive Embryo'; or again: 'methodize what you have to say handsomely, not mingling things of different tribes together.'[2] These instructions are from one of the numerous guides to good breeding that were offered to an eager public after the Restoration. How far such books, which were often translated or adapted from Continental originals, reflect actual practice amongst the most refined of society, or how far their precepts were followed by the young and socially ambitious, must remain conjectural. Though the demand for these manuals seems to have been high, information about their readers (apart from the plagiarizing compilers of other

---

[1] p. 73.
[2] *Galateo of Manners* [an anonymous translation of Giovanni della Casa's *Galateo*], (1703), pp. 105 and 108.

[ 14 ]

courtesy-books) is very scanty. Dudley Ryder, a law-student in the Middle Temple, records that he 'met with' a second-hand copy of Pierre d'Ortigue's *L'art de plaire dans la conversation*, and thought it well written, 'with a good many very just and polite reflections'.[1] But Ryder, who came of a non-conformist linen-draper's family, was painfully conscious of his need for 'polish', and he and his cousin, another young man of social aspirations, had already discovered many of Ortigue's precepts for themselves: 'We talked about story-telling and the necessity of it for conversation and the difficulty of doing it well. He [the cousin] has to this end thought over stories and wrote down hints of them.'[2] To the same end Ortigue considers at length how we can prepare ourselves for good society; he concludes that we should analyse conversations that we have taken part in, and recall at night the best things we have heard, or uttered, during the day. The keeping of a commonplace-book was as necessary for the good speaker as for the good writer. Such advice and such efforts might well tend to produce rather studied and bookish ways of speaking. So that as literature absorbed contemporary speech-habits and grew more relaxed and easy, conversation, at least among certain sections of society, came to meet it.

Authors and conversationalists alike pursued the same essentially social virtues – ease, liveliness and clarity – and abjured the same anti-social vices. Jargon and hard words were forbidden. Any ambiguity or obscurity, anything which might puzzle and irritate one's audience, was considered thoroughly objectionable: 'nothing is more unpolite than to be obscure.'[3] For the sake of his hearers or readers a man must be immediately intelligible, taking care to avoid repetition and circumlocution. If called upon to 'give an account of your self to *inquisitive* or *Learned* men; let your answers be *direct* and *concise*, It is both your *Wisdome* and your *kindness* to come to the point at first.'[4] While the brief aside is approved as an essential feature of

---

1 *The Diary of Dudley Ryder, 1715–1716*, ed. W. Matthews (1939), p. 75. Ortigue's work was first published in 1690.
2 Ibid., p. 270.
3 James Forrester, *The Polite Philosopher* (Dublin, 1734), p. 16.
4 Richard Lingard, *A Letter of Advice to a Young Gentleman* (Dublin, 1670), p. 11.

lively conversation, the rambling and bewildering digression, what the age usually intends by the word 'parenthesis', is frowned upon. 'Nothing', declares Shenstone with jocular exaggeration, 'tends so much to produce drunkenness, or even madness, as the frequent use of parentheses in conversation.'[1] It is therefore highly commendable to earn the title of 'an enemy to Parentheses', and the French nobleman so described, Pierre d'Ortigue, is significantly said to combine the qualities of an excellent prose stylist and a very well-bred man.[2]

The arts of writing and conversing have always come most intimately together in the private letter. At the beginning of one of his early letters to Henry Cromwell Pope testifies to the quality of his friendship by invoking, without further ceremony, a well-known definition of the epistolary style: 'To make use of that freedom and familiarity of style which we have taken up in our Correspondence, & which is more properly talking upon Paper, than Writing. . . .'[3] In the late seventeenth and early eighteenth centuries a great deal of literature, and not only literature in prose, could accurately be described as 'talking upon Paper'. This is largely because writers after the Restoration, whether journalists or divines, essayists or members of the Royal Society preparing their reports, were all keenly aware of their audience. Moreover, they were eager to accommodate themselves to that audience. It was no longer acceptable to tease, astonish and bewilder one's readers, as Nashe had done, and as Sterne was to do later. The reader must be quietly put at his ease, by the kind of calculatedly off-hand approach that Dryden makes in the first paragraph of his Preface to *Fables Ancient and Modern*, or by the relaxed, easy-going, yet delicately controlled sentences of Sir William

---

[1] William Shenstone, 'On Writing and Books', *Works in Verse and Prose* (1764–9), vol. II, p. 201.
[2] *The Art of Pleasing in Conversation*, trans. John Ozell (1736), vol. I, p. xiv. Cf. vol. I, p. 103: 'A man should banish equivocal terms and transpositions, and never use parentheses but thro' necessity and with judgment.'
[3] 25 November 1710, *Correspondence*, vol. I, p. 105. Pope had used the same formula to Caryll, 31 July 1710 (*Correspondence*, vol. I, p. 94), and Broome, one of his assistants in the Homer translation, employed it in writing to his co-assistant Fenton (*Correspondence*, vol. II, p. 346).

Temple's essays. Lord Shaftesbury, another gentleman-author like Temple, finds it natural at the end of his *Characteristicks* to apologize to his readers as though to a group of acquaintances: 'If, contrary to the Rule and Measure of Conversation, I have drawn the Company's Attention towards me thus long, without affording them an Intermission, during my Recital. . . .'[1] Prose works were therefore judged to be most successful when they most closely approximated to good, slightly disciplined talk, when, that is, they were characterized by a kind of premeditated negligence. It was even permissible to err a little on the side of negligence and verbosity. Dudley Ryder considers that Locke 'writes with the greatest clearness I ever met with in any man. His style is pretty diffused and prolix, it seems to have come from him without any study or choice of words, but to have writ his thoughts down as they presented themselves to him in different lights, much such a language as a man that is full of a subject and had a command of words would use in conversation.'[2] This is the criterion of good expository prose style that was to find its most memorable expression in Hazlitt's essay 'On Familiar Style' and Coleridge's definition of the 'very best' kind of prose, such as Southey's, where 'you read page after page, understanding the author perfectly, without once taking notice of the medium of communication; – it is as if he had been speaking to you all the while'.[3]

The poet, too, must cherish the conversational virtues of clarity, ease, and conciseness. And there is no reason why the use of rhyme should be a hindrance to him in this task. Dryden claimed that rhyme strikes us as disagreeably artificial only 'when the poet either makes a vicious choice of words, or places them, for rhyme sake, so unnaturally as no man would in ordinary speaking; but when 'tis so judiciously ordered that the first word in the verse seems to beget the second, and that the next, till that becomes the last word in the line which, in the negligence of prose, would be so; it must then be

---

[1] Anthony Ashley Cooper, 3rd Earl of Shaftesbury, *Characteristicks of Men, Manners, Opinions, Times*, 2nd ed. (1714), vol. III, p. 335.
[2] *Diary*, p. 75.
[3] *Coleridge's Miscellaneous Criticism*, ed. T. M. Raysor (1936), p. 423.

granted, rhyme has all the advantages of prose besides its own'.[1] In this instance Dryden's prose might be thought a shade too negligent and breathless; if so, it draws attention to one of the 'advantages' of rhyme, namely that it checks the habit of digressiveness and discourages 'parentheses'. The couplet, sometimes only too predictably, knows where it is going. Blank verse, on the other hand, may tempt the weak-willed poet to indulge in a distressing garrulity: 'Blank verse will therefore, I fear, be too often found in description exuberant, in argument loquacious, and in narration tiresome'.[2]

Pope, early in his career, was responsive to the pressure of conversational norms upon the writer of verse. In a well-known letter of 1710, outlining his ideas on versification, he censured expletives, and for a significant reason: 'I wou'd except against all Expletives in Verse, as Do before Verbs plural, or ev'n too frequent use of Did & Does, to change the Termination of the Rhime; *all these being against the usual manner of Speech* & meer fillers up of unnecessary syllables.'[3] When he was revising his poems for his first collected edition, the *Works* of 1717, Pope carefully weeded out the expletives that he had previously overlooked. The joke in the *Essay on Criticism* – 'While *Expletives* their feeble Aid *do* join' (line 346) – made caution doubly necessary; no fewer than ten offending words were removed from the text of that very poem.

In compiling his list of the 'Niceties' of versification Pope, as Professor Tillotson has noted, seems to have been drawing here and there on Edward Bysshe's *Art of English Poetry*, a manual for practising poets first published in 1702.[4] Under the heading 'Rules conducing to the Beauty of our Versification' Bysshe announces that 'it is a fault to make *Amazed* of three Syllables, and *Loved* of two; instead of *Amaz'd* of two, and *Lov'd* of one'. The 'fault' consists in

---

[1] Dedication of *The Rival Ladies* (1664), *Essays*, vol. I, p. 7.
[2] Johnson, 'Life of Akenside', *Lives of the Poets*, vol. III, pp. 417–18.
[3] To Henry Cromwell, 25 November 1710, *Correspondence*, vol. I, p. 107. The phrase I have italicized was omitted in the more polished version of his prosodic programme which Pope claimed to have sent to the critic William Walsh in 1706: see *Correspondence*, vol. I, pp. 22–5.
[4] Geoffrey Tillotson, *Pope and Human Nature* (Oxford, 1958), p. 187, note 2.

running counter to current pronunciation, in being affectedly poetical, and it had been condemned before, perhaps most roundly in 1685 by Robert Wolseley, in his Preface to the Earl of Rochester's adaptation of Fletcher's *Valentinian*. Having defended Rochester from the charge of 'bawdry' levelled by the Earl of Mulgrave in the course of his *Essay on Poetry*, Wolseley carries the war into the enemy's camp, and demonstrates that by writing his *Essay* in verse Mulgrave has proved himself no poet at all. Wolseley quotes an unfortunate couplet:

> That Author's Name has undeserved Praise
> Who pall'd the Appetite he meant to raise.

'In the first place,' he enquires, 'What does that *ed* in *undeserved* do there? I know no businesse it has, unlesse it be to crutch a lame Verse and each [i.e. eke] out a scanty Sence, for the Word that is now us'd is *undeserv'd*.' Mulgrave should take note that 'the *eds* went away with the *forto's* and the *untils*, in that general Rout that fell on the whole Body of the *thereons*, the *thereins*, and the *therebys*. . . .' The language of poetry has been reformed and purged. A counter reformation is out of the question, for the new conception of poetic style, as Wolseley proceeds to show, is 'grounded on the Authority of *Horace*, who tells us in his Epistle *de Arte Poeticâ*, That present Use is the final Judge of Language (the Verse is too well known to need quoting), and on the common Reason of Mankind, which forbids us those antiquated Words and obsolete Idioms of Speech whose Worth time has worn out . . . ; for what is grown pedantick and unbecoming when 'tis spoke will not have a jot the better grace for being writ down'.[1] If poetry, as Horace requires, is to be brought to the bar of present usage, tested against current speech-habits, then it follows that for Edward Bysshe such elisions as *am'rous*, *'tis*, *we're*, *can't*, and *let's*, are all 'allowable in our Poetry'. The general tendency of Bysshe's recommendations is to encourage poets working at least in the lowlier 'kinds' to proclaim their allegiance to the forms of contemporary speech. The pastoral is traditionally the

---

[1] *Critical Essays of the Seventeenth Century*, ed. Joel E. Spingarn (Oxford, 1908–9), vol. III, pp. 26–7.

proper, humble form in which to launch a poetical career, and in his *Pastorals* of 1709 Pope elides with enthusiasm: *'tis, I'll, am'rous, lab'rer, quiv'ring,* even *vi'lets.* By doing so he ensures that the language of the poems is never quaintly archaic and affected, while their 'numbers' come close to being 'the smoothest, the most easy and flowing imaginable'.[1]

Eliding of syllables, removing of expletives, and avoidance of antiquated words and obsolete idioms go some way towards reducing the gap between verse and speech. The gap remains, and must remain, unless poetry is to abandon its very nature and forsake the multiplicity of 'advantages' which, according to Dryden, it may and should enjoy. In Augustan verse the gap is at its narrowest in Swift's 'Humble Petition of Frances Harris', which the editor of *The Oxford Book of English Talk* has deliberately printed as a piece of prose in order to emphasize its remarkable closeness to actual speech.[2] No poem of Pope's could endure this treatment, but then there is no good reason why it should. For Pope, over a large part of his output, enjoys the best of both worlds, suggesting the presence of the speaking voice without dissipating the substance and energy of his lines, without any of the slackening of pressure consequent on Swift's brilliant realism. When Pope gives us what purports to be actual speech he is characteristically economical. At the beginning of the *Epistle to a Lady* a single sentence allegedly 'once let fall' by Martha Blount (' "Most Women have no Characters at all" ') immediately creates a witty manner and an intimate tone. At the end of the same *Epistle* the poet himself lets fall a brief and delicate aside:

> Be this a Woman's Fame: with this unblest,
> Toasts live a scorn, and Queens may die a jest.
> This Phœbus promis'd (I forget the year)
> When those blue eyes first open'd on the sphere.

> (281–4)

The tactful gallantry of 'I forget the year' is set off by its more

---

[1] Pope's 'Discourse on Pastoral Poetry' (1717), Twickenham Edition, vol. I, p. 29.
[2] James R. Sutherland (ed.), *The Oxford Book of English Talk* (Oxford, 1953), pp. 182–5 and 449.

formal surroundings, and in its turn imparts a slightly mock-heroic flavour to 'Phœbus' and 'the sphere'. This quality of gay seriousness informs the whole of the concluding address to Martha Blount, and reveals the poet as no less wittily charming and good-humoured than the lady herself:

> The gen'rous God, who Wit and Gold refines,
> And ripens Spirits as he ripens Mines,
> Kept Dross for Duchesses, the world shall know it,
> To you gave Sense, Good-humour, and a Poet.

In these closing lines of the *Epistle* Pope has perfected a style in which, twenty years earlier, he had first handled the theme of feminine good humour:

> But, Madam, if the Fates withstand, and you
> Are destin'd *Hymen*'s willing Victim too,
> Trust not too much your now resistless Charms,
> Those, Age or Sickness, soon or late, disarms;
> *Good Humour* only teaches Charms to last,
> Still makes new Conquests, and maintains the past.[1]

The similarities between this and the later *Epistle* – particularly the mock-serious Latinism of 'the Fates withstand' – serve to enhance the differences. This address is more formally polite ('But, Madam, . . .'), the tone a trifle didactic for the occasion. We miss the lightness of touch, the sense that the person addressed is herself gathered into the poem.

Pope's epistolary verse, since it is a matter of *talking* upon paper, is continually tending towards the dramatic, as when the poet, imitating Horace, reports to his friend the tribulations that beset a writer in London:

> My Counsel sends to execute a Deed:
> A Poet begs me, I will hear him read:
> In Palace-Yard at Nine you'll find me there –
> At Ten for certain, Sir, in Bloomsb'ry-Square –

---

[1] 'To a Young Lady, with the Works of Voiture' (first published 1712), lines 57–62. Pope later retitled the poem 'Epistle to Miss Blount', without making it clear which of the two Blount sisters was intended. The original 'Lady' may have been a figment of his imagination. See Twickenham Edition, vol. VI, p. 65.

Before the Lords at Twelve my Cause comes on –
There's a Rehearsal, Sir, exact at One. –
"Oh but a Wit can study in the Streets,
"And raise his Mind above the Mob he meets."
Not quite so well however as one ought;
A Hackney-Coach may chance to spoil a Thought,
And then a nodding Beam, or Pig of Lead,
God knows, may hurt the very ablest Head.

(Epistle II ii 92–103)

The friend's contempt for the mob, conveyed by the scornful alliteration ('And raise his Mind above the Mob he meets') is played off against the bland reasonableness of the poet's reply: 'Not quite so well however as one ought.' The adroit placing of 'however' gives just the right touch of gentle dissent, so that the poet calmly re-emerges from the bustle of affairs as that recognizably Horatian figure, the urbane and witty companion. His wit manifests itself partly in the unexpectedly abstract 'Thought', since hackney coaches usually spoil more material things; partly in the ingenuity with which he has imitated Horace. The Latin 'hac lutulenta ruit sus' ('that way rushes a mud-bespattered sow') is punningly metamorphosed, in terms of the contemporary London street-scene, into a falling 'Pig of Lead'.

In almost all the editions of Pope's Imitations of Horace which appeared during his lifetime the Latin original faces its English version across the page, and invites detailed comparison. But ultimately more important than all the local felicities is the fact that in sustained passages Pope has re-created, by his tone and style, something of Horace's very attractive poetic personality. For it was a large part of Horace's appeal in the early eighteenth century that he was, evidently, a very sociable man. He 'had the nicest Tast of Conversation, and was himself a most agreeable Companion'.[1] In his Epistles and Satires he is unassumingly content to handle the language and situations of everyday life, concealing his artistry beneath a manner that appears relaxed, and, in its occasional abrupt transitions, spontaneous and improvised. Not only do several of the

---

[1] *The Tatler*, no. 268.

satires, either wholly or in part, profess to be transcripts of the spoken word; Horace also modestly refers to his ethical pieces as *sermones*, that is to say discourses, discussions, or simply and literally 'Speeches'.[1] Pope was careful to emphasize this conversational aspect of Horace in his first public tribute to the Latin poet:

> *Horace* still charms with graceful Negligence,
> And without Method *talks* us into Sense.
>
> (*Essay on Criticism* 653-4)

'Graceful Negligence' sums up the whole art of pleasing in conversation, so that Horace can be acclaimed the best of courtesy-writers: 'One cannot read any book I believe more fit to learn one the polite way of writing and conversing than Horace, and one cannot be too familiar with him.'[2] The agreeable companion in Horace comes out most delightfully in his brief and graceful letter to Albius Tibullus (Epistle I iv), with its blend of compliment, advice, and self-mockery; in the invitation to Torquatus (Epistle I v), and in the neatly-turned letter of introduction on behalf of Septimius (Epistle I ix), a poem whose tact particularly recommended it to Augustan taste. Matthew Prior adapted it as an epistle to Harley, and it was translated and warmly praised by Steele in the *Spectator*.[3]

In a later number of the *Spectator*, Ambrose Philips discusses the writing of verse-epistles. He distinguishes two main types; first, the Ovidian, comprising 'Love-Letters, Letters of Friendship, and Letters upon mournful Occasions', a genre to which Pope makes a major contribution with his *Eloisa to Abelard;* secondly, the Horatian, or 'Familiar, Critical, and Moral' epistles. Philips believes that to succeed in the second type one must be 'a Master of refined Raillery, and understand the Delicacies, as well as the Absurdities of Conversation'.[4] In other words the poet must be an experienced conversationalist, since it was necessary to be a 'Master of refined

---

[1] This literal equivalent is offered by Thomas Sprat in his 'Life and Writings of Mr Abraham Cowley', *Critical Essays*, ed. Spingarn, vol. II, p. 136.

[2] *Diary of Dudley Ryder*, p. 78.

[3] Prior, *Works*, vol. I, pp. 394-5; *The Spectator*, no. 493.

[4] *The Spectator*, no. 618.

Raillery' in order to be truly qualified for polite society. Raillery was fashionable: 'according to the humour of this Age, our Conversation runs much upon *Raillery*.'[1] Like other fashionable things it was affected by the vain and the frivolous, the cynical and the mischievous, and thereby degraded. Men congratulated themselves on employing witty raillery when they were merely being derisive, when they indulged in buffoonery, even when they stooped to mimicry of physical mannerisms and infirmities. Women, if we accept Swift's inventory of 'The Furniture of a Woman's Mind', were yet more guilty:

> For Conversation well endu'd;
> She calls it witty to be rude;
> And, placing Raillery in Railing,
> Will tell aloud your greatest Failing;
> Nor makes a Scruple to expose
> Your bandy Leg, or crooked Nose.[2]

Courtesy-writers and commentators on the social scene made strenuous efforts to discriminate polite raillery from this kind of abusiveness, to distinguish, that is, between Railing and Raillery.

Railing is unsatisfactory because its direct attack is artistically crude, unpolished, lacking in witty refinement. Raillery, therefore, will be distinguished in the first place by its indirectness, by an ingenious obliqueness of method; hence it will often be found to employ irony. When the term raillery is carried over into literary criticism it is often simply used to denote ironical praise, the technique of the mock encomium. Steele refers to the 'Ironical Commendation of the Industry and Charity' of procuresses which 'makes up the Beauty of the inimitable Dedication to the *Plain Dealer*, and is a Master-piece of Raillery on this Vice'.[3] By this definition Pope's masterpieces of raillery are his *Epistle to Augustus* and his ironical essay on Ambrose Philips's pastoral verse.[4] Although

---

[1] *The Rules of Civility* [an anonymous translation of Antoine de Courtin, *Nouveau Traité de la Civilité* (Paris, 1671)], 3rd ed. (1678), p. 261.
[2] Lines 17–22; *Poems*, p. 416.
[3] *The Spectator*, no. 266.
[4] *The Guardian*, no. 40.

this kind of 'manifest, but ingenious derision' commends itself to the satirist because it possesses the great virtue of indirectness, it is too keen a weapon for the conversationalist: 'in this sense there is not much difference betwixt *raillying*, and railing, only railing is deliver'd bluntly without the trouble of Ornaments.'[1] Ingenuity is necessary, but it is not enough. To obliqueness of method must be added inoffensiveness of motive. Conversation certainly requires liveliness, pungency, even perhaps a little tartness, but not at the risk of upsetting the ease of the company, of putting anyone 'out of countenance'. True refined raillery consists of 'agreeable smart-nesses, accompanied with mirth and gayety, which divert without offending people, and without breaking in upon that character of *urbanity* which . . . we ought never to lay aside'.[2]

At its furthest remove from derisive railing, therefore, raillery will be not only innocent of all malice, diverting people without in the least offending them, but also positively complimentary. It can take the form of an ingeniously good-natured speech in which an apparent reproof or piquancy turns out to be illusory and harmless, so that the final effect is wholly one of panegyric. This, the very opposite of the *Spectator*'s 'Ironical Commendation', is for Swift the true meaning of the term:

> Raillery is the finest Part of Conversation; but, as it is our usual Custom to counterfeit and adulterate whatever is dear to us, so we have done with this, and turned it all into what is generally called Repartee, or being smart. . . . It now passeth for Raillery to run a Man down in Discourse, to put him out of Countenance, and make him ridiculous, sometimes to expose the Defects of his Person, or Understanding. . . . The *French*, from whom we borrow the Word, have a quite different Idea of the Thing, and so had we in the politer Age of our Fathers. Raillery was to say something that at first appeared a Reproach, or Reflection; but, by some Turn of Witun expected and surprising, ended always in a Compliment, and to the Advantage of the Person it was addressed to.[3]

---

[1] *The Rules of Civility*, pp. 262–3.
[2] Ortigue, *Art of Pleasing in Conversation*, vol. I, p. 347.
[3] 'Hints towards an Essay on Conversation', *Prose Works*, vol. IV, p. 91. See also Swift's poetical epistle 'To Mr Delany', lines 29–40, where he pays tribute to Voiture's mastery of 'that Irony which turns to Praise': *Poems*, p. 216.

Fulsome flattery is open to precisely the same objections as railing; it is embarrassing and crude. And it is suspect, whereas Swift's kind of indirect praise will be acceptable because its very obliqueness subtly flatters the intelligence of the recipient. Further, though the 'Reproach, or Reflection' turns out to be a mere fiction, it has the passing effect of suggesting the speaker's independence and manliness; he is no fawning parasite. So this type of raillery often employs a rough and downright manner of delivery. Steele quotes admiringly a verbal exchange between 'the late Duke of B[uckingha]m' and 'the late Earl of O[rrer]y':

> *My Lord*, (says the Duke, after his Libertine Way) *you will certainly be D—d. How my Lord!* says the Earl, with some Warmth. *Nay*, said the Duke, *there's no Help for it, for it is positively said, Cursed is he of whom all Men speak well.* This is taking a Man by Surprize, and being welcome when you have so surpris'd him. The Person flatter'd receives you into his Closet at once; and the sudden Change in his Heart, from the Expectation of an Ill-wisher, to find you his Friend, makes you in his full Favour in a Moment.[1]

Considerably wittier is a deft compliment that Swift paid to Robert Harley in July 1711, shortly after Harley had been made Lord Treasurer:

> I said, there was something in a treasurer different from other men; that we ought not to make a man a bishop who does not love divinity, or a general who does not love war; and I wondered why the queen would make a man lord treasurer who does not love money. He was mightily pleased with what I said.[2]

This perfectly satisfies Swift's own definition of raillery, and fully justifies his evident satisfaction in reporting the incident to Stella. The conclusion of Pope's *Epistle to Cobham* is a less ingenious variant of the same device. In this *Epistle*, where Pope expounds his doctrine of the Ruling Passion, he is unable to make the usual sharp contrast between his satiric victims and the entirely worthy recipient of his verse-letter, for each individual, without exception, is controlled by

---

[1] *The Tatler*, no. 17, where further examples of this technique of 'true panegyric' are given; see also no. 208.
[2] *Journal to Stella*, ed. Harold Williams (Oxford, 1948), vol. I, p. 307.

his Ruling Passion. So the brief final paragraph begins by seeming to link Cobham quite deliberately ('And you! . . .') with the band of fools and sinners whose death-bed scenes have been brilliantly sketched in the preceding lines:

> And you! brave COBHAM, to the latest breath
> Shall feel your ruling passion strong in death:
> Such in those moments as in all the past,
> "Oh, save my Country, Heav'n!" shall be your last.

The reader, if not greatly startled by the turn the last line takes, is at least agreeably surprised, and appreciates that it is paradoxically in this common factor of the ruling passion that Cobham's uniqueness lies. An apparent limitation is converted into a real virtue.

The raillery of Pope's address to Cobham, like that of his *Guardian* essay on pastoral, is characterized by singleness of purpose; the one terminates in unqualified compliment, the other in equally unqualified complaint. Between these extremes lie many ways of being agreeably smart, ways of blending praise and blame in varying proportions. Not far from the positive, flattering end of the spectrum is the method employed by 'Callisthenes', who, says Steele,

> rallies the best of any Man I know, for he forms his ridicule upon a Circumstance which you are in your Heart not unwilling to grant him, to wit, that you are Guilty of an Excess in something which is in it self laudable. He very well understands what you would be, and needs not fear your Anger for declaring you are a little too much that thing. The Generous will bear being reproached as Lavish, and the valiant, rash, without being provoked to resentment against their Monitor.[1]

The Marquise de Lambert would seem to have a closely related if not identical technique in mind when she writes that 'Raillery . . . touches lightly on little Faults, to give the more Force to great Qualities.'[2] Rather more distant from Swiftian raillery was that practised by Charles Sackville, sixth Earl of Dorset, and described

---

[1] *The Spectator*, no. 422.
[2] Anne Thérèse, Marquise de Lambert, *Advice from a Mother to her Son and Daughter*, trans. William Hatchett (1729), p. 37.

for us by Matthew Prior, who was for many years Dorset's friend and protégé:

> while he said things severe enough, he rather surprised than hurt the Person he assailed, and brought himself always off so with the Mention of some greater Merit to compensate the Foible he attacked in the same Person, that by a Turn imperceptible his Satyrs slid into Panegyric which appeared the finer as it seemed less meant; but this is a perfection so hard to attain, and a thing so clumsey if a Man aimes at and misses it, that it is safer and better not to attempt it.[1]

In such cases the wound is quickly healed by the praise that follows. Or the rallier may choose to withhold commendation, and alleviate the pain of rebuke by appearing to implicate himself:

> *Minutius* has a Wit that conciliates a Man's Love, at the same time that it is exerted against his Faults. He has an Art of keeping the Person he rallies in Countenance, by insinuating that he himself is guilty of the same Imperfection. This he does with so much Address, that he seems rather to bewail himself, than fall upon his Friend.[2]

All discussions of this wide middle area of raillery agree that reproof must be aimed at slight defects only; that it must be delivered in a good-humoured tone, so that no offence can be taken because plainly none is intended; and that the victim of the joke, surprised by mirth, should be able to join in the laugh against himself. One writer can speak for all: 'The raillery which is consistent with good-breeding, is a gentle Animadversion on some Foible, which while it raises a Laugh in the rest of the Company, doth not put the Person rallied out of Countenance, or expose him to Shame and Contempt. On the contrary, the Jest should be so delicate, that the Object of it should be capable of joining in the Mirth it occasions.'[3] The company will not be disturbed or discomposed by raillery, but rather drawn together in genial high spirits, without any sacrifice of liveliness and gaiety.

---

[1] 'Heads for a Treatise upon Learning' (*c.* 1721), *Works*, vol. I, p. 585.
[2] *The Spectator*, no. 422.
[3] Fielding, 'An Essay on Conversation' (*c.* 1742), in his *Miscellanies* (1743), vol. I, p. 174. On the representativeness of this piece see Henry K. Miller, *Essays on Fielding's 'Miscellanies': a Commentary on Volume One* (Princeton, 1961), pp. 174–80.

The benefits which the satirist can derive from conversational raillery are nowhere more clearly defined than in Dryden's 'Discourse concerning Satire' of 1693. This essay is addressed to that acknowledged master of spoken raillery and Horatian satire, Charles Sackville, Earl of Dorset; Dryden very properly begins by gently rallying the noble Lord on his literary reticence, having in advance drawn the sting of his rebuke by warm praise of Dorset's literary talents. And it is with a renewed consciousness of Dorset's manifold abilities that Dryden undertakes his well-known defence of 'the manner of Horace in low satire'. Conceding Juvenal's success in his chosen mode of witty declamation, Dryden argues that 'still the nicest and most delicate touches of satire consist in fine raillery. This, my Lord, is your particular talent, to which even Juvenal could not arrive.' These delicate touches of satire correspond to the gentle animadversions of refined raillery: 'Neither is it true that this fineness of raillery is offensive. A witty man is tickled while he is hurt in this manner, and a fool feels it not.' And when he goes on to congratulate himself on the portrait of Zimri in *Absalom and Achitophel*, we find that Dryden discovers in that passage the virtues usually looked for in raillery: 'he for whom it was intended was too witty to resent it as an injury. If I had railed, I might have suffered for it justly: but I managed my own work more happily, perhaps more dexterously. I avoided the mention of great crimes, and applied myself to the representing of blindsides, and little extravagancies.'[1] It is true that Dryden has exposed Zimri's follies rather than his vices, but it is an exposure made in such forthright terms ('Stiff in Opinions, always in the wrong', 'Buffoon', 'Blest Madman') that it goes far beyond 'blindsides, and little extravagancies'. In paying his respects to Dorset and Horace, Dryden has been led to distort his own achievement. He redresses the balance, and comes much closer to describing his preferred satirical manner, when in the next paragraph but one of the 'Discourse' he claims that 'Juvenal has railed more wittily than Horace has rallied'.

---

[1] *Essays*, vol. II, pp. 136–7. Cf. the address 'To the Reader' prefacing *Absalom and Achitophel*: 'there's a sweetness in good Verse, which Tickles even while it Hurts. . . . I have but laught at some mens Follies, when I coud have declaim'd against their Vices.'

By 1728, when Edward Young published in collected form his seven satires on the *Love of Fame*, witty railing no longer had a great deal to commend it. The first two decades of the eighteenth century had seen Horace established as the type of the satirist, largely through the precepts and practice of the periodical essayists, with their winning tone and their eagerness to follow Horace's example by including in their discourse 'not only all the rules of morality, but also of civil conversation'.[1] Steele's amiable *persona* Isaac Bickerstaff is benign, playful, self-depreciating, and consequently truly Horatian. In his Preface to *Love of Fame*, therefore, Young makes Dryden's points about fine raillery over again, but with a more specific appeal to conversational experience, and without Dryden's ultimate preference for Juvenal. He also reveals that the adjective 'delicate', which Dryden used, and which is indeed inseparable from any discussion of raillery, is now passing into the literary-critical vocabulary; *delicate satire*, or *delicacy*, is to literature what raillery is to conversation:

> *Laughing Satire* bids the fairest for success. The world is too proud to be fond of a serious Tutor: And when an Author is in a passion, the laugh, generally, as in conversation, turns against him. This kind of Satire only has any delicacy in it. Of this delicacy *Horace* is the best master: He appears in good humour while he censures; and therefore his censure has the more weight, as supposed to proceed from Judgment, not from Passion.[2]

Horace and delicacy are now synonymous and supreme.

This equivalence of Horatian 'delicacy' and polite raillery is also accepted by Fielding. Just before giving his own definition of raillery ('a gentle Animadversion on some Foible. . . .') he cites Persius's famous description of the satirical method favoured by Horace:

> Omne vafer vitium ridenti Flaccus amico
> Tangit, et admissus circum praecordia ludit.[3]

---

[1] Dryden, 'A Discourse concerning Satire', *Essays*, vol. II, p. 128.
[2] *Love of Fame, The Universal Passion*, 2nd ed. (London, 1728), sig. A4ʳ.
[3] Satire I, 116–17. In Dryden's translation of this passage, Horace 'with a sly insinuating Grace, /Laugh'd at his Friend, and look'd him in the Face'.

Pope, too, interpreted these lines as relating Horace's satire closely to the sort of intimate situation, a dialogue between friends, in which raillery could flourish. He observed to Spence that 'the best time for telling a friend of any fault he has is while you are commending him, that it may have the more influence upon him. And this I take to be the true meaning of the character which Persius gives of Horace,' and which Pope went on to quote.[1] Horace's method appears at its disarming best in the letter to Iccius (Epistle I xii), where the poet teases his friend for repining at his lot, and then suggests that Iccius enjoys true prosperity because he is blessed with good health and austere taste, and is devoted to the cause of virtue; what began as gentle animadversion ends in dignified and serious compliment, just as Dorset's satirical comments 'by a Turn imperceptible . . . slid into Panegyric'. Pope repeated his observation three years later, in order to explain to Spence the subtleties of a couplet in the newly-completed Fourth Book of *The Dunciad*:

> Let Freind affect to speak as Terence spoke,
> And Alsop never but like Horace joke.
>
> (223–4)

'Those two lines', Pope commented, 'have more of satire than of compliment in them, though I find they are generally mistaken for the latter only. It goes on Horace's old method "Ridenti Flaccus amico" of telling a friend some less fault while you are commending him. . . . I scarce meet with anybody that understands delicacy.'[2] The verb 'affect' is explicitly satirical, and the reference to Alsop's jokes more covertly so; his jests were often not in the best of taste, and therefore not always Horatian. But to describe the lines as having 'more of satire than of compliment in them' seems an exaggeration, perhaps born of despair at not being properly understood. For Freind and Alsop are exalted by the classical exemplars they are paired with, and the couplet is part of the speech of 'Aristarchus', namely Richard Bentley, the 'mighty Scholiast, whose

---

[1] Spence, §540. Professor Osborn dates this remark 'summer? 1739'.
[2] Spence, §336.

unweary'd pains/Made Horace dull, and humbled Milton's strains'.[1] Bentley's dismissive scorn for two learned but more polite opponents is tantamount to any right-minded man's commendation.

Dryden, too, quoted Persius on Horace in the 'Discourse concerning Satire', and vouched for his accuracy. Persius, he says, 'concludes with me that the divine wit of Horace left nothing untouched; that he entered into the inmost recesses of nature; found out the imperfections even of the most wise and grave, as well as of the common people; discovering, even in the great Trebatius, to whom he addresses the first satire, his hunting after business, and following the Court. . . .'[2] Dryden is referring to the poem that was to form the basis of Pope's first published Imitation of Horace, *To Fortescue* (*Satire II i*), and his comment points to yet another layer in the complex opening paragraph of Pope's version. As Horace had in some bewilderment approached the lawyer Trebatius, so Pope respectfully solicits the help of his legal adviser:

> There are (I scarce can think it, but am told)
> There are to whom my Satire seems too bold,
> Scarce to wise *Peter* complaisant enough,
> And something said of *Chartres* much too rough.
> The Lines are weak, another's pleas'd to say,
> Lord *Fanny* spins a thousand such a Day.
> Tim'rous by Nature, of the Rich in awe,
> I come to Council learned in the Law.
> You'll give me, like a Friend both sage and free,
> Advice; and (as you use) without a Fee.

Here is the 'laughing Satire' which Edward Young had claimed as distinctively Horatian. Praise and blame are skilfully compounded, as in the best raillery. Pope's Counsel is a learned man and a generous friend, but the poet is also making a veiled reproach. Warburton, by no means the least acute of Pope's commentators, took the point; of the crucial seventh line ('Tim'rous by Nature, of the Rich in awe') he observed that 'the delicacy of this does not so much lie in the ironical application of it to himself, as in its seriously characterizing the Person for whose advice he applies'.[3] This is the

---

[1] *Dunciad* IV, 211–12.    [2] *Essays*, vol. II, p. 129.    [3] *Works*, vol. IV, p. 53.

raillery employed by Steele's 'Minutius', the man who administers a rebuke by 'insinuating that he himself is guilty of the same Imperfection', seeming 'rather to bewail himself, than fall upon his Friend.' Pope has brilliantly re-created the style of Horace, who 'laugh'd at his Friend, and look'd him in the Face', for beneath the incredulity of 'I scarce can think it, but am told' lurks the smile of a man who has taken the measure of his interlocutor. Among those to whom Pope's satire seems too bold is the very man he is addressing. It is the Friend's natural timorousness that leads him both to disapprove of, and to exaggerate, the boldness of Pope's satire, though even his disapproval is cleverly converted by the poet into a vehicle for additional, and as it were unintentional, satire:

> F. Better be Cibber, I'll maintain it still,
> Than ridicule all Taste, blaspheme Quadrille,
> Abuse the City's best good Men in Metre,
> And laugh at Peers that put their Trust in Peter.
> Ev'n those you touch not, hate you.
> P. What should ail 'em?
> F. A hundred smart in Timon and in Balaam.
>
> (37–42)

The sensitivity of such readers of satire is at best moral squeamishness (as in the Friend), at worst, in those who smart, the touchiness of the guilty. And as the Friend is timorous by nature, so also he stands in awe of the rich, reminding the poet that wealth can hire assassins:

> F. Alas young Man! your Days can ne'r be long,
> In Flow'r of Age you perish for a Song!
> Plums, and Directors, Shylock and his Wife,
> Will club their Testers, now, to take your Life!
>
> (101–4)

The timorous man is thus made to utter the most scathing and personally abusive lines of the entire poem, so throwing into relief the poet's lofty idealism. For it is this cynical warning which at once draws from the poet the climactic declaration: 'What? arm'd for Virtue when I point the Pen. . . .' And that, in its turn, eventually persuades the Friend to admit the ethical and responsible nature of

[ 33 ]

the satirist's activities. Pope pleads that his poems are not 'lawless' libels and satires,

> But grave *Epistles*, bringing Vice to light,
> Such as a *King* might read, a *Bishop* write,
> Such as Sir *Robert* would approve –
> *F.* Indeed ?
> The Case is alter'd – you may then proceed.

Even here, at the moment of his conversion, the Friend reveals his fundamental weakness by eagerly accepting Walpole's approval as the clinching argument in the poet's favour. The implications of the legal phraseology are brought out by one of Pope's letters: 'The *case is altered* was not more a maxim of Plowden, when the Court was concerned, than it is of the public when any favourite . . . comes into consideration with them.'[1] Like Trebatius, Pope's lawyer 'follows the Court'; like Horace, Pope fixes on his Friend a look which is shrewdly appraising.[2]

At the beginning of *To Fortescue*, then, Pope appears as the witty companion who takes up a pose appropriate to raillery; to see the poet as adopting in these lines the *persona* of an ingenuous *naïf* is to lose some elements of their wit and dramatic tension. There might, however, seem to be a stronger case for reading the opening of Pope's next published Imitation, *To Bethel* (*Satire II ii*), in terms of a created *persona*, for its assertions and attitudes are completely disowned by the time we reach the end of the poem. Yet this too is the sort of reversal that is commonly encountered in raillery, and the poem offers a variant of the insinuation technique that we have seen in its predecessor. The pose which Pope now adopts is perhaps a little more difficult to see through, because of his very considerable modification of the Latin text. Horace simply claims to be giving a direct transcript of a long speech by the countryman Ofellus:

---

[1] To Broome, November 1724, *Correspondence*, vol. II, pp. 271–2.
[2] Warburton gave this *Satire* the convenient sub-title 'To Mr Fortescue' in the 1751 *Works*, but Pope had written to his friend William Fortescue shortly after the poem was published explaining that 'though, when I first began it, I thought of you; before I came to end it, I considered it might be too ludicrous, to a man of your situation and grave acquaintance, to make you Trebatius . . .': *Correspondence*, vol. III, p. 351.

Quæ virtus & quanta, boni, sit vivere parvo,
(Nec meus hic *Sermo*, sed quem præcepit Ofellus
Rusticus, *abnormis* sapiens, *crassaque Minerva*)
Discite non inter lances, *mensasque nitentis*,
Cum stupet *insanis acies fulgoribus*, & cum
Acclinis falsis animus meliora recusat;
Verum hic *impransi* mecum disquirite.[1]

Here all but the explanatory parenthesis is spoken by Ofellus. Pope, however, transfers the whole of this opening statement to himself, and in doing so converts Horace's quiet dissociation from Ofellus's message ('Nec meus hic Sermo') into an explicit disavowal. Only after ten introductory lines is the speech of Hugh Bethel, Pope's equivalent for Ofellus, reported to the assembled company by the poet himself:

What, and how great, the Virtue and the Art
To live on little with a chearful heart,
(A Doctrine sage, but truly none of mine)
Lets talk, my friends, but talk before we dine:
Not when a gilt Buffet's reflected pride
Turns you from sound Philosophy aside;
Not when from Plate to Plate your eyeballs roll,
And the brain dances to the mantling bowl.
    Hear Bethel's Sermon, one not vers'd in schools,
But strong in sense, and wise without the rules.
    Go work, hunt, exercise! (he thus began)
Then scorn a homely dinner, if you can.

Pope is the cordial and good-humoured host. He suggests a general topic for conversation, and remains himself impartial; the doctrine of frugality is urbanely admitted to be a wise one even while it is being disowned. The Augustan reader, with his dislike and fear of being lectured at ('in private Conversation . . . the Talent of Haranguing is, of all others, most insupportable'),[2] is put at his

---

[1] 'What and how great, my friends, is the virtue of frugal living – now this is no talk of mine, but is the teaching of Ofellus, a peasant, a philosopher unschooled and of rough mother-wit – learn, I say, not amid the tables' shining dishes, when the eye is dazed by senseless splendour, and the mind, turning to vanities, rejects the better part; but here, before we dine, let us discuss the point together.'

[2] Swift, 'Hints towards an Essay on Conversation,' *Prose Works*, vol. IV, p. 93.

ease, disarmed by the poet's geniality and politeness. Once an audience has been gained by the poet's show of undemanding worldliness, that audience can be invited to hear Bethel's exhortation to temperate living – only to find that when Bethel has concluded his speech the 'real' Pope steps forward:

> His equal mind I copy what I can,
> And as I love, would imitate the Man.
>
> (131–2)

Taking over the remainder of Ofellus's speech, Pope proceeds to extol his own equanimity and way of life. He and his guests will dine modestly on broccoli and mutton, fish from the Thames, home-grown fruit, and so on. Pope contrives to seem at once a follower or disciple of Bethel (which is a handsome tribute to his friend) and a man who has been confirmed in temperance from his earliest years: 'My Life's amusements have been just the same,/Before, and after Standing Armies came' (153–4). The suave, light-hearted disclaimer, 'A Doctrine sage, but truly none of mine', proves to have been no more than a piece of genteel equivocation, designed to allay the reader's fears by creating the sympathetic image of an Epicurean poet. Here then is another example of the type of raillery by which a man makes a false confession of his failings instead of directly reproaching others (the table-companions, and, by extension, many of Pope's readers) with their weaknesses. It is probable that Pope was tempted to diverge from Horace in order to repeat the success of *To Fortescue*; the comparable social situation at the beginning of the later poem ('Lets talk, my friends . . .') suggests the convivial atmosphere in which raillery is appropriate.[1] But there was at least one good English precedent for Pope's satirical stratagem. *Absalom and Achitophel* opens with a similar kind of subterfuge, in that Dryden pretends to a witty libertinism that serves to draw in the Restoration gentleman-reader and is then gradually abandoned as the poem proceeds.

---

[1] It is worth noting that *To Bethel* was not first published as a separate folio, which was Pope's usual practice, but appeared in a joint volume with the second edition of *To Fortescue* in 1734.

At the beginning of this satire Pope assumes that the average sensual reader will find his pretended Epicureanism congenial, and will also be prepared to enjoy some mild raillery at Hugh Bethel's expense. This new thread of raillery reinforces the image of the urbane poet and further ensnares the reader, giving him a false sense of polite security. Bethel is teased, to use Steele's phrase, for 'an Excess in something which is in it self laudable';[1] being earnest and serious-minded he is reproached with solemnity. The request that we should 'Hear Bethel's Sermon' prepares us for a speech more hortatory, more formal, certainly more doctrinaire than a blasé man of the world would utter. Bethel admits to using a pulpit manner:

> Preach as I please, I doubt our curious men
> Will chuse a *Pheasant* still before a *Hen*.
>
> (17–18)

He is made to sound over-emphatic, thanks to Pope's liberal italics, and is equipped with an aggressive, finger-wagging manner:

> By what *Criterion* do ye eat, d'ye think,
> If this is priz'd for *sweetness*, that for stink?
>
> (29–30)

His vocabulary, here as elsewhere, is far from being conventionally polite: 'do the feat', 'stench', 'dev'lish dear', 'keep a pother', 'sowse the Cabbidge'. Presumably even the banal savagery of the couplet on the Wortley Montagus –

> *Avidien* or his Wife (no matter which,
> For him you'll call a dog, and her a bitch)
>
> (49–50)

– is intended to be in character. But the reader who begins by feeling superior to this down-to-earth wisdom ends, if Pope's tactics are successful, by being converted to Bethel's point of view, and by seeking, like the poet, to 'imitate the Man'. The conversion is certainly made easier when the austere frugality which seems to be Bethel's text at the start turns conveniently into a more acceptable 'Temperance' at

---

[1] *The Spectator*, no. 422.

line 67. As in fine raillery, the initial teasing has been absorbed in approval of Bethel's seriousness. Ofellus is harsh, even fanatical, to the end, so that our acceptance of his teaching remains, as Horace intends, guarded and qualified;[1] Bethel's attitude, fully endorsed by Pope in poetry and practice, is soundly moral.

One of the advantages of delicate satire is that it offers a possible solution to what both Pope and Swift recognized as the satirist's greatest technical problem, the difficulty of entrapping the reader, of implicating him in the satirical attack. A further advantage is that the poet can make oblique or mildly bantering commendations, as of Cobham and Bethel, which help to sustain the 'private' Horatian role of the urbanely witty gentleman; more important, these artful commendations provide a positive balance to the satiric strokes, but without any sudden wrenching of the prevailing tone, without any breaking of continuity. In these ways 'delicacy' makes for dramatic tension, and effects of great subtlety and complexity beneath what may at first appear smoothly, even prosaically, polite. Not that the smooth politeness is without its own special importance. At the beginning of *To Bethel* and *To Fortescue*, and throughout the *Epistles* to Burlington and Martha Blount, the predominantly sociable manner, that of a man born to converse and write with ease, is a guarantee that the poet is companionable and out-going. A man so experienced in the arts of pleasing in conversation is no mis-anthropist, will never run satirically amuck. And the style makes a satirical contribution, being in itself a condemnation of anti-social behaviour, whether of pedants and antiquarians who turn their backs on society, or of Timon and Atossa, who fly in society's face. The poet, by contrast, is pleasantly sociable, his verse suggesting the give and take of informal talk in which agreement and qualifica-tion are politely offered:

> Yes, you despise the man to Books confin'd,
> Who from his study rails at human kind;
> Tho' what he learns, he speaks and may advance
> Some gen'ral maxims, or be right by chance.

---

[1] W. S. Anderson, 'The Roman Socrates: Horace and his Satires', in *Critical Essays on Roman Literature: Satire*, ed. J. P. Sullivan (1963), pp. 32 and 34.

The coxcomb bird, so talkative and grave,
That from his cage cries Cuckold, Whore, and Knave,
Tho' many a passenger he rightly call,
You hold him no Philosopher at all.
    And yet the fate of all extremes is such,
Men may be read, as well as Books too much.
To Observations which ourselves we make,
We grow more partial for th'observer's sake. . . .[1]

Such a manifestly reasonable man, a man who eschews extremes, deserves our attention.

---

[1] *Epistle to Cobham* 1–12.

# The Complete Gentleman

Horace reveals himself in his poetry as a master of raillery, and an amiable companion of great men. In short, he is perfectly well-bred: 'He shews the *Gentleman* even whilst he reads the most serious Lectures of *Philosophy*'.[1] By keeping his reader (and victim) in countenance, Horace is able to strike suddenly and woundingly under the reader's guard. It is much easier to ward off the direct frontal assault of a piece of invective. For one thing, the blows are less well aimed. In such poems as Oldham's *Satyrs upon the Jesuits* the author is too passionate to control his material effectively; he dissipates his strength instead of concentrating it. Pope remarked to Spence that 'Oldham is a very undelicate writer. He has strong rage, but 'tis too much like Billingsgate.'[2] Further, the railing satirist lays himself open to the charge of impure motives. It has long been a commonplace that excessive rage may be actuated by guilt, or may even betray a secret fascination with the object attacked: 'Nothing gives so sharp a Point to one's Aversion, as good Breeding; as, on the contrary, ill Manners often hide a secret Inclination.'[3] The well-bred satirist can vex mankind without losing his temper. His indignation will not cloud his judgment; he will remain in control of himself, of his satirical weapons, and, most important, of his victims.

---

[1] John Boswell, *A Method of Study: or, an Useful Library*, vol. I (1738), p. 273.
[2] Spence, §473.
[3] Colley Cibber, *The Non-Juror* (1718), p. 52. Cf. the character Snarl in Thomas Shadwell's *The Virtuoso* (1676), described in the list of *dramatis personae* as 'an old pettish Fellow, a great Admirer of the last Age, and a Declaimer against the Vices of this, and privately very vicious himself'.

The polite and unruffled manner of Pope's *Epistles to Several Persons* deceives us into believing that Timon and Sir Balaam and Peter Walter, though they are forms of eighteenth-century life, are also in some sense merely the creatures and creations of Pope. He is their omniscient prosecutor.

In everyday life the Augustan gentleman aimed to display a similar self-command, and to maintain a similarly unostentatious control over the social situation. Pope was being thoroughly orthodox when he observed that 'true politeness consists in being easy oneself and making everybody about one as easy as we can.'[1] 'Easy' behaviour is valued as the outward sign of a mind content with itself, free from nagging cares and divided aims, and of a mind in command of itself, unperturbed by the small accidents or tactlessnesses of conversation, willing to give way when relatively unimportant matters are at stake. A man so self-possessed will dispense 'ease' wherever he comes, and this, on the authority of no less a person than Locke, is a very considerable talent: 'He that knows how to make those he converses with easie without debasing himself to low and servile flattery, has found the true art of living in the World, and being both welcome and valued every where.'[2]

Augustan society sought to attain this coveted 'ease' by a number of negative precautions. Exaggerated respect for the forms of etiquette should be avoided; to insist on trifling ceremonies may be more embarrassing than polite. It is only the sycophantic courtier who 'bows, and bows again'.[3] But if 'Excess of Ceremony is troublesome . . . Rudeness is offensive, and brutish';[4] better be starched and civilized than rough and coarse. Brutish, too, are profanity and obscenity, lying and slander. Such things lower man's dignity and are so obviously beneath a gentleman that courtesy-manuals do not waste much space in denouncing them. More careful attention is paid to sins of social pride, to dogmatism or 'positiveness', and to egotism. Such pride is at its most virulent in the

---

[1] Spence, §539.
[2] John Locke, *Some Thoughts Concerning Education*, 5th ed. (1705), p. 258.
[3] Pope, 'The Fourth Satire of Dr. John Donne . . . Versifyed', line 176.
[4] Constable, *Conversation of Gentlemen*, p. 191.

[ 41 ]

pedant, a creature at the furthest remove from the polite gentleman. Citing the classics has to be done with discretion, even among friends, while in mixed company recondite jokes and private jargon are anathema. For to be pedantic is to overrate '*any* kind of knowledge we pretend to'.[1] If we can take a wider view we shall admit that such specialised knowledge is at best incomplete and inadequate, at worst trivial and irrelevant.

The pedant, awkwardly unsociable, is likely also to be obstinate in the defence of his overrated knowledge. Wrangling and disputing are the most determined enemies of ease. Therefore, 'avoid Disputes as much as possible. . . . But if you are at any time obliged to enter on an Argument, give your Reasons with the utmost Coolness and Modesty,' so that 'should you be pinched in your Argument, you may make your Retreat with a very good Grace: You were never positive, and are now glad to be better informed.'[2] An argumentative habit of mind was usually blamed upon a faulty educational system that trained boys to chop logic, to split hairs, and to indulge in contradiction for contradiction's sake. It seemed to many, and not least to Pope and his fellow-members of the Scriblerus Club, that logic was a debater's weapon for beating down opponents, rather than a tool for the discovery of truth.[3] Gilbert Burnet recommended that the study of logical method should occupy no more of a pupil's time than a single week, and went on: 'All disputing about philosophy I condemn; the perfection whereof when acquired, is to make a youth vainly subtile, and contentiously jangling. . . .'[4] Behind these attitudes lies the fear of a renewal of civil hostilities. A game of ombre at Hampton Court, like hunting and shooting in Windsor Forest, is a socially approved outlet for aggressive tendencies:

> The shady Empire shall retain no Trace
> Of War or Blood, but in the Sylvan Chace,

---

[1] Swift, 'On Good-Manners and Good-Breeding', *Prose Works*, vol. IV, p. 215; my italics.
[2] Eustace Budgell, *Spectator* no. 197.
[3] See *Memoirs of . . . Martinus Scriblerus*, ed. Charles Kerby-Miller (New Haven, 1950), pp. 122–3 (ch. vii); and Addison, *Spectator* no. 239.
[4] *Thoughts on Education* (written *c.* 1668, published 1761), p. 71.

[ 42 ]

The Trumpets sleep, while chearful Horns are blown,
And Arms employ'd on Birds and Beasts alone.

*(Windsor-Forest* 371-4)

A violent argument, on the other hand, sounds dangerously like an echo of the religious controversies of the seventeenth century, and the Civil War to which they led. It was not for nothing that Butler created Sir Hudibras both pedant and logician, and devoted so much of his narrative to verbal and physical combats.

'Ease', then, is principally secured by avoiding all strident assertions of individualism. Dogmatism and pedantry are as foolish as singularity in dress or manners: 'how extravagant soever a mode may be, a man would yet be still more extravagant, if he refused to comply with it. Shall he alone offer to withstand the general consent of his country?'[1] Thus it was difficult for Pope not to write satirically of Richard Bentley, a 'verbal critic' who used 'thou' and 'thee' in conversation, and wore a particularly large-brimmed hat. Bentley was as vulnerable to attack as Morose, in Jonson's *Silent Woman*, who had been routed by Truewit, Dauphine and Clerimont, those forerunners of the Augustan witty gentleman.[2] In their demand for compliance with the mode French, Italian and English courtesy-writers are as one. Individualism, however, was more particularly frowned on in England, where it had expressed itself as religious 'enthusiasm' and the Puritan doctrine of the inner light, and could be held responsible for the political turmoil of the 1640s. The Puritan, at least in popular conception, was a kind of pedant in religion, whereas the gentleman's virtue, like his clothes, 'sits easy about him'.[3]

Thomas Sprat, discussing Horace's polite style, perceived that the same criteria could be applied to men's writing and conversation as to their 'behaviour and carriage'; in both cases 'that is most

---

[1] Ortigue, *Art of Pleasing in Conversation*, vol. I, p. 55.
[2] Dryden commented that Truewit was 'the best character of a gentleman which Ben Jonson ever made': *Essays*, vol. I, p. 151 (and cf. p. 74). During the period 1660-1725 *The Silent Woman* was, not surprisingly, the most popular of Jonson's plays on the London stage. Pope considered it the best English comedy: Spence, §486.
[3] *The Tatler*, no. 5.

courtly and hardest to be imitated, which consists of a Natural easiness and unaffected Grace, where nothing seems to be studied, yet everything is extraordinary.'[1] This graceful negligence, since it is so difficult to imitate successfully, helps to keep the title of 'gentleman' agreeably exclusive. While fops, country squires, and the bourgeoisie are standing upon punctilios, they find themselves out of date: 'The Fashionable World is grown free and easie; our Manners, sit more loose upon us.'[2] And they sit more gracefully. Though young people and country squires might choose to be boisterously jovial, and Puritans to be unsmiling, the true gentleman will avoid both vehemence and glumness, while allowing himself to indulge in elegant mirth. Rabelais is rather too uproarious for the taste of Edward Young. He has 'a particular art of throwing a great deal of Genius, and Learning into frolick, and jest; but the Genius, and the Scholar is all you can admire; you want the Gentleman to converse with, in him.'[3] The ideal, as always, is Horace.

The gentleman's demeanour must express serenity and cheerfulness. His behaviour must be characterized by 'decency' and 'decorum', terms which in the early eighteenth century were free from any restrictive and straight-laced associations. Cicero had maintained that *honestum* (virtue) and *decorum* are inescapably linked, so that the 'decency' or gracefulness of an action is a sign of its moral value: 'whatever Becomingness there is in any Action, it immediately arises from the Honesty of it.'[4] It will also follow that a virtuous action, to be acclaimed truly virtuous, must be seen to be 'decorous'; without decorum a potential virtue degenerates into its opposite vice:

> Courage in an ill-bred Man, has the Air, and scapes not the Opinion of Brutality: Learning becomes Pedantry; Wit Buffoonry; Plainness Rusticity; Good Nature Fawning. . . . Good qualities are the Substantial Riches of the Mind, but 'tis good Breeding sets them off. . . .

---

[1] 'Life and Writings of Cowley', *Critical Essays*, ed. Spingarn, vol. II, pp. 136–7.
[2] Addison, *Spectator* no. 119.
[3] Preface to *Love of Fame* (1728), sig. a1ʳ.
[4] *Tully's Offices*, trans. Thomas Cockman, 3rd ed. (1714), p. 68 (*de Officiis* I xxvii). Cockman consistently translates *honestum* as *honesty*.

A graceful Way and Fashion, in every thing, is that which gives the Ornament and Liking.[1]

So when Pope begins the third part of the *Essay on Criticism* by laying down his 'Rules for the *Conduct* of *Manners* in a Critic', he acknowledges that truths must be conveyed, and critical judgments enforced, with suitable good manners:

> 'Tis not enough your Counsel still be *true*,
> *Blunt Truths* more Mischief than *nice Falshoods* do;
> Men must be *taught* as if you taught them *not*;
> And Things *unknown* propos'd as Things *forgot*:
> Without *Good Breeding*, *Truth* is disapprov'd;
> *That* only makes *Superior* Sense *belov'd*.      (572-7)

Tact, decorum, and a sense of the social hierarchy must regulate the critic's conduct.

In the humdrum affairs of daily life, the decency with which a trivial action is performed may elevate that action into something of real worth, for 'in most cases the manner of doing is of more Consequence, than the thing done; And upon that depends the Satisfaction or Disgust wherewith it is received'.[2] It is with this meaning of gracious behaviour that the word *decorum* makes its sole appearance in Pope's verse, in the prologue to Horace's story of the Town Mouse and the Country Mouse:

> O charming Noons! and Nights divine!
> Or when I sup, or when I dine,
> My Friends above, my Folks below,
> Chatting and laughing all-a-row,
> The Beans and Bacon set before 'em,
> The Grace-cup serv'd with all decorum:
> Each willing to be pleas'd, and please,
> And even the very Dogs at ease!
> Here no man prates of idle things,
> How this or that Italian sings,
> A Neighbour's Madness, or his Spouse's,
> Or what's in either of the *Houses*:
> But something much more our concern,
> And quite a scandal not to learn:

---

[1] Locke, *Thoughts Concerning Education*, pp. 143-4. Cf. *The Spectator*, no. 292.
[2] Locke, *Education*, p. 144.

[ 45 ]

Which is the happier, or the wiser,
A man of Merit, or a Miser?
Whether we ought to chuse our Friends,
For their own Worth, or our own Ends?
What good, or better, we may call,
And what, the very best of all?[1]

This idyllic scene follows a vivid account (by Swift) of the fret and
bustle of London politics, and points a contrast which will be more
humorously defined in the mouse-fable that concludes the poem. At
the poet's 'Country Seat' good fellowship reigns, for each man considers the 'ease' of his neighbours. The topics discussed at table are
neither too abstruse and technical, nor too mean and trivial. The
fare (unlike what is apparently being offered at the opening of *To
Bethel*) is frugal enough to be no distraction to talk that is serious
without being solemn.

The pervasive contentment of this scene owes not a little to
social distinctions; the poet's friends are placed at the top of the
table, his dependents below. Augustan writers on manners un-
questioningly accept the traditional tripartite division of society. We
must, says Swift, 'suit our behaviour to the three several degrees of
men; our superiors, our equals, and those below us';[2] the assump-
tion, here as elsewhere, is that writer and readers stand contentedly
in the middle rank. A man should know and acknowledge his social
level, but at that level can enjoy full freedom of movement. The
ideal is a maximum of social stability, together with a maximum of
'ease' and equality on each level of the hierarchy. Hence the importance of raillery, the only acceptable way of shining in company,
the only permissible form in which individualism can manifest itself.
Courtesy-writers describe it as the 'sauce to discourse', the 'delicious
Seasoning of Society', because it keeps up the liveliness of the
gathering; at the same time it draws the conversational circle
intimately together by uniting its members, including the victim of
the jest, in laughter. In fact, of course, it largely draws together

---

[1] *Satire II vi* 133–52. Swift had 'imitated' the first part of Horace's satire in 1714; the
whole poem, completed by Pope, was published in 1738.
[2] 'On Good-Manners and Good-Breeding', *Prose Works*, vol. IV, p. 213.

[ 46 ]

those who are already close in spirit, since it assumes a like-mindedness, an equality of perceptiveness and intelligence, in the conversational group. One of the earliest comprehensive definitions of raillery, by Richard Flecknoe, leaves no doubt as to its class basis: it 'differs from *Gybing*, as gentle smiles from scornfull laughter, and from rayling as Gentlemens playing at foyls, from Butchers and Clowns playing at Cudgels. Tis nothing bitter, but a poignant sauce of wit, for curious pallats, not for your vulgar Tasts.' Like jousts and tournaments, it is 'a sport onely for your nobler sort'; 'the common People' must be content to be mere railers, since they are 'much of the nature of those Beasts who cannot play, but they must fall to scratching and biting strait'.[1] Raillery, then, both excludes and unites. There can be real equality only among equals, since there must also be firm stratification if society is not to lapse into anarchy.

It is one of the functions of decorum to make communication between the strata of society as agreeable as possible, while never denying that the strata exist. The word 'decorum' therefore comprehends the sort of tactful good sense which adjusts words and deportment to the occasion, and to the status of the person who is being addressed:

> There is a certain Modesty, and becoming Decorum observ'd, in all the Words and Actions of a *Gentleman*, which evidence his good Breeding. He disposes all he does and says, in their just and proper Places, with a due Regard to, and Observation of all those Circumstances, the not observing whereof, makes our Civility unpracticable. He observes the Circumstances of Age and Condition, the Quality of the Person with whom he converses, the Time and the Place of his Conversation. To be defective in these things, renders humane Actions disagreeable and ungrateful, tho the Intentions be good and laudable.[2]

For a gentleman to practise decorum presupposes that he is keenly aware of social status. He will pay respect and deference (without servility) to his superiors, and towards his inferiors will show amiable condescension and courtesy. In Prior's opinion the ideal

---

[1] *Enigmaticall Characters* (1658), pp. 30–1.
[2] *A Discourse Concerning the Character of a Gentleman* (Edinburgh, 1716), pp. 10–11.

had been realized, once again, by the Earl of Dorset, whose 'Behavior was Easie and Courteous to all; but Distinguished and Adapted to each Man in particular, according to his Station and Quality.'[1]

Eighteenth-century *decorum* thus comes very close to what modern literary criticism, following Dr I. A. Richards, has learnt to call *tone*: the expression of the speaker's attitude to his listeners, the manifestation of his 'sense of how he stands towards those he is addressing'.[2] For many Augustan authors this awareness of, and adaptation to, their readers was fostered both by society's concern with good-breeding and by the study of rhetoric, with its detailed attention to the expectations and responses of a particular audience. It was also called into play by such essentially social forms of literature as the dialogue and the epistle. When an eighteenth-century author is talking upon paper he is rarely talking to himself. In Pope's Epistles and the more dramatic of his Satires we find extraordinarily delicate adjustments of the tone of voice to the 'Circumstances of Age and Condition, the Quality of the Person with whom he converses'. At the close of the *Epistle to Bolingbroke* (*Epistle I i*) that nobleman is rallied, with just a touch of audacity, on his shortcomings as Pope's mentor. But to Lord Burlington, on a more public occasion, Pope is respectfully polite, without being distant:

> You show us, Rome was glorious, not profuse,
> And pompous buildings once were things of Use.
> Yet shall (my Lord) your just, your noble rules
> Fill half the land with Imitating Fools. . . .
>
> (*To Burlington* 23–6)

The tone of the masterly third line is created partly by the placing of the politely deferential '(my Lord)', partly by the sequence 'your just, your noble rules'; the voice falls on 'noble' in such a way as to suggest that the poet is choosing his words of praise with due care, and to underline the pun (these architectural rules have been devised by a nobleman) which seasons the tribute with wit and prevents it from cloying.

---

[1] *Works*, vol. I, pp. 248–9.    [2] *Practical Criticism* (1929), p. 182.

Finally, the sense of *decorum* as adaptability can be extended so as to include the accommodating of ourselves to the interests and inclinations of our companions. According to Pierre d'Ortigue, to be able to 'insinuate your self into opposite humours', to chime in with another's mood, is a matter for congratulation: 'we may call that man happy, that has this suppleness of humour.' Ortigue himself possessed this faculty, though he was too modest to say so: 'He would assume any Character he had a mind to,' says his editor; 'he was a *Proteus*.'[1] An eighteenth-century Proteus will talk trivially to the trivial-minded, rationally to the philosophical, and 'can even condescend to Horses and Dogs with Country Gentlemen.'[2] Such a versatile man is the antithesis of the intractable pedant or dogmatic individualist. He is self-effacing and unassertive, his personality almost submerged. We have reached here an extreme to which social consideration for others can go, and it is improbable that anyone ever attained this degree of pliancy, unless for dubious ends. Nevertheless a consideration and respect for the feelings and opinions of other underlies many aspects of eighteenth-century life besides manners. The exterior of a Queen Anne or Georgian town-house is modest and not at all flamboyant, the points of interest on its façade confined to the door-way and fan-light, and to the wrought ironwork of lamp-holder and link-extinguisher. The house-front, harmonious in itself, is subdued to the larger harmony of the terrace or square.[3] And the gentleman will be unostentatious in death as in life; the typical eighteenth-century memorial tablet, with its reticence of statement and decoration, respects the neighbouring dead.

Among the assets of the adaptable man is his fund of general knowledge, a knowledge both of books and humankind. Some part of this he will acquire by wide experience–'he should be no Stranger

---

[1] *Art of Pleasing in Conversation*, vol. II, p. 39, and vol. I, p. xvi.
[2] Fielding, 'Essay on Conversation,' *Miscellanies*, vol. I, pp. 160–1.
[3] According to Sir John Summerson, the houses in Great Queen Street, Holborn, built in the late 1630s, 'were reputed, in the eighteenth century, to constitute "the first regular street in London". They laid down the canon of street design which put an end to gabled individualism. . . .': *Georgian London*, revised ed. (Harmondsworth, 1962), p. 34.

to Courts and to Camps'[1] – by travel, and by mixing in polite society. But he must also prepare himself for society by reading and study, by collecting his own thoughts, and (in his commonplace book) the best of other people's. 'If you would pass muster abroad, you must have a general Knowledge and Tast of Things; you must furnish out a little *Lab'ratory* in your Head, glean Occasional Intimations and Notions, and treasure up Materials for every Turn.'[2] Though a gentleman would not wish to speak by rote, at least he will have thought over the topics that are likely to occur in the best conversational circles. And so will a well-bred lady; Belisa, one of the characters in *The Art of Pleasing in Conversation*, remarks:

> I am now methinks qualified to speak of History, and of the most noted Historians: but my notions are not sufficiently clear concerning the nature of the Passions, of Vices and Virtues . . . a thing which is every moment talkt of in company. I don't want to be thorough mistress of it, but I shou'd be glad to be able to deliver my opinion upon it with some sort of exactness.[3]

The ideal is the universal man (and less commonly the universal woman), the man who is not a specialist in any one subject, but who has a smattering of many, always including the truly gentlemanly pursuits of painting, sculpture, architecture, and gardening. The Duchess of Marlborough, who was nothing if not critical, wrote after visiting her grandson-in-law, the third Duke of Bedford: 'He spoke on every subject that offered with perfect good sense, was as civil as anybody can be without being troublesome and in the most obliging manner, not pressing any point too far. . . .'[4] Widely rather than deeply read, modestly allusive rather than prone to uttering quotations, the gentleman wears his learning lightly. Prior observed of the Earl of Dorset that 'He perfected His Judgment by Reading and Digesting the best Authors, tho' He quoted Them very seldom'.[5] Sir William Temple's *Essays* were deservedly popular as models both

---

[1] *The Guardian*, no. 34.
[2] Samuel Parker, *Sylva. Familiar Letters upon Occasional Subjects* (1701), p. 73.
[3] Vol. II, pp. 149–51; cf. p. 223.
[4] Gladys Scott Thomson, *Letters of a Grandmother, 1732–1735* (1943), pp. 33–4.
[5] *Works*, vol. I, p. 249.

for prose style and for a 'Gentleman-like Use of Learning in Conversation'.[1]

Pope, in his role of urbane gentleman, appears to carry his learning as easily as any. The *Epistle to Burlington* alludes to familiar items of classical mythology, and refers explicitly to two well-known works of modern literature, *Gulliver's Travels* and *Don Quixote*, works which also happily suggest that Pope's *Epistle* keeps the best satirical company. An esoteric poet would be an impolite poet, and one who forfeited the right to censure the extravagances of tasteless prodigals. So the *Epistle*'s essential vocabulary of landscape-gardening and the visual arts is kept to a minimum, and is never allowed to become too technical. Artists' names are not arrogantly paraded:

> On painted Cielings you devoutly stare,
> Where sprawl the Saints of Verrio or Laguerre. . . .

Professor Tillotson has alerted us to Pope's subtleties with the innocent-seeming word 'or'.[2] Here its function is to imply that Pope is too much the modest amateur to be able to differentiate between these very similar artists; not that it greatly matters, for each of these painters, Pope also implies, is as vulgar as the other. When the poet conducts us on our inspection of Timon's study he warns us that

> For Locke or Milton 'tis in vain to look,
> These shelves admit not any modern book.

Here the 'or' simply intensifies the hopelessness of the search; neither writer will be found. Milton and Locke are modern classics, standard reading for gentlemen. They are much praised and quoted in the *Spectator*, and Pope's imaginary companion looks for them on the shelves as evidence that Timon is as well-bred as himself. If Timon is indifferent to such authors, the Dunces are actively hostile. Elkanah Settle reminds his 'sons' that

> 'Tis yours, a Bacon or a Locke to blame,
> A Newton's genius, or a Milton's flame.
> (*Dunciad* III 215–16)

---

[1] Constable, *Conversation of Gentlemen*, p. 51.
[2] Geoffrey Tillotson, *On the Poetry of Pope*, 2nd ed. (Oxford, 1950), pp. 150–1.

Bentley had mutilated Milton in his edition of 1732. The Heads of Houses at Oxford, scholars still committed to the outworn disputatious logic of Aristotle, had met in 1703 'to censure Mr Locke's Essay on Human Understanding, and to forbid the reading it'.[1] For Pope there was nothing to choose between this short-sighted bigotry and the happy ignorance of the inhabitants of Grubstreet, men like the poetaster James Ralph, who 'was wholly illiterate, and knew no Language not even *French*: Being advised to read the Rules of Dramatick Poetry before he began a Play, he smiled and reply'd, *Shakespear writ without Rules.*'[2]

Pope's ideal critic is an ideal gentleman: 'tho' Learn'd, well-bred', one whose politeness prevents his erudition from degenerating into pedantry. More important still, he is candid and truthful: 'and tho' well-bred, sincere'.[3] The poet's awareness of the possible discrepancy between exterior breeding and inner worth (conveyed with characteristic economy by the single word 'though') finds a parallel in the distinction frequently made at the end of the seventeenth century between good breeding and good nature. The negative function of the former needs to be balanced and supplemented by the positive energies of the latter. Sir William Temple observes succinctly:

> Good Nature is seen in a Disposition to say and do, what one thinks will please or profit others.
> Good Breeding in doing nothing one thinks will either hurt or displease them.[4]

This formulation marks a new and important stage in the development of the idea of the gentleman. Benevolence and the Christian virtues are beginning to displace the nonchalant self-sufficiency that

---

[1] Pope's note on *Dunciad* IV 196: 'Each fierce Logician, still expelling Locke'.
[2] Note on *Dunciad* (A) III 159.
[3] *Essay on Criticism* 635.
[4] 'Heads, designed for an Essay on Conversation', *Works* (1720), vol. I, p. 313. These notes were first published by Swift, in Temple's *Miscellanea*, Part III (1701), pp. 317–36.

was preached and practised in the Renaissance. The gentleman's conduct must now be judged by the qualities of character it reveals, not by its courtly trappings. The distinction which Temple so neatly states was especially convenient for the satirist and the reformer, a useful way of emphasizing that Restoration gentlemen and fine ladies, though conventionally well-bred, were not always well-disposed. Pope concedes that Belinda is perfectly ladylike in her handling of her male admirers:

> Favours to none, to all she Smiles extends,
> Oft she rejects, but never once offends.
> *(Rape of the Lock* II 11–12)

There is no doubt that the unoffending Belinda is, by Temple's definition, well-bred; but the rather formally 'extended' smiles scarcely amount to his complementary 'Disposition to . . . please or profit others'. Nor does anything that could be definitely called good nature emerge from the rest of her portrait:

> Yet graceful Ease, and Sweetness void of Pride,
> Might hide her Faults, if *Belles* had Faults to hide:
> If to her share some Female Errors fall,
> Look on her Face, and you'll forget 'em all.

Pope's basic criticism of Belinda's world is that in its vanity and self-satisfaction it is too little concerned for other people; complacency is the enemy of good nature. Thalestris, who embodies the values of this world in their most angular and aggressive form, incites the heroine to vengeance by conjuring up a fearful vision of social ruin:

> Methinks already I your Tears survey,
> Already hear the horrid things they say,
> Already see you a degraded Toast,
> And all your Honour in a Whisper lost!
> How shall I, then, your helpless Fame defend?
> 'Twill then be Infamy to seem your Friend!
> (IV 107–12)

At that last satirical touch the surface of the polite world disintegrates.

[ 53 ]

The forms and ornaments of good breeding are obviously of little worth unless they are the outward tokens of inner good nature. 'Becomingness' must be grounded in 'Honesty'. Steele points out that the man who can be considered perfectly qualified for good company is one 'in whom a general good Will to Mankind takes off the Necessity of Caution and Circumspection'.[1] One of the clearest indications of a gentleman's goodwill to mankind is his affability or 'ease of access', a sweetness of disposition that goes beyond mere courtesy and is the very opposite of haughtiness. Affability creates 'a hope in those who speak to us, that they may easily approach us, and speak what and as oft as they please.'[2] The tone of the *Epistle to Burlington* suggests that this noble Lord must be affable to Pope, who can address him in so relaxed a way, engaging him in conversation as an intellectual equal, if not quite as a social one. Timon, however, is unapproachable:

> My Lord advances with majestic mien,
> Smit with the mighty pleasure, to be seen:
> But soft – by regular approach – not yet –
> First thro' the length of yon hot Terrace sweat,
> And when up ten steep slopes you've dragg'd your thighs,
> Just at his Study-door he'll bless your eyes.

Timon has sacrificed the ease of his visitors to his autocratic demand for a 'regular approach' to his presence. The 'ill judged and inconvenient' linking of house and garden (as Pope calls it in his note on this passage) is contrived to produce the sort of frustrating formality that the proud but basically insecure man requires, and the affable man will dispense with. Timon is all for ceremony. His dinner is 'a solemn Sacrifice, perform'd in state'; his guests eat to the accompaniment of ringing salvers, in a 'Temple' of a dining-room. What passes for politeness in his Villa is the negation of true civility, which seeks to promote the ease of the company, and of true complaisance, which 'smooths Distinction, sweetens Conversation, and makes every one in the Company pleased with himself'.[3] His lavish hospitality is

---

[1] *The Tatler*, no. 45.  [2] S. C., *The Art of Complaisance* (1673), p. 36.
[3] *The Guardian*, no. 162.

a display of 'civil Pride' – a contradiction in terms as flagrantly absurd as serving one's guest with the food he most dislikes:

> In plenty starving, tantaliz'd in state,
> And complaisantly help'd to all I hate,
> Treated, caress'd, and tir'd, I take my leave,
> Sick of his civil Pride from Morn to Eve.

Timon stands civility on its head. Here, to our amusement, even the poet is infected by the prevailing topsy-turvydom. For the story of Tantalus ('tantaliz'd in state'), and the particular phrase 'starving in plenty', were regularly used to describe the pitiful condition of the avaricious man surrounded by his money-bags.[1] The gentleman-poet finds himself degraded to the status of an anti-social miser. With Timon everything is out of place. The religious atmosphere appropriate to the Chapel stiflingly pervades the dining-room, while the Chapel itself is an annexe of the salon. The Brobdingnagian scale of the establishment reduces Timon to the stature of a puny insect, and thus breaks *decorum* in a strictly architectural sense of that word: 'the keeping of a due Respect between the *Inhabitant* and the *Habitation*'.[2] In Timon's garden 'the suff'ring eye inverted Nature sees'; those gentlemen who follow Nature suffer in sympathy with her at the sight of trees clipped into sculpted shapes, while the genuine statues, instead of being artistically disposed, are massed in plantations. The true gentleman has good taste, while Timon, with his squirting Cupids, sprawling Saints, and spewing Tritons, is ostentatiously vulgar.

The *Epistle to Burlington* insists that a lack of taste is consequent upon a lack of sense. The poem is indeed rather over-explicit on this point, especially in the passage about Sense being more needful than Expense (lines 39–46). Such a plain statement, put into Lord Burlington's mouth, seems superfluous after the sardonic account of the

---

[1] 'Perhaps the story of *Tantalus* was invented solely to paint the nature of a covetous person, who starves amidst plenty, like *Tantalus* in the midst of water': *The Odyssey of Homer*, trans. Pope, Fenton, and Broome (1725–6), Book XI, note to line 709. See also Cowley, 'Of Avarice', *Essays*, pp. 436–42.

[2] 'T.N.' [Richard Neve], *The City and Countrey Purchaser, and Builder's Dictionary* (1703), p. 126; Neve is explaining what Vitruvius meant by *decor*.

Fools who slavishly follow his designs, even to the detriment of their health:

> Or call the winds thro' long Arcades to roar,
> Proud to catch cold at a Venetian door;
> Conscious they act a true Palladian part,
> And if they starve, they starve by rules of art.

Here is architectural senselessness in full spate. Its horticultural counterpart is Timon's ingenious siting of his lake on the wrong side of the house, so as to improve 'the keenness of the Northern wind', and Benjamin Styles's decision to expose his home to all weathers by cutting 'wide views thro' Mountains to the Plain'.[1] The gentleman does not commit such blunders, because he is careful to 'consult the Genius of the Place in all'. Thus, in his building and planting he is directed by the same principle that guides him in his social affairs, where he consults the 'genius', the distinctive quality and condition, of each of his friends and associates. To observe decorum is much the same thing as to follow Nature. Moreover, this sort of accommodatingness and adaptability, based on a keen regard for the total environment, may also be properly designated as Good Sense, which is defined by Dr Johnson as 'a prompt and intuitive perception of consonance and propriety.'[2] So having advised us to consult the Genius of the place Pope proceeds, almost tautologically:

> Still follow Sense, of ev'ry Art the Soul,
> Parts answ'ring parts shall slide into a whole,
> Spontaneous beauties all around advance,
> Start ev'n from Difficulty, strike from Chance;
> Nature shall join you, Time shall make it grow
> A Work to wonder at – perhaps a STOW.

And the joint appeal to Sense and Nature is capped by a concise statement of the principle of decorum:

> Ev'n in an ornament its place remark,
> Nor in an Hermitage set Dr. Clarke.

---

[1] Lines 75–6; see Pope's note on this couplet and the annotation in the Twickenham Edition, vol. III (ii), p. 144.
[2] 'Life of Pope', *Lives of the Poets*, vol. III, p. 216.

The rallying-cries of any age will tend to overlap to the point of synonymity, and in the early eighteenth century Sense and Nature are often scarcely distinguishable from one another. Two examples from the *Tatler* may suffice: 'Senecio', the type of the good-natured old man, 'never converses but with Followers of Nature and good Sense'; and one of the characters in a dialogue on duelling humorously remarks, 'I am of Opinion . . . that Fashion governs a very Pretty Fellow; Nature, or common Sense, your ordinary Persons, and sometimes Men of fine Parts.'[1] Terms as interchangeable as these are in some danger of being emptied of their meaning. Pope has succeeded, I think, in giving them weight and substance (and what better place than a poem on architecture and gardening to achieve such solidity?) by pointing to specific examples of senselessness and impropriety, and by indicating, more positively, how Nature should be respected:

> But treat the Goddess like a modest fair,
> Nor over-dress, nor leave her wholly bare.

Sense and Nature usher in yet another of the presiding deities, Moderation.

Just as true good breeding must be rooted in good nature, so taste must have a foundation deeper than sense, a foundation of morality. Pope believed that in his choice of pictures, prints and other ornaments 'a Man not only shews his Taste but his Virtue'.[2] Or, in the case of Timon and his like, his want of Virtue. The prodigal, at the beginning of the *Epistle to Burlington*, buys 'Statues, dirty Gods, and Coins'; he accepts the dirt as a guarantee of antiquity (though it is probably faked), but the gods may well be 'dirty' because their poses are indecent. A man who makes his money in wicked ways will dispose of it in foolish ones. Sir Visto succumbs to a demonic whisper – ' "Visto! have a Taste!" ' – and squanders his 'ill got wealth'. And Bubo's descent into vulgarity is a punishment for his 'aukward pride', a disagreeable combination of social and moral failings. These examples cluster at the opening of the

---

[1] Nos. 45 and 39.
[2] Letter to Ralph Allen, 30 April 1736, *Correspondence*, vol. IV, p. 13.

*Epistle*, but it is in the description of Timon's Chapel that Pope makes his unanswerable charges against the tastelessness which betrays moral inadequacy. There the silver bell summons us, in the most consummate piece of self-contradiction, 'to all the Pride of Pray'r'; the 'light quirks of Musick' are superbly improper, and the painted ceilings depict a very doubtful sort of Paradise, where the sprawling Saints display their charms:

> On gilded clouds in fair expansion lie,
> And bring all Paradise before your eye.
> To rest, the Cushion and soft Dean invite,
> Who never mentions Hell to ears polite.

Timon, then, does not merely offend against aesthetic canons, for the environment he has created for himself is an expression of his pride, and panders to sloth and lasciviousness. Hence the climax of the visit, the final intolerable insult, takes place in the dining-room, where ease, geniality and fellowship should reign. The episode of Timon's 'solemn Sacrifice' is a brief variation on the theme of the uncomfortable dinner-party, and Pope's allusion to a familiar satirical situation reinforces his point that more is at stake here than the False Taste of an English Timon.[1] Such a dinner-party is a travesty of genuine hospitality and an affront to human dignity, since it strikes at all the social values which are enshrined in the act of feasting together. Timon's dinner represents primarily a failure in human relations, and only secondarily a failure in taste. He conflates the two chronologically distinct aspects of his Athenian namesake, being at one and the same time lavishly ostentatious (' "What sums are thrown away!" ') and harshly misanthropic: 'What his hard Heart denies,/His charitable Vanity supplies'. It is fitting that Timon should disappear from the poem in this rather sumptuous oxymoron, 'charitable Vanity'. For by a final irony, which goes a little way towards setting his moral world upright again, his self-centred magnificence is discovered to be providentially directed to good and positive ends. His ostentation 'supplies' a means of livelihood to a household

---

[1] See Horace, Satire II viii; Juvenal, Satire v; Boileau, Satire iii, and Rochester's 'Timon, a Satyr' (based on Boileau).

of musicians, servants and labourers: 'Yet hence the Poor are cloath'd, the Hungry fed.'

Cicero believed that the rich man is entitled to aim at Magnificence. His house should be an adequately 'pompous' indication of his wealth, but its size is finally justified only because the privilege of wealth brings with it a duty to society: 'he must keep up the Laws of Hospitality, and entertain Multitudes of all sorts of Persons. . . . For a fine and large House that gives Entertainment to no Body, serves but to reproach and upbraid its Owner.'[1] Timon's hospitality is not worthy of the name. His Villa is a showpiece and nothing more, whereas the true landowner is mindful of his local and national obligations. The man 'who plants like BATHURST . . . makes his Neighbours glad, if he encrease';[2] these neighbours who are pleased at his prosperity are, we presume, other landlords and gentlemen-farmers, his social equals. Meanwhile his social inferiors, the 'chearful Tenants' of his farms, rest contented in their humbler sphere and 'bless their yearly toil'. Pope's exemplary noblemen are leavening agents; they diffuse happiness. Having begun by considering Lord Bathurst in relation to his social equals and inferiors, the poet deliberately completes the pattern by showing Lord Burlington enjoying the esteem of his royal masters. So Burlington achieves both the professional and the social triumphs of his most illustrious architectural predecessors, especially the triumphs of Vitruvius, who had found an imperial patron for his treatises on architecture in Augustus Caesar:[3]

> You too proceed! make falling Arts your care,
> Erect new wonders, and the old repair,
> Jones and Palladio to themselves restore,
> And be whate'er Vitruvius was before:
> Till Kings call forth th' Idea's of your mind,
> Proud to accomplish what such hands design'd,
> Bid Harbors open, public Ways extend,
> Bid Temples, worthier of the God, ascend;
> Bid the broad Arch the dang'rous Flood contain,
> The Mole projected break the roaring Main;

---

[1] *Tully's Offices*, trans. Cockman, p. 101 (Book I xxxix).
[2] *Epistle to Burlington* 178ff.
[3] Robert Morris, *An Essay in Defence of Ancient Architecture* (1728), p. viii.

Back to his bounds their subject Sea command,
And roll obedient Rivers thro' the Land;
These Honours, Peace to happy Britain brings,
These are Imperial Works, and worthy Kings.

Pope's own lengthy annotation of this passage brings out its satirical undertones. Burlington's Temples will be 'worthier' than some of the recently erected Churches, whose foundations had proved to be insecurely laid. Many public ways 'were hardly passable, and most of those which were repaired by Turnpikes were made jobs for private lucre, and infamously executed, even to the entrances of London itself.' But with Burlington presiding over the programme of civic works, there is no cause for undue pessimism. He will re-create the splendours of Renaissance Italy, and re-establish the English neo-classicism of Inigo Jones. He will inaugurate an architectural revival comparable with that in Rome at the time of Augustus, a revival embracing both the beautiful and the useful, both temples and highways. Pope's address to Burlington appropriately echoes similar accounts of Roman greatness by Horace and Virgil; first (though here Pope has completely reversed the mood of the original) Horace's brief catalogue of public works:

> debemur morti nos nostraque: sive receptus
> terra Neptunus classes Aquilonibus arcet,
> regis opus, sterilisve palus diu aptaque remis
> vicinas urbes alit et grave sentit aratrum,
> seu cursum mutavit iniquum frugibus amnis
> doctus iter melius.[1]

The second and more famous passage is the prophecy of Anchises in Book VI of the *Æneid*. Dryden's translation of Anchises's speech concludes: 'These are Imperial Arts, and worthy thee'; by appropriating this line Pope in his turn prophesies that Hanoverian England

---

[1] *Ars Poetica* 63–8: 'We are doomed to death – we and all things ours; whether Neptune, welcomed within the land, protects our fleets from northern gales – a truly royal work – or a marsh, long a waste where oars were plied, feeds neighbouring towns and feels the weight of the plough; or a river has changed the course which brought ruin to corn-fields and has learnt a better path.' Horace is referring to the building of the Julian Harbour on the Campanian Coast, the draining of the Pomptine marshes, and the straightening of the course of the Tiber to prevent floods. I am indebted to Professor Norman Callan for drawing my attention to this Horatian parallel.

will become the true descendant of Augustan Rome. His vision is dominated by a classical sense of control; natural forces are held in check, 'contained', made 'obedient' in the service of agriculture and navigation. It is a vision, too, of an inclusive and firmly-established hierarchy, yet a hierarchy suffused with movement; the sea roars dangerously in the background while man extends his rule over the material kingdom and raises new and worthier temples to God. Energy and order coexist.

The *Epistle to Burlington*, published in December 1731, was the first of Pope's major Epistles, and preceded all the extant *Imitations of Horace*. The patriotic confidence of its concluding lines looks back to *Windsor-Forest*, and will not appear in Pope's work again. He is as ready to identify himself with 'happy Britain' as he had been in the earlier poem, where English oaks rush into the floods, where *'Augusta*'s glitt'ring Spires increase', and villas rise on the banks of the Thames. But in 1713, with a Tory Government in office, the political scene was far more congenial to Pope than in 1731, when it was dominated by Walpole's seemingly impregnable administration. Pope's rather unexpected nationalism in the *Epistle* was perhaps something of a concession to Lord Burlington's Whiggish sympathies. Two years after the poem was published he joined the Opposition over the Excise question, but at the time of its composition political honours were still being conferred on him by George II, no doubt in order to persuade him to remain politically faithful to the Court. More important, the Palladian movement itself, of which Burlington had now become leader, was particularly associated with the Whig oligarchs, and (an important factor in its success) was strongly patriotic in feeling. As Sir John Summerson has reminded us, its initial intention 'was not so much to celebrate Palladio as Inigo Jones and the movement was, in its earliest years, quite specifically an Inigo Jones cult'.[1] Among the decaying works of art which Burlington and Kent restored were two important buildings by Jones, the Barber-Surgeons' Hall, and St. Paul's, Covent Garden. Finally,

[1] 'The Classical Country House in 18th-Century England', *Journal of the Royal Society of Arts*, vol. CVII (1959), pp. 549-50. See also the account of William Benson's house at Wilbury Park, Wiltshire, in Christopher Hussey, *English Country Houses: Early Georgian, 1715-1760*, 2nd ed. (1965), pp. 121-5.

in spite of his reservations about the new churches and turnpikes Pope's tone reveals that he largely shares the optimistic and expansive spirit of the 1720s. He is looking forward to yet more of the very considerable activity that this decade had already seen: substantial development of the inland waterway system, plans for extending road communications, and heavy investments in land improvement schemes. Defoe's *Tour Thro' the Whole Island of Great Britain* (1724–7) is a sustained tribute to the new buoyancy and energy, though even Defoe experienced some difficulty in keeping pace with developments. In the Preface to the third volume of the *Tour* he lists the most important buildings, public and private, that have appeared 'in and about *London*' during the past year; they include 'Mr *Guy*'s Hospital in *Southwark* . . . several new Steeples and Churches', and 'a little City of Buildings, Streets and Squares . . . at the West End of *Hanover* and *Cavendish* Square . . . . If all these Additions are to be found in the small Interval between the publishing the second Volume and this of the third, and that in so narrow a Compass, what may not every subsequent Year produce?'[1] For once, Pope and Defoe share the same attitude.

It is true that since 1713 and *Windsor-Forest* Pope had seen with horror how the mounting rubbish of Grubstreet threatened to overwhelm England's literary culture. But in the realms of architecture and gardening it seemed to Pope that Burlington's prestige and Bathurst's plantations constituted very impressive bulwarks against the pride and show of a Timon, so that the poet could be less fearful about this part of the national scene. According to *Windsor-Forest* the miseries of the Civil War and the rigours of William III had been dispelled by a bounteous Queen Anne, bestowing on her country the 'Blessings of a peaceful Reign'. In the *Epistle to Burlington*, similarly, the aberration of Timon's Villa is seen merely as an interlude; the insult which he offers to Nature will be avenged, and 'laughing Ceres' will 're-assume the land'. The future is secure in the hands of the gentleman-builder and the gentleman-farmer, while their virtues and achievements are chronicled by their fellow triumvir, the gentleman-poet.

---

[1] *Tour*, ed. G. D. H. Cole (1927), vol. II, pp. 535–6.

# CHAPTER FOUR

# Rural Virtue

*Windsor-Forest* ends with a vision of '*Albion*'s Golden Days', a new era of peace and prosperity. In the *Epistle to Burlington*, too, peace will bring both architectural and agricultural blessings to a happy Britain, when such absurdities as Timon's Villa and gardens are no more:

> Another age shall see the golden Ear
> Imbrown the Slope, and nod on the Parterre,
> Deep Harvests bury all his pride has plann'd,
> And laughing Ceres re-assume the land.

We recognize here the familiar attributes of the idyllic Golden Age: luxuriant crops and abundant harvests; the absence (in this case the obliteration) of proud, ambitious, and selfish passions; and a prevalent joyousness. The golden ears of corn represent substantial riches, unlike the tawdry splendours of Timon's buffet or the 'gilded clouds' of his chapel ceiling. With their assured dignity Pope's lines convey the full triumph of Nature's restoration. But it is a triumph in which Art also joins. Ceres is the goddess both of natural growth and of cultivation, and here gives her blessing to a new attitude towards the English landscape, and to a new conception of the English garden. For the progression from parterre to wheatfield, the submergence of Timon's barren symmetries beneath useful cultivation, brilliantly summarizes the evolution of garden design during Pope's lifetime. In that evolution Pope had a not inconsiderable share, as satirist of the clichés of formalism, as advocate and exponent of subtler principles of garden planning, and as consultant to his aristocratic friends and neighbours. The confident tone of these four evocative lines owes something to the poet's own participation in the change of taste he describes.

During the seventeenth century the garden was treated architecturally and sculpturally, so that garden and house together made a joint assertion of the desirability of discipline and the value of Reason and Order. Trees and shrubs were clipped to statues. Walls of hornbeam or trimmed yew were provided with niches to be filled with busts and terms. The intricacies of the *parterre de broderie*, a garden plot in which scroll patterns were marked out in yellow sand, red tile-dust, and black filings, mirrored the figurations of the carpets within. From inside the house the view was of a scene as civilized and almost as intimate as the drawing-room itself. The intimacy was secured in part by the inescapable presence of the boundary wall, making the formal garden seem an extension of the living accommodation of the house; in part by the remoter presence, beyond that wall, of the wilder parts of the gentleman's estate. The formal garden was a well-ordered haven of tranquillity.

Sir William Temple, writing in 1685, remarks that among the English 'the Beauty of Building and Planting is placed chiefly in some certain Proportions, Symmetries or Uniformities; our Walks and our Trees ranged so, as to answer one another, and at exact Distances.'[1] Timon, in whose garden grove nods at grove, is fifty years behind the times. For Temple is already hinting at other and richer possibilities. Having praised Moor Park, Hertfordshire, as the perfection of the regular garden (it was the model for his own Moor Park in Surrey), he admits that a wholly irregular garden 'may, for ought I know, have more Beauty than any of the others'; there follows Temple's famous observation about Chinese gardens, where a harmonious effect is obtained by unobtrusive subtleties of contrast and balance. Coming nearer home, he notes that in the temperate parts of France and the Netherlands, 'where I take Gardening to be at its greatest Height', the gardens are more spacious than in England and can afford to have 'some Parts Wild, some Exact'.[2]

---

[1] 'Upon the Gardens of Epicurus,' *Works* (1720), vol. I, p. 186.
[2] Ibid., p. 181.

The French delighted in the utmost intricacies of the parterre. They contrived porticoes and colonnades of clipped and trained elms, and boasted that their art had 'abundantly out-done Nature'.[1] But it was the French, too, who admitted some irregularity (usually in distant corners of their gardens), who allowed an occasional path to wind sinuously, and began to open the prospect by abolishing the boundary wall. At Versailles André Le Nôtre sent avenues out to the horizon, and proclaimed the magnificence and conspicuous waste of Louis XIV.

An extensive prospect is not merely a gratifying token of social status and political power; it also helps to create what Addison called the Pleasures of the Imagination. In order that the sense of sight may be fully satisfied the eye must be at liberty: 'in the wide Fields of Nature, the Sight wanders up and down without Confinement, and is fed with an infinite variety of Images, without any certain Stint or Number.' This argument leads Addison to give the same preference to Continental gardens as was given by Temple, and for the same reasons, their spaciousness and 'wildness': 'our *English* Gardens are not so entertaining to the Fancy as those in *France* and *Italy*, where we see a large Extent of Ground covered over with an agreeable mixture of Garden and Forest, which represent every where an artificial Rudeness, much more charming than the Neatness and Elegancy which we meet with in those of our own Country.' The English gardener is circumscribed; it is impracticable 'to alienate so much Ground from Pasturage, and the Plow, in many Parts of a Country that is so well peopled, and cultivated to a far greater Advantage'.[2] Addison's happy solution is to turn English cultivation to a greater advantage still. As he perceives, the farmer is, all unintentionally, an artist: 'The Husband-man . . . is employed in laying out the whole Country into a kind of Garden or Landskip, and making every thing smile about him, whilst in reality he thinks of nothing but of the Harvest, and Encrease which is to arise from it.' The husbandman, therefore, instinctively follows Nature, whose

---

[1] Louis Liger, *The Retir'd Gardener*, trans. George London and Henry Wise, 2nd ed., revised Joseph Carpenter (1717), p. 406.
[2] *The Spectator*, no. 414.

'Works . . . are at the same time both useful and entertaining.'[1]
This in turn makes him (again unwittingly) a candidate for the
highest artistic honours: 'omne tulit punctum qui miscuit utile
dulci.'[2] It is an easy step to suggest that the ideal English gardener
will be a rather more self-conscious and artful husbandman, and
will undoubtedly also qualify for Horace's esteem. To meet the objection that England cannot accommodate lavish pleasure-grounds
Addison rhetorically enquires:

> But why may not a whole Estate be thrown into a kind of Garden by
> frequent Plantations, that may turn as much to the Profit, as the
> Pleasure of the Owner? A Marsh overgrown with Willows, or a
> Mountain shaded with Oaks, are not only more beautiful, but more
> beneficial, than when they lie bare and unadorned. Fields of Corn
> make a pleasant Prospect, and if the Walks were a little taken care of
> that lie between them, if the natural Embroidery of the Meadows were
> helpt and improved by some small Additions of Art, and the several
> Rows of Hedges set off by Trees and Flowers, that the Soil was
> capable of receiving, a Man might make a pretty Landskip of his own
> Possessions.[3]

Use and Beauty (Pope's synonyms for the Addisonian Profit and
Pleasure) can gain no admittance to the pompous and arid symmetries of Timon's gardens. They must look elsewhere:

> Who then shall grace, or who improve the Soil?
> Who plants like BATHURST, or who builds like BOYLE.
> 'Tis Use alone that sanctifies Expence,
> And Splendour borrows all her rays from Sense.
>
> (*To Burlington* 177–80)

Pope remarks that the 'ample Lawns' of such landed men as Lord
Bathurst 'are not asham'd to feed/The milky heifer and deserving
steed', while their woodlands, though richly beautiful and giving
profitable shade, are destined to a more public and exalted end:

> Whose rising Forests, not for pride or show,
> But future Buildings, future Navies grow:

---

[1] *The Spectator*, no. 387.
[2] Horace, *Ars Poetica* 343: 'He has won every vote who has blended profit and pleasure.'
[3] *The Spectator*, no. 414.

Let his plantations stretch from down to down,
First shade a Country, and then raise a Town.

The mark of the good poem, according to Horace, is that it simultaneously delights and instructs its reader. To the making of such a poem both Nature and Art must contribute:

Natura fieret laudabile carmen an arte,
quaesitum est: ego nec studium sine divite vena,
nec rude quid prosit video ingenium: alterius sic
altera poscit opem res et coniurat amice.[1]

The eighteenth century paid far more than lip-service to Horatian rules, and was more than willing to mould its landscape as well as its poetry under their guidance. Addison takes the last part of this passage as the motto of his *Spectator* paper on gardening, for he believes that the garden designer, who is concerned with Nature in an even more direct and immediate way than the poet, must carefully reconcile the claims of Art and Nature if he is to create something at once pleasurable and profitable. And so must the architect of country houses:

To build, to plant, whatever you intend,
To rear the Column, or the Arch to bend,
To swell the Terras, or to sink the Grot;
In all, let Nature never be forgot.

(*To Burlington* 47-50)

Pope's own poetic art, like the skill of the landscape-gardener, draws no attention to itself. Here, with delicate fancifulness, he portrays the architect raising a column as if he were rearing a young shoot, and bending the curves of an archway as if he were training the branches of a fruit-tree. Architecture is as 'natural' an activity as gardening; its columns and curves 'follow' and imitate those of Nature. So the golden rule for builder and planter is the same:

Consult the Genius of the Place in all;
That tells the Waters or to rise, or fall,

---

[1] *Ars Poetica* 408-11: 'Often it is asked whether a praiseworthy poem be due to Nature or to art. For my part, I do not see of what avail is either study, when not enriched by Nature's vein, or native wit, if untrained; so truly does each claim the other's aid, and make with it a friendly league.'

Or helps th'ambitious Hill the heav'n to scale,
Or scoops in circling theatres the Vale,
Calls in the Country, catches opening glades,
Joins willing woods, and varies shades from shades,
Now breaks or now directs, th'intending Lines;
Paints as you plant, and, as you work, designs.

The gentleman-gardener, who plants and prepares the ground-work, has virtually exchanged roles with the Genius of the place, who presides over the general design, 'calls in' the adjacent country, and, priest-like, 'joins willing woods' in a ceremony of marriage.[1] The result of such perfect co-operation can be stated briefly:

Nature shall join you, Time shall make it grow
A work to wonder at – perhaps a STOW.

The ideal has been successfully realized in Lord Cobham's gardens at Stowe, as laid out by Charles Bridgeman.

Under the leadership of Bridgeman, Stephen Switzer, and William Kent, garden planning in the 1720s and '30s moved towards a satisfying synthesis of Beauty and Use, of Art and Nature. Some formal design was still customary near the house itself, but it was a formality much subdued and simplified. Elaborate topiary work was discredited, thanks in part to Pope's satirical essay in the *Guardian*, where such verdant sculpture is gaily shown to be neither natural nor sensible, since it is so costly to maintain. Pope's catalogue of tonsured greens includes 'a Quick-set Hog shot up into a Porcupine, by its being forgot a Week in rainy Weather'.[2] In the poet's own garden at Twickenham no trees were cut to statues, the central area was occupied by a smooth lawn, and paths wound through the outlying parts. But art was still much in evidence; 'mounts' were constructed to provide agreeable prospects and variety of contour, and regularly planted, but not quite symmetrically balanced, groves of trees flanked the emphatic central axis (Plate I). Judged by the excessively naturalistic standards of the later eighteenth century, Twickenham,

---

[1] Warburton, in a perceptive note on this passage, pointed out the implications of 'joins willing woods': *Works*, vol. III, pp. 273–4.
[2] *The Guardian*, no. 173.

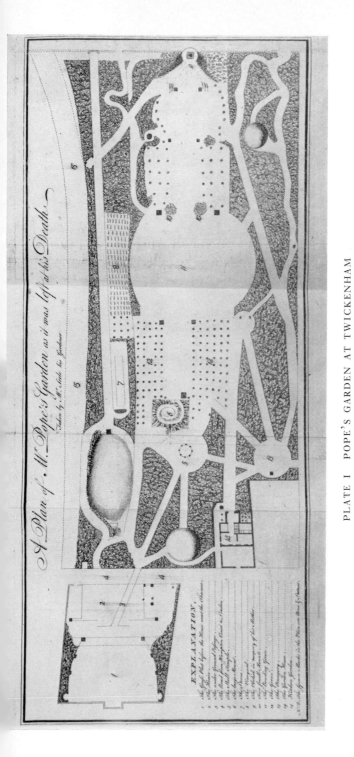

PLATE I   POPE'S GARDEN AT TWICKENHAM

The most important features of the layout are the underground passage (3), the shell temple (5), the large mount (6), the obelisk to the memory of the poet's mother (9), two small mounts (10), the bowling green (11) and grove (12).

Bridgeman's Stowe, even Kent's garden for General Dormer at Rousham, Oxfordshire, all appear conservative. In fact these gardeners have already travelled a long way from those earlier symmetries and artificialities which 'abundantly out-did Nature'. French designers, for example, consistently held that the garden area nearest the house should be laid out in rich, embroidered parterres, while the simple grass plot, the meanest and plainest of the several types of parterre, should be reserved for more remote spaces. At Rousham, however, Kent chose to site a bowling-green immediately North of the house, where it serves, with the minimum of formality, as a terrace overlooking the River Cherwell and the pastoral scene in the meadows beyond.

Here, at Rousham, the line of demarcation between garden and farmland is unobtrusive; but as Switzer justly observed, a river or stream 'can't always be had'. More amenable is the sunk fence, a device that was introduced to England in the same year (1712) as Addison's papers on the Imagination, in the course of a translation of a French gardening treatise:

> Grills of Iron are very necessary Ornaments in the Lines of Walks, to extend the View, and to shew the Country to Advantage. At present we frequently make Thorough-Views, call'd *Ah, Ah*, which are Openings in the Walls, without Grills, to the very Level of the Walks, with a large and deep Ditch at the Foot of them, lined on both Sides to sustain the Earth, and prevent the getting over, which surprizes the Eye upon coming near it, and makes one cry, *Ah! Ah!* from whence it takes its Name. This Sort of Opening is, on some Occasions, to be preferred, for that it does not shut up the Prospect, as the Bars of a Grill do.[1]

The ha-ha, as it came more conveniently to be called, was adapted from the art of fortification. As this quotation implies, it was used somewhat cautiously by French gardeners to extend the view at the ends of alleys and walks, the remainder of the garden being still cut off from the surrounding country by high walls. Its possibilities would seem to have been first realized by Bridgeman, in whose hands

---

[1] A.-J. Dezallier d'Argenville, *The Theory and Practice of Gardening*, trans. John James (1712), p. 77.

it became the major technical device for opening the prospect. By 1724 he had used the ha-ha in the gardens of Houghton, and, very freely, at Stowe. Since the sunk fence 'conceals the Bounds' of an estate,[1] it liberates the eye and promotes the pleasures of the visual imagination. And by masking the dividing line between garden and open parkland or pasture the ha-ha also implements Addison's scheme of throwing the whole estate into a kind of garden. Meadows and coppices, with a little trimming and modelling, can be absorbed into a total picturesque design, and a man, as Addison suggested, can 'make a pretty Landskip of his own Possessions'. The ha-ha is another manifestation of the Augustan talent for creative compromise. The opened prospect is beautiful because it includes the useful parts of the estate, its woodlands and cornfields. At the same time Nature, in the shape of the milky heifer and deserving steed, is kept at an unembarrassing distance by the concealed Art of the sunk fence.

The River Cherwell is not merely an important pictorial element in the composition of Rousham, for it has very practical advantages: 'The best Fences for Pleasure and Profit, are Running Ditches, or Rivers; for they afford Water for Cattle, and Fish for your Table, and at the same Time, a most delightful View; with this additional Satisfaction, that they never want Reparation.'[2] The 'usefulness' of a garden was never beneath the designer's notice. Even the most ornamental pool was expected to provide fish, or at least an excuse for fishing, and one of Kent's sketches for the artificial 'river' at Chiswick House shows a gentleman placidly dangling his line. In making this strong practical emphasis the gardener was following classical doctrine. Pope's *Guardian* essay begins with the descriptions in Homer and Virgil of representative gardens of the Ancients, consisting 'intirely of the useful Part of Horticulture, Fruit Trees, Herbs, Water, &c'. Pope's brief account was filled out in 1728 by a detailed study, *The Villas of the Ancients Illustrated*; its author, Robert Castell, was a young protégé of the Earl of Burlington, who financed the handsome publication and to whom it was dedicated.

---

[1] *Epistle to Burlington* 56.
[2] Giles Jacob, *The Country Gentleman's Vade Mecum* (1717), p. 8.

From the evidence supplied by the descriptive letters of Pliny the Younger, supplemented by the writings of Varro and Columella, Castell concludes that there were three main types of Roman villa, distinguished according to the degree of economic self-sufficiency enjoyed by the owner. Thus the *villa urbana*, the country house designed as a place in which to retire briefly from the turmoil of city life, could be planned without regard to 'any thing relating to Agriculture or Pasturage'.[1] Of this kind is Pliny's villa at Laurentinium, described in his letter to Gallus (Epistle II xvii). This house provides 'a convenient, tho' not sumptuous, Reception for my Friends'. The garden is stocked with fig-trees and vines, but since the house is only a temporary residence it is entirely dependent on the neighbourhood for its other provisions. Fuel is supplied from the woods nearby, while 'other Conveniencies may be had from *Ostia*. To a frugal Man what a Village affords . . . would be sufficient.' Nor is there any shortage of the less exotic fish: 'the Sea indeed does not abound in choice Fish; yet it produces Soles and the best Prawns. My *Villa* even exceeds in the Plenty of the inland Country, principally in Milk.'[2] The descendants of Laurentinium are Burlington's own Chiswick House, and Lady Suffolk's Marble Hill. Pope's Thames-side villa, unlike Pliny's, is his permanent home, but like Pliny Pope can offer his guests home-grown or local produce, plentiful though not sumptuous fare:

> Content with little, I can piddle here
> On Broccoli and mutton, round the year;
> But ancient friends, (tho' poor, or out of play)
> That touch my Bell, I cannot turn away.
> 'Tis true, no Turbots dignify my boards,
> But gudgeons, flounders, what my Thames affords.
> To Hounslow-heath I point, and Bansted-down,
> Thence comes your mutton, and these chicks my own:
> From yon old wallnut-tree a show'r shall fall;
> And grapes, long-lingring on my only wall,

---

[1] Castell, p. 2.

[2] Castell, pp. 3, 10, and 15. The English equivalent of the *villa urbana* is considered more fully on pp. 178–80 below.

And figs, from standard and Espalier join:
The dev'l is in you if you cannot dine.

(*To Bethel* 137–48)

Pope's villa is a centre of hospitality, and is enmeshed in, because it is very dependent upon, the agricultural life of the neighbourhood.

Pliny's summer residence in Tuscany, described in his letter to Apollinaris (Epistle V vi), was an altogether more rural affair, a *villa rustica* rather than a *villa urbana*. Castell infers from the letter that there was a farm near the main dwelling-house, able to supply all the needs of the master and his household. The plan of the estate, as he reconstructs it, includes 'Meadows, Vineyards, Woods, plowed Land'; Pliny can pass the time in hunting game or enjoying the prospect over a varied agricultural scene.[1] In Addisonian phrase, the whole estate has been thrown into a kind of garden, and Pliny's residence is the ancestor of what came to be known as the 'ferme ornée'. By his contemporaries Philip Southcote was credited with introducing the ornamented farm to England, so realizing the Addisonian ideal. His Woburn Farm, near Weybridge, was begun in 1734, and Southcote recorded that Pope had expressed his admiration of the estate.[2] But this style of 'Rural and Extensive Gardening' had been vigorously advocated as early as 1718 by Stephen Switzer, in his *Ichnographia Rustica*. By 1742, when he published an 'Appendix' to that work, it seemed to Switzer that he could look back on his campaign with justifiable pride:

> This Taste, so truly useful and delightful as it is, has also for some time been the Practice of some of the best Genius's of *France*, under the Title of *La Ferme Ornée*. And that *Great-Britain* is now likely to excel in it, let all those who have seen the Farms and Parks of *Abbs-Court*, *Riskins*, *Dawley-Park*, now a doing, with other Places of the like Nature, declare: In all which it is visible, that the *Roman* Genius, which was once the Admiration of the World, is now making great advances in *Britain* also.[3]

Switzer liked to parade his knowledge of ancient and modern authors, and he perhaps hoped that these examples of the 'Farm-like Way of

---

[1] Castell, pp. 96–8 and 124–6.    [2] Spence §615, and pp. 422 ff.
[3] *An Appendix to Ichnographia Rustica*, pp. 8–9.

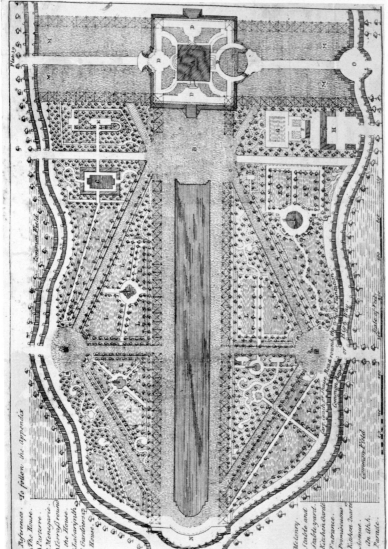

PLATE II
LORD BATHURST'S
ESTATE AT RICHINGS
PARK

'The Plan annex'd . . .
is a regular Epitomy
of a much larger
Design portraited and
lay'd out, by the
Right Honourable the
Lord Bathurst at
Riskins near Coln-
brooke. . . .'
*Appendix to Ichno-*
*graphia Rustica,* p. 9.
The principal features
are the house (A),
parterre (B) and
terrace (D), 'Promis-
cuous Kitchen
Quarters' (L), and a
ha-ha (N) beyond the
central canal.

Gardening' would gain in significance and prestige from their associations with Pope. For Switzer's 'Dawley-Park' (or, as its owner fashionably preferred to call it, Dawley Farm) was the rural retreat of Lord Bolingbroke after his return to England in 1725. Here he superintended the hay-making, and declared his allegiance to agriculture by having his hall painted with 'Trophies of Rakes, spades, prongs, &c.'.[1] Of Riskins (Richings Park, near Slough), the seat of Lord Bathurst, Switzer adds that it is laid out 'upon the Plan of the *Ferme Ornée*, and the Villa's of the Ancients', and he endorses Pope's praise of Bathurst for allowing his ample lawns to be used for pasture: 'the Lawns round about the House are for the feeding of Sheep, and the insides of the Quarters [i.e. the garden-plots] for sowing of Corn, Turnips, &c. or for the feeding of Cattle.'[2] Beauty is not neglected amid so much attention to Use, for labyrinths and little copses occupy odd angles of the design, while statues and fountains grace the intersections of the paths (Plate II). Switzer's remaining example is the 'delightful *Abs-court*' celebrated by Pope in his Imitation of Horace's second Epistle of the second Book, published in 1737. As at Richings the farm-land appears to have been an integral part of the overall garden layout. Abscourt, near Walton-on-Thames, was a property of the Earl of Halifax, and when Pope wrote his Imitation it was leased to Anthony Browne. Pope reasons that a tenant who uses the resources of the estate he rents may properly be said to own it:

> If there be truth in Law, and *Use* can give
> A *Property*, that's yours on which you live.
> Delightful *Abs-court*, if its Fields afford
> Their Fruits to you, confesses you its Lord.
>
> (*Epistle II ii* 230–33)

Such a tenant is much to be preferred to a landlord of the wrong sort. The 'new men' in society, financiers and others, purchase estates but fail to live off the land:

> Heathcote himself, and such large-acred Men,
> Lords of fat *E'sham*, or of Lincoln Fen,

---

[1] Pope to Swift, 28 June 1728, *Correspondence*, vol. II, p. 503.    [2] *Appendix*, p. 9.

Buy every stick of Wood that lends them heat,
Buy every Pullet they afford to eat.[1]

The art of these two short passages is inconspicuous, as befits an imitation of Horace's plain style, and Pope makes his contrasts with little fuss. In the lines on Abscourt generosity and abundance are just hinted at by the running-on of the lines: 'if its Fields afford/ Their Fruits to you . . .'; in the second passage 'lends' wittily transfers the niggardliness of the owners to their domestic fuel. Finally, the effectiveness of 'Buy every Pullet they afford to eat' depends on a subdued pun which keeps the 'possible other case' in our minds. Heathcote and his like can afford, financially speaking, to buy their poultry, but the verb *afford* was regularly used, as in the Abscourt passage, to describe the natural yield of an estate. If the large-acred men had really used their acres, instead of merely possessing them, their grudging expenditure would have been unnecessary.[2]

The 'ferme ornée' is perhaps the most complete realization of a widespread desire to unite profit with pleasure. Even in the royal garden at Richmond, Bridgeman 'dared to introduce cultivated fields'.[3] The result is that gardening becomes 'inextricably wove' with 'Agriculture . . . and all the Business and Pleasures of a Country Life'.[4] Some gentlemen might prefer the Pleasures of hunting to the Business of farming. Others might be preoccupied with the details of estate finance. But many, including the largest landowners, were bound to their estates by ties that were neither frivolous nor mercenary. The first Earl of Bristol, though he spent enormous energy on political affairs in the capital, confessed to a deep affection for his Suffolk house, 'peaceful blessd Ickworth (ye sweet center of my humble soul), being ye most innocent quiet place it knows in all

---

[1] Lines 240–3. Sir Gilbert Heathcote, Governor of the Bank of England, bought the Lincolnshire estate of Normanton about 1729.

[2] Pope's concern in this *Epistle* with Property and Use is further discussed in chapter VII, section iii.

[3] Horace Walpole, 'The History of the Modern Taste in Gardening', in I. W. U. Chase, *Horace Walpole : Gardenist* (Princeton, 1943), p. 24. Bridgeman was working at Richmond in the early 1730s: ibid., p. 140.

[4] Switzer, *The Nobleman, Gentleman, and Gardener's Recreation* (1715), p. iv.

ye world'.[1] The country seat was the fixed centre of the landed family, the outward sign of its social, financial and political standing, the custodian of its traditions and its family papers. Moreover, no large estate was complete without its home farm, usually situated close to the house, and able to supply much of the food and drink consumed in the household. The Duke of Chandos had his own beer brewed at Cannons; his brewer was also responsible for making soap and candles from the fat of the pigs reared on the estate.[2] For any landowner the financial advantages of such measures would be considerable. For smaller men than the Duke of Chandos they might be decisive. Defoe believed that many gentlemen, especially those with estates yielding less than £500 a year, were living above themselves and running steadily into debt. His remedy, given with his customary zest for practical detail, is to turn to better account the peculiar advantages of the gentleman's situation; these are:

> that he payes no rent, that his park having some meddow grounds within the pale, few parks are without it, affords him grass and hay for his coach horses and saddle horses, which goes also a great way in the expence of the family; besides that, he has venison perhaps in his park, sufficient for his own table at least, and rabbits in his own warren adjoyning, pidgeons from a dove house in the yard, fish in his own ponds or in some small river adjoyning and within his own royalty, and milk with all the needfull addenda to his kitchen, which a small dary [sic] of 4 or 5 cows yields to him.[3]

Defoe is urging the gentry to re-create the third of Castell's categories of Roman villa, the completely self-sufficient country house. For Varro the only kind of villa that deserves the name is a closely-knit complex of master's dwelling and farm-house; the estate of which it is the focus is not merely a self-contained unit, but can even export its surplus produce. Such an estate will have its own mill and bake-house, its orchards and rabbit-warren, fish-ponds and apiary, and a vivarium, or park, stocked with deer, wild goats and

---

[1] *The Diary of John Hervey, First Earl of Bristol*, ed. S. H. A. Hervey (Wells, 1894), p. 54.
[2] C. H. C. and M. I. Baker, *The Life and Circumstances of James Brydges, First Duke of Chandos* (Oxford, 1949), p. 184.
[3] *The Compleat English Gentleman*, ed. Karl D. Bülbring (1890), p. 247.

[ 75 ]

boars.[1] But there were many sound eighteenth-century arguments in favour of resourcefulness and economic independence which must have carried more weight than classical precedent. The uncertain state of communications and the possibility of crop failures made it essential to have granaries and barns large enough to store at least a year's supply of corn, malt, oats, and so on. The traditional rapacity of the middleman, and the rigging of markets, were advanced as strong reasons for attempting to achieve the Varronian ideal. Other land-owners, it is suggested, should follow the example of those gentlemen who 'provide every Thing within themselves, for the Support of their Families, by agreeing [i.e. contracting] with some Tenant for whatever they want all the Year round, at a Set-price; or by reserving so much Land as is sufficient to answer that End; and they have their own Slaughter-houses, Granaries, and Store-Rooms for all their necessary *Provisions*, independent of the several Trades in their Neighbourhood.'[2]

The smaller country house tends therefore to be indistinguishable from a substantial farm-house, and to be inseparable from its rural environment. An engraving of Easington (or Eastington) House, Gloucestershire, made by Joannes Kip about 1709, depicts a house without either elaborate gardens or private landscaped park (Plate III). The only gesture towards formality is made by four rows of young trees on the entrance front. For the rest, 'rough country roads come almost up to the house; farm buildings stand in the courtyard; sheep are dipped only a few yards from the house'.[3] In such a situation it is impossible for the gentleman to remain as 'independent of the several Trades in [his] Neighbourhood' as the extremist opponent of middlemen would like him to be. The country house will rather become the hub of a whole village community,

---

[1] Castell, *Villas of the Ancients*, pp. 55–78.
[2] *An Essay to Prove, that Regrators, Ingrossers, Forestallers . . . are Destructive of Trade* (1718), pp. 20–1. The statutes against regrating and engrossing continued to be invoked from time to time, but with little success. They were repealed in 1772, in the cause of free trade.
[3] W. G. Hoskins, *The Making of the English Landscape* (1955), p. 134. See also John Steegman, *The Artist and the Country House* (1949), plates 4 and 21.

*Earsington the Seat of Nathaniel Stevens Esq.*

PLATE III EASINGTON HOUSE, GLOUCESTERSHIRE, IN 1709

but that community in its turn may well achieve something approaching economic viability. The gentleman, as village squire, will be the most important single contributor to the workings of the community, but he will also enjoy the greatest measure of independence within it. He can have his clothes made up by the village tailor and his horses shod by the blacksmith; he may sell some of his own cows and sheep to the local market, and pasture the cattle and horses of his neighbours for a small fee. If he is wealthy enough he will act as the local banker and money-lender.

It was among the landed gentry who maintained these traditional links with, and responsibilities towards, their local communities that Pope found some of his closest friends: John Caryll, Hugh Bethel and later the philanthropic Ralph Allen. And, as we have seen, it was to the 'useful' and social aspects of the great estates that Pope directed attention; the cheerful tenants of such landowners as Bathurst 'bless their yearly toil'. Pope seems to have believed (wrongly) that he himself belonged to a branch of one of the landed Roman Catholic families, for in the *Epistle to Arbuthnot* he supplied a genealogical note to this effect: 'Mr *Pope*'s Father was of a Gentleman's Family in *Oxfordshire*, the Head of which was the Earl of *Downe*, whose sole Heiress married the Earl of *Lindsey*.'[1] With more justification he saw himself living something like the life of a country gentleman in his Twickenham Villa. For by the same argument that he uses about the tenant of delightful Abscourt Pope is the true Lord of his rented property. Because he *uses* his miniature estate he attains independence:

> In *South-sea* days not happier, when surmis'd
> The Lord of thousands, than if now *Excis'd*;
> In Forest planted by a Father's hand,
> Than in five acres now of rented land.
>
> (*To Bethel* 133–6)

In the Horatian original of this poem (*Satire II ii*) the speaker, Ofellus, has formerly cultivated his own land. He is now reduced to

---

[1] Note to line 381. See George Sherburn, *The Early Career of Alexander Pope* (Oxford, 1934), p. 30.

the status of tenant-farmer, though without any damage to his Stoical principles. This change of fortune appears in an ingeniously altered form in the Imitation, where Bethel represents Ofellus in his earlier freeholding capacity, and Pope himself fills the role of tenant. The effect is to assimilate the poet at Twickenham to the genuine countryman in Yorkshire. Pope even adopts Bethel's downrightness of tone and language: 'The dev'l is in you if you cannot dine.' The lines in which he describes his home-spun hospitality have been notorious ever since Matthew Arnold used them to demonstrate that Pope is a 'classic of our prose'. But a sturdy prosiness, in keeping with the down-to-earth manner of Bethel's 'Sermon', would seem to be precisely what Pope was aiming at; and the sense of the poet's 'engagement' with his environment ('To Hounslow-heath I point, and Bansted-down') makes an essential contribution to the image of the countryman. We are led to believe that Pope, like his way of life and his poetry, is modest and straightforward.

Simplicity, integrity, and plain-dealing, the qualities of the ideal country gentleman, were embodied in the unpretentious and conservative architecture of the gentleman's country house. In its internal design, however, the smaller country house was being modified in an important direction, a direction in which the palatial buildings of the aristocracy were already rapidly moving. Though its ground-plan remained the 'H' form so common in the early seventeenth century, the central section of the 'H' was now frequently treated not as a spacious hall for entertaining guests but as an entrance vestibule to receive and impress visitors. Behind the vestibule, as in the larger houses, would be an elegant saloon, flanked with smaller parlours and dining-rooms. Space is no longer available for large-scale entertainment; the gentleman dines with his family or a few acquaintances. Not that lack of space was the only curb on hospitality. Many gentlemen found it necessary to cut down their expenditure in the country in order to arrive fashionably in town for the season, or simply in order to combat the rising cost of living and a heavy burden of taxation. The land tax, a rate levied on landed property, was maintained at the unpopularly high figure of four shillings in the pound whenever the Government found itself in financial difficulties. Catholics and non-jurors among the gentry were penalized for their religious beliefs by being double-taxed. It was a general complaint that income from rents was no longer keeping pace with expenses. A contemporary economist observed that 'Gentlemen . . . now pay on the Par above 20 times as much for every thing as was paid for the same Things about four Centuries ago, whilst their Rents are not above four times as much as they were then'; hence they find 'they can't live so well and hospitably on the same Estates, as their Ancestors did, who had vastly less Income from them'.[1] The aristocracy, less disturbed by these economic considerations, was not inclined to be socially out-going. It kept increasingly to itself after the Restoration, its hospitality largely confined to members of its own circle who were paying set visits. The first Earl of Bristol entertained, and was entertained by, his aristocratic kinsmen and acquaintances; the only poet to visit him had the social distinction of being Physician in Ordinary to the King. This was Dr Samuel Garth, who promised to celebrate the charms of the Earl's country seat, 'if ever he wrote any more in verse'.[2] At the beginning of the eighteenth century Matthew Prior was obliged to confess that the Earl of Dorset's dinner-table 'was one of the Last, that gave Us an Example of the Old House-keeping of an ENGLISH Nobleman. A Freedom reigned at it, which made every one of his Guests think Himself at Home: and an Abundance, which shewed that the Master's Hospitality extended to many More, than Those who had the Honor to sit at Table with Him.'[3] Hospitality was an outmoded virtue. Joseph Hall had announced in 1598 that 'Hous-keping's dead';[4] men continued to mourn its passing for a century and a half.

When Pope mentions his own or others' hospitality he usually also glances back to some earlier and more generous age. He writes to Hugh Bethel that his house at Twickenham 'is like the house of a Patriarch of old, standing by the highway side and receiving all

---

[1] Jacob Vanderlint, *Money Answers All Things* (1734), pp. 93 and 17.
[2] *Diary of John Hervey*, p. 65.
[3] *Works*, vol. I, p. 254.
[4] *Virgidemiarum*, Book V, Satire ii, line 1. Quotations from Hall, in this and the following chapter, are from his *Collected Poems*, ed. A. Davenport (Liverpool, 1949).

travellers';[1] he tells William Fortescue, in a similar vein, 'I shall dye of Hospitality, which is a Fate becoming none but a Patriarch or a Parliament man in the Country'.[2] In *To Bethel* the picture of the hospitable poet is completed by a double allusion to the 'house-keeping' of Homeric Greece and of Elizabethan England:

> My lands are sold, my Father's house is gone;
> I'll hire another's, is not that my own,
> And yours my friends? thro' whose free-opening gate
> None comes too early, none departs too late;
> (For I, who hold sage Homer's rule the best,
> Welcome the coming, speed the going guest.)
>
> (155–60)

Pope appears to be quoting here an inscription over the East door of Montacute House, Somerset:

> Through this wide op'ning Gate
> None come too Early none Return too Late.[3]

Pope's rather recondite invocation of the spirit of Elizabethan largesse gives way to a more public and accessible allusion; the final line of the passage in *To Bethel* quotes Pope's own translation (or, more accurately, that of one of his assistants) of a Homeric *sententia*:

> True friendship's laws are by this rule exprest,
> Welcome the coming, speed the parting guest.
>
> (*Odyssey* XV 83–4)

Yet behind the specific 'rule' stated in Homer's line there lies the wider context of the *Odyssey* as a whole, for that poem is greatly concerned with the ethics of hospitality. Pope wishes to remind us of a narrative in which only base and evil persons close their doors against strangers, or abuse the welcome they themselves receive,

---

[1] 9 August 1726, *Correspondence*, vol. II, p. 386.

[2] 23 August 1735, *Correspondence*, vol. III, p. 486.

[3] The Custodian, Mr J. A. Brock, has very kindly checked the text of the inscription; it would seem to be contemporary with the House, which was built 1588–1601. Pope might have seen Montacute, or heard about these lines, when he was visiting Lord Digby at Sherborne, some ten miles away, in the summer of 1724: see *Correspondence*, vol. II, p. 192, note 1, and pp. 236 ff.

whereas noble characters constantly display 'all the openness of ancient hospitality'.[1]

Pope, on his own testimony, is generous but not lavishly ostentatious. He holds the middle place between the extremes of inhospitality and profuseness represented by Cotta and his son in the *Epistle to Bathurst*. The portrait of the elder Cotta, moving smoothly from amused tolerance to sombre comedy, is a fine example of Pope's skill in modulating tone and feeling.

> Old Cotta sham'd his fortune and his birth,
> Yet was not Cotta void of wit or worth:
> What tho' (the use of barb'rous spits forgot)
> His kitchen vy'd in coolness with his grot?
> His court with nettles, moats with cresses stor'd,
> With soups unbought and sallads blest his board.
> If Cotta liv'd on pulse, it was no more
> Than Bramins, Saints, and Sages did before;
> To cram the Rich was prodigal expence,
> And who would take the Poor from Providence?
>
> (179–88)

The poet concedes that Cotta is endowed with wit and worth, though 'worth' here, as frequently elsewhere in Pope, is a matter rather of 'fortune' than of any moral qualities. But at least the vegetarian who lays aside barbarous spits may justly claim to be more innocent and civilized than his neighbours, while in economic terms Cotta would seem to be the ideally self-sufficient country gentleman. In living off his own cresses and nettles, however, he is also living entirely for himself. So the pretence of justifying his behaviour by reference to Bramins, Saints and Sages obliquely makes the first serious charge against him, as the single point of likeness, living on pulse, throws into prominence all the points of difference. More seriously, Cotta's refusal to 'cram the Rich' is the right decision taken for the wrong reason ('prodigal expence'), and the passage brings us up short with his bleak indifference to the fate of the Poor. Cotta's smug rejection of social responsibility is seen to fit neatly into a pattern established by contemporary Saints and Sages:

---

[1] Note (by Broome) to Book I line 157 of Pope's *Odyssey*.

Perhaps you think the Poor might have their part?
Bond damns the Poor, and hates them from his heart:
The grave Sir Gilbert holds it for a rule,
That "every man in want is knave or fool:"
"God cannot love (says Blunt, with tearless eyes)
"The wretch he starves" – and piously denies:
But the good Bishop, with a meeker air,
Admits, and leaves them, Providence's care.

(101–8)

Cotta shames his fortune and his birth by failing to relieve the poor
and to honour his social obligations. What should be a healthy
landlord-tenant relationship has gone sour. The benighted traveller,
that traditional, Homeric object of hospitality, is denied admission.
Pope can no longer regard Cotta's behaviour with ironic detach-
ment:

Like some lone Chartreux stands the good old Hall,
Silence without, and Fasts within the Wall;
No rafter'd roofs with dance and tabor sound,
No noontide-bell invites the country round;
Tenants with sighs the smoakless tow'rs survey,
And turn th'unwilling steeds another way:
Benighted wanderers, the forest o'er,
Curse the sav'd candle, and unop'ning door;
While the gaunt mastiff growling at the gate,
Affrights the beggar whom he longs to eat.

(189–98)

Pope has forged here some interesting links with Elizabethan satire.
The Chartreux simile, and the 'slaughter'd hecatombs' with which
Cotta's son prodigally atones for his father's thrift (line 203), refer
back to Donne's second Satire, which Pope had versified as early as
1713:

In Halls
Carthusian Fasts, and fulsome Bacchanals
Equally I hate. Mean's blest. In rich men's homes
I bid kill some beasts, but no Hecatombs,
None starve, none surfeit so.[1]

---

[1] Lines 105–9. Pope's version of the immediately preceding line also anticipates the
Cotta passage: 'Where are those Troops of Poor that throng'd before/The good old
Landlords hospitable Door?'

[ 82 ]

Cotta's smokeless chimneys are the sure sign of an inhospitable household. Joseph Hall, after announcing the death of house-keeping, goes on to describe the plight of the traveller who sees 'Faire glittering Hal[l]s to tempt the hopefull eye', only to find that the proud exteriors have nothing within. All is 'dumbe and silent . . . The marble pauement hid with desart weede':

> Looke to the towred chymneis which should bee
> The wind-pipes of good hospitalitie,
> Through which it breatheth to the open ayre,
> Betokening life and liberall welfaire,
> Lo, there th'vnthankfull swallow takes her rest. . . .[1]

The description of Cotta's hall, with its concentration of negatives ('No rafter'd roofs . . . No noontide-bell . . . smoakless . . . unop'ning'), forcefully implies the hospitality that ought to be in evidence. Cotta's Fasts should be Feasts. But the terms of the description also suggest that such hospitable activity is part of an older way of life that the ascetic Cotta has renounced. The 'dance and tabor' belong to a rapidly vanishing rural England, so that in the end we are not so much shown what Cotta's house might be, as left to contemplate, nostalgically, what it must have been in more liberal times.

It seemed to Pope that the spirit of hospitality survived only among a few old-fashioned country gentlemen. One such was John Caryll, to whom Pope wrote on 28 December 1717:

I am strongly inclined to think there are at this very day at Grinsted, certain antique charities and obsolete devotions yet in being: that a thing call'd Christian cheerfullness, ([not] incompatible with Christmass pies and plum-broth) whereof frequent is the mention in old sermons and almanacs, is really kept alive and in practice at the said place: That feeding the hungry, and giving alms to the poor, do yet make a part of good housekeeping in a latitude not more remote from London than forty miles.[2]

---

[1] *Virgidemiarum*, Book V, Satire ii. Other Elizabethan and Jacobean comments about the significance of smoking chimneys are cited in Davenport's edition of Hall, p. 242, and in L. C. Knights, *Drama and Society in the Age of Jonson* (1937), p. 114, note 4.
[2] *Correspondence*, vol. I, p. 457.

In fact many landowners gave alms to the poor, and often continued to do so even when they were hard pressed by creditors and forced to curtail their other expenses.[1] But it was easy, and increasingly common, to attribute the poverty of the working-classes entirely to their idleness, and to excuse oneself from undertaking charitable works by citing the provisions of the Poor Law. Lady Petre, for example, advises that left-over scraps of meat should be 'kept together in a Dole-tub and two or three times a week with brown bread and small beer bee given to poore parishioners att the dore. Beef broth, or any other superfluitys may be added to this, which is more for necessary ostentation sake, than for true charity, for here in England every parish is obliged to maintaine their owne poore. . . . Such as rove about without passes are vagabonds and to relieve these is to encourage idleness and debauchery.'[2] The poor, if not the care of Providence, are certainly the care of the parish. Lady Petre's words reflect the change which the Act of Settlement of 1662 had brought to the administration of the Poor Law. This Act, says Trevelyan, 'was the condition on which the upper and middle classes consented to fulfil their duty, that had now become traditional, of maintaining the impotent poor.' Under its terms local authorities could 'prevent a labourer from moving into a parish, even if he had obtained employment within its bounds, if they feared that he might some day in the future come upon its poor-rate'.[3] Single able-bodied men, unless they were suspected of being dissidents and potential rioters, were not usually discriminated against, but the Act was commonly invoked against those who might constitute a drain on the parish funds, against men with large families, and against the very young and the infirm. Unemployed labourers and their families were hunted from parish to

---

[1] See G. E. Mingay, *English Landed Society in the Eighteenth Century* (1963), p. 275.
[2] Dom John Stéphan, 'Notes on Household Management in the 18th Century: Transcript of a MS Note-Book', *Notes and Queries*, vol. CCIV (1959), p. 171. Dom Stéphan identifies the author of this notebook as Lady Petre, of Thorndon Hall, Essex, and deduces that it was compiled about 1740 for the guidance of her friend the Duchess of Norfolk.
[3] G. M. Trevelyan, *England under the Stuarts*, 19th ed. (1946), p. 435.

parish; men at the point of death were removed to avoid funeral expenses; pregnant women were carried over the parish boundary. The integrity and independence of the local community was not maintained without human cost.

The administration of the Poor Law was largely in the hands of the gentry, since it was from their ranks that most Justices of the Peace were recruited. Among his other duties a Justice was expected to supervise road repairs and to license alehouses, to fix wages and to serve on Commissions and Boards of Trustees. The local gentry were often informally called upon to arbitrate in disputes; Dryden's honoured kinsman sends former enemies home in friendship and saves them 'th' Expence of long Litigious Laws'.[1] Steele sums up the social responsibilities of the landowner:

> There is no Character more deservedly esteemed than that of a Country Gentleman, who understands the Station in which Heaven and Nature have plac'd him. He is Father to his Tenants, and Patron to his Neighbours, and is more superior to those of lower Fortune by his Benevolence than his Possessions. . . . His Life is spent in the good Offices of an Advocate, a Referee, a Companion, a Mediator, and a Friend. His Council and Knowledge are a Guard to the Simplicity and Innocence of those of lower Talents, and the Entertainment and Happiness of those of equal.[2]

This is an idealized picture, for Steele is endeavouring to recall men to a true sense of their place in the community. Too often the gentleman understood the station in which heaven and nature had placed him only too well, for it was a station which happily avoided the hardships of the one beneath it, and the anxiety and restless ambition of the one above. The country gentleman's life could so easily be one of sheltered contentment that some gentlemen were understandably reluctant to disturb their peace by accepting onerous and time-consuming local duties. Cowley says that if he had to decide which members of society enjoyed the greatest measure of personal liberty he would 'pitch upon that sort of People whom King *James* was wont to call the Happiest of our Nation, the Men placed in the Countrey

---

[1] 'To my Honour'd Kinsman, John Driden', line 11.  [2] *The Tatler*, no. 169.

by their Fortune above an High-Constable, and yet beneath the trouble of a Justice of Peace, in a moderate plenty. . . .'[1] Pope was not being ironical when he expressed concern that Hugh Bethel was 'in danger of being Sheriff', for the Sheriff's was an even more 'troublesome' office, in Cowley's sense, than that of the Justice.[2] The duties and expenses of such posts were steadily increasing with the growth of population, and an effective system of local government, administered by paid officials, had yet to be evolved. Among the upper classes, therefore, reaction to this state of affairs led publicly to the imposing of such harsh conditions as those of the Act of Settlement, and privately in many cases to a quiet withdrawal from public responsibilities. In this respect Dryden's kinsman is to be honoured because he is so exceptional.

He is also honoured for his part in national politics. As a Member of Parliament he steers 'betwixt the Country and the Court', furthering the public interest, but never gratifying the whims of 'the Great'. In helping to preserve a balance of political forces he is a true patriot, and Dryden compares his role to that of Britain in European politics. During the early years of the eighteenth century the country gentlemen in the House of Commons were proud of their influence, and boasted of their power to make or ruin statesmen. It was their violent reaction to the Excise Bill of 1733 which obliged Walpole to withdraw the measure. This was at a time when the Opposition party, with which Pope was becoming more and more closely associated, was extolling the virtues of simplicity and independence, pitting them against the venality, luxury and corruption of Walpole's administration and the Court which backed it. Led by Bolingbroke, the Opposition championed the cause of British Liberty in the pages of the *Craftsman*, and the poets added their voices to those of the essayists. Thomson's *Liberty*, published in instalments during 1735 and 1736, and Richard Glover's *Leonidas* (1737), a poem which met with Pope's strong political approval,

---

[1] 'Of Liberty,' *Essays*, p. 386.
[2] Letter to Bethel, 27 November 1739, *Correspondence*, vol. IV, pp. 205–6. On the sheriff's duties see J. H. Plumb, *Sir Robert Walpole: the Making of a Statesman* (1956), p. 47.

celebrated virtues that appeared to be threatened with extinction. Like rural hospitality, these virtues were out of date. At the end of 1736 Pope writes to Swift that he has made the acquaintance of the new generation of Opposition politicians, particularly George Lyttleton and Henry Hyde, Lord Cornbury, 'young men, who look rather to the past age than the present, and therefore the future may have some hopes of them. . . . Two or three of them have distinguish'd themselves in Parliament, and you will own in a very uncommon manner, when I tell you it is by their asserting of Independency, and contempt of Corruption.'[1] Given the atmosphere of the 1730s Pope's decision to imitate Horace's second Satire of the second Book can be seen as at least in part a political decision. Bethel's 'Sermon' laments the passing of 'old Simplicity' (line 36), and firmly associates the gluttony and extravagance he denounces with Court circles: 'Let me . . . to crack live *Crawfish* recommend,/ I'd never doubt at Court to make a Friend.' Since it was a stock joke that a politician forgets his friends once hardship or political disgrace overtakes them, Pope's behaviour is an implicit rebuke to such self-seeking:

> But ancient friends, (tho' poor, or out of play)
> That touch my Bell, I cannot turn away.

Luxury, in the eyes of the Opposition, is the prerogative of the Court. Bethel, who exhorts us to remain 'blest with little', finds his disciple Pope 'content with little' at Twickenham.

Pope's association with the Opposition perhaps helped to deepen his gloomy concern with England's political sickness; it did not blind him to the shortcomings of the Opposition party itself. In the disillusioned fragment 'One Thousand Seven Hundred and Forty' the vaunted independence of the gentry turns out to be an ignorant parrotting of the official 'Patriot' line:

> As for the rest, each winter up they run,
> And all are clear, that something must be done.
> Then urg'd by C[artere]t, or by C[artere]t stopt,
> Inflam'd by P[ulteney], or by P[ulteney] dropt;

---

[1] To Swift, 30 December 1736, *Correspondence*, vol. IV, p. 51.

> They follow rev'rently each wond'rous wight,
> Amaz'd that one can read, that one can write:
> So geese to gander prone obedience keep,
> Hiss if he hiss, and if he slumber, sleep.
> Till having done whate'er was fit or fine,
> Utter'd a speech, and ask'd their friends to dine;
> Each hurries back to his paternal ground,
> Content but for five shillings in the pound,
> Yearly defeated, yearly hopes they give,
> And all agree, Sir Robert cannot live.          (29–42)

The pattering lines, with their deliberately mechanical balance and repetition, imitate the puppet-like behaviour of the M.P.s, who expend their energy in aimless fulmination against Walpole, and in empty rallying-cries: 'something must be done', 'Sir Robert cannot live'. Their 'paternal ground' is merely a refuge for their ineffectiveness.

Yet for all his reservations Pope has a strong sense of what a nineteenth-century reviewer called the 'rural stabilities'.[1] If sincerity, sturdy independence of mind, hospitality, and an awareness of man's obligations to his fellows are to be found anywhere in England, they will be found only outside London, outside the 'corrupt & corruptible world within the Vortex of the Court & City'.[2] The vortex image is an apt one, for the combined pull of fashion, high finance, and political power was strong, and to counteract it the delights and advantages of the country had to be strongly urged. The second Earl of Nottingham could not take it for granted that his eldest son would want to live on the family estate: 'I have appointed my gardens, cow-yards and a building opposite my stable to be finished. These things being done the habitation will be convenient and pleasant and may induce Daniel to live in the country, which I hope he will love, and mind his own affairs and estate, which is part of a gentleman's calling.'[3] Pope's house and garden at

---

[1] Unsigned review of Byron's *Letter to Murray, on . . . Bowles' Strictures on Pope*, in *The Edinburgh Monthly Review*, vol. V (1821), p. 617.

[2] Pope to Bathurst, 28 April 1741, *Correspondence*, vol. IV, p. 342.

[3] H. J. Habakkuk, 'Daniel Finch, 2nd Earl of Nottingham: His House and Estate,' in *Studies in Social History*, ed. J. H. Plumb (1955), p. 172.

Twickenham, though far from being a country estate, achieved in their own modest way a synthesis of Art and Nature, Use and Beauty. They stood outside the vortex of London, enshrining the rural virtues. Here guests were assured of a warm welcome, here ease and independence flourished. Pope told Spence that 'Lord Bolingbroke's usual health after dinner is "Amicitiae et Libertati",' and added that he would like to adapt the motto as an inscription to be placed over his own door, so publicly and solemnly dedicating his home to Liberty and Friendship.[1]

---

[1] Spence, §279.

# CHAPTER FIVE

# Courtly Vice

In the Preface to his edition of Shakespeare, published in 1725, Pope boasted of having evolved a 'shorter and less ostentatious method of performing the better half of Criticism (namely the pointing out an Author's excellencies) than to fill a whole paper with citations of fine passages, with *general Applauses*, or *empty Exclamations* at the tail of them'. Pope's new method has all the merits of simplicity and economy; 'fine passages' are indicated by the editor's marginal commas, while a striking scene is heralded by a star printed at its head. Some of Pope's editorial preferences – the Dover Cliff speech in *King Lear* and the quarrel scene in *Julius Cæsar*, for example – faithfully reflect the prevailing climate of critical opinion; others would seem to represent a deliberate effort to reassess plays unjustly neglected by Pope's contemporaries, as when he selects five passages from *Antony and Cleopatra*. But in many cases Pope is evidently responding to the satirist in Shakespeare. Thus in *As You Like It* he marks Touchstone's summary of his life at Court: 'I have trod a measure, I have flatter'd a lady, I have been politick with my friend, smooth with mine enemy, I have undone three taylors. . . .'[1] Quite as predictably he marks also Corin's complementary vindication of the way of life enjoyed by the shepherd: 'I earn that I eat; get that I wear; owe no man hate, envy no man's happiness; glad of other men's good, content with my harm. . . .'[2] This firm statement looks back to the exiled Duke's first and famous speech in the forest of Arden, where the opposition

---

[1] Act V scene iv, lines 44 ff.    [2] Act III ii 77 ff.

between Court and country has already been sharply focused: '. . . are not these woods/More free from peril than the envious court?'; of this speech, too, Pope approves. Again, in *Cymbeline* he commends Belisarius's passionate and sustained defence of a quiet rural life as against the miseries and uncertainties of court and city.[1] Pope's editorial choices remind us of the well-established links between pastoral and satirical poetry, and point forward to his own creation, in *To Bethel*, of a poem that is at once satire and pastoral.

Not only does Pope celebrate the virtues of hospitality and simplicity, plain-living and plain-speaking. He also exploits the traditional contrast between the rural and the urban, playing off one way of life against the other. Rural innocence may conveniently be defined by negatives drawn from the habits of the city and, more especially, of the Court, that quintessence of artificial urban existence. A country life is neither vexed by legal disputes, nor undermined by subterfuge, nor unsettled by the passions of greed and ambition. So Pope's evocation of the delights of his 'Country Seat' ('O charming Noons! and Nights divine! . . .') is enhanced by the preceding account of 'Those Cares that haunt the Court and Town'.[2] For the man who is unwillingly caught up in those cares will long, no less fervently than Horace's Country Mouse, for escape to peace and freedom. In Pope's version of Donne's fourth Satire the poet at last finds release from the Courtier's importunities:

> In that nice Moment, as another Lye
> Stood just a-tilt, the *Minister* came by.
> Away he flies. He bows, and bows again;
> And close as *Umbra* joins the dirty Train. . . .
>   Bear me, some God! oh quickly bear me hence
> To wholesome Solitude, the Nurse of Sense:
> Where Contemplation prunes her ruffled Wings,
> And the free Soul looks down to pity Kings.

(174 ff.)

The Court, for Pope as for his satirical predecessors, is everything that the country is not. Its least objectionable representative,

---

[1] Act III iii; Pope sets commas beside the first fifty-five lines of this scene.
[2] *Satire II vi* 132.

[ 91 ]

the Town Mouse, is conceited and affected. Though he takes an ill-founded pride in his politeness, he is dogmatic, and therefore not well-bred:

> Our Courtier walks from dish to dish,
> Tastes for his Friend of Fowl and Fish;
> Tells all their names, lays down the law,
> "*Que ça est bon! Ah! goutez ça!*
> (*Satire II vi* 200–3)

The Country Mouse values his 'Liberty'; he is frugal, but also 'right hospitable', whereas the Town Mouse lives for himself and the present moment:

> "Consider, Mice, like Men, must die,
> "Both small and great, both you and I:
> "Then spend your life in Joy and Sport,
> "(This doctrine, Friend, I learnt at Court.)

The frivolity and extravagance of courtiers is in complete contrast to the way of life of the modest country gentleman. Indeed the courtier may (incredibly) have renounced such a way of life, and chosen to exchange his paternal acres for the doubtful benefits of ostentatious apparel and a striking equipage. The '*British* Youth' who flock to the Royal Drawing-Room, the centre of the Court's social life, are attired

> In Hues as gay, and Odours as divine,
> As the fair Fields they sold to look so fine.
> (*Donne IV* 216–17)

They have sacrificed their moral and political independence to gain what is in reality a 'splendid Livery',[1] and have given up their economic independence for the remote possibility of a 'place' at Court:

> Wants reach all States; they beg but better drest,
> And all is *splendid Poverty* at best.
> (*Donne IV* 224–5)

The Court beggar in his finery had been observed by other Elizabethan satirists besides Donne, whom Pope is here following.

---

[1] *Epistle to Murray* (*Epistle I vi*) 33.

Joseph Hall describes the typical gallant as having 'So little in his purse, so much vpon his backe:/So nothing in his maw.'[1] And a hundred years later he was observed by others than Pope, whose phrase 'splendid Poverty' is in fact a quotation from one of Edward Young's outbursts against court life.[2] The courtier may have purchased his false splendour by selling his birthright; he will certainly maintain it by living on credit. Touchstone brags of having 'undone three taylors', and Belisarius condemns those who satisfy their vanity by rustling 'in unpaid-for silk'. The beau with a tailor's bill in his pocket or on his book-press is a stock figure of Augustan satire, and Narcissa, we remember, 'paid a Tradesman once to make him stare'.[3] Luxury is bought at the price of other men's anxiety and ruin. Even when, with the increasing prestige and articulateness of the middle classes, the gay hues and personal ornaments became grounds for urgent complaint by eighteenth-century drapers and tailors and wig-makers, credit could still be freely obtained, and men could go on augmenting the number of their financial dependents. In 1740 the estate of Lord Weymouth was found to be encumbered with unpaid bills and arrears of wages amounting to 'probably not less than £30,000'.[4] When Pope exclaims, with self-satisfaction,

> I was not born for Courts or great Affairs,
> I pay my Debts, believe, and say my Pray'rs,
>
> (*To Arbuthnot* 267–8)

he is drawing attention as much to debtors in high life as to his own financial honesty.

The Court, and the fashionable 'Town' set associated with it, are characterized by duplicity and false appearances. Their finery is not paid for, and their good breeding throws a veil over their selfish pride. The appropriate language to describe the Court is the language

---

[1] *Virgidemiarum*, Book III, Satire vii, lines 20–21.
[2] *Love of Fame*, Satire I, line 245.
[3] Pope, *Epistle to a Lady* 56.
[4] H. J. Habakkuk, 'The English Land Market in the Eighteenth Century', in *Britain and the Netherlands*, ed. J. S. Bromley and E. H. Kossmann (1960), p. 163. £30,000 would be roughly equivalent to £300,000 today.

of paradox; the appropriate rhetorical figure is the oxymoron. Robert Gould satirized the 'Rabble of Nobility'; Edward Young saw a Court peopled only by 'smiling Care', 'well-bred Hate' and 'servile Grandeur', and Pope's contemptible figures of the 'livery'd Lord', *'noble Serving-Man'* and 'well-drest Rabble' are created in the same well-established and inevitable stylistic pattern.[1] By this device the satirist can thrust on our notice the dichotomy between impressive appearance and the base reality beneath. Or, more expansively, he may treat the theme of appearance and reality by contemplating that great shrine of dissimulation, the female dressing-room. There we may compare

> Sappho at her toilet's greasy task,
> With Sappho fragrant at an ev'ning Mask:
> So morning Insects that in muck begun,
> Shine, buzz, and fly-blow in the setting-sun.
>
> (*To a Lady* 25–8)

In spite of the touch of Swiftian realism ('greasy task'), the first couplet here seems to be offering a generous, if slightly amused, admiration of its subject. But the second, with its precisely-managed sequence of verbs, brings rapidly before us Sappho's social brilliance, her contribution to the idle buzzing chatter of the masquerade, and (in 'fly-blow') her delight in its malicious gossip. The pivotal phrase, 'that in muck begun', is nicely ambiguous. It seems at first merely to emphasize the transition from morning dishabille to evening elegance, but as we proceed to observe and evaluate Sappho's conduct we realize that the phrase indicates continuity rather than contrast: insects which begin life in dirt will always behave dirtily. The fragrance may transcend its greasy beginnings, but it cannot disguise Sappho's moral squalor. And it is a fragrance assumed for the sake of a 'Mask', an entertainment symbolic of all the hypocrisies of town life. (The country has its more innocent amusements of dances and assemblies.) Pope's point is made succinctly, and with much less heat than Swift usually generates on this topic.

---

[1] Gould, 'The Sketch, a Satyr', *Works* (1709), vol. II, p. 333; Young, *Love of Fame*, Satire I, lines 245–6; Pope, *Donne IV* 197 and 199, and *Epistle to Bolingbroke* 111; cf. *Epistle to Murray* 99–100.

In the course of re-moulding Donne's fourth Satire Pope intensifies the jibes about feminine 'painting'. To conclude his account of the importunate Courtier Donne comments drily that 'wiser then all us,/He knows what Lady is not painted'. Pope adds a realistic detail by introducing a contemporary beauty preparation ('whitewash') which also punningly alludes to the Gospel denunciation of hypocrites as whited sepulchres:

> And last (which proves him wiser still than all)
> What Lady's Face is not a whited Wall?
> (150–1)

Later in the poem, when Pope amplifies Donne's image of the courtiers as pirates boarding the ladies, he produces a brilliant 'imitation' of his original, re-creating the Elizabethan scene as an eighteenth-century comedy of manners. Here is Donne:

> Now
> The Ladies come. As Pirats, which do know
> That there came weak ships fraught with Cutchanel,
> The men board them; and praise (as they think) well,
> Their beauties; they the mens wits; both are bought.
> Why good wits ne'r wear scarlet gowns, I thought
> This cause, These men, mens wits for speeches buy,
> And women buy all reds which scarlets die.
> He call'd her beauty limetwigs, her hair net:
> She fears her drugs ill lay'd, her hair loose set.
> (187–96)

Pope concerns himself only with the first half of this passage:

> Painted for sight, and essenc'd for the smell,
> Like Frigates fraught with Spice and Cochine'l,
> Sail in the *Ladies*: How each Pyrate eyes
> So weak a Vessel, and so rich a Prize!
> Top-gallant he, and she in all her Trim,
> He boarding her, she striking sail to him.
> "*Dear Countess*! you have Charms all Hearts to hit!"
> And "*sweet Sir Fopling*! you have so much wit!"
> Such Wits and Beauties are not prais'd for nought,
> For both the Beauty and the Wit are *bought*.
> (226–35)

[ 95 ]

On this occasion the Biblical allusion (the 'weaker vessel' of St
Peter's First Epistle) merely contributes to the surface wit. A more
significant addition is Pope's 'Frigates', which was current slang for
women of easy virtue,[1] so that the pun neatly uncovers the mer-
cenariness beneath the fine trim of the ladies. The exclamatory 'so
rich a Prize!' in the same way makes the men's predatoriness more
explicit than it is in Donne. The elaborate rhetorical patterning of
Pope's verse, and his persistent balancing of the half-lines, male
against female, mimes the minuet-like progression of this court
ritual, until the formality is brutally shattered by the emphatic
'*bought*'. Had Pope followed Donne in his amused speculation as to
'Why good wits ne'r wear scarlet gowns. . . .' he would have
muffled the reverberations of this key-word. For '*bought*' does not
simply mean that the Countess has acquired her charms by means
of bought perfumes and cosmetics (spice and cochineal) while Sir
Fopling has picked up his wit at second-hand from books and plays.
The fine lady and the witty gentleman (we can take Beauty and Wit
in the last line as personal nouns) are *bought* because they have been
bribed and corrupted, and their sexual skirmishing barely conceals
their hope of further winnings in the game of Court politics: they do
not praise 'for nought'.

The piratical fortune-hunter sacrifices all considerations to his
own gain, and remains supremely indifferent to the needs of others:
'For 'tis the Genius of a true *Courtier* not to lend a Hand, or part
with a Farthing to one that wants every thing.'[2] Full of self-seeking,
the Court was also full of shifts and stratagems, encouraging the
secretive, claustrophobic atmosphere so skilfully realized in Donne's
Satire. Place-hunting was a matter of course, as was the bribing of
electors and journalists. Appropriately enough it was from the
Secret Service funds, which were exempted from detailed account-
ing, that many of the political manoeuvres were financed. Shaftesbury presents a cautionary sketch of life 'in the highest Sphere of

---

[1] Cf. Pope's *Sober Advice from Horace*, line 62: 'Who trades in Frigates of the second
Rate.'
[2] Tom Brown, *Amusements Serious and Comical* (1700), p. 13.

human Affairs'. His account, its head-long speed suggesting the mad haste of the events, may remind us of Pope's narrative of the last days of Sir Balaam:

> First a general Acquaintance. – Visits, Levees. – Attendance upon the *Great* and *Little*. – Popularity. – A Place in Parliament. – Then another at Court. – Then Intrigue, Corruption, Prostitution. – Then a higher Place. – Then *a Title*. – Then a Remove. – A *new* MINISTER! – Fractions at Court. – Ship-wreck of *Ministrys*. – The *new*: The *old*. – Engage with *one*: piece up with *t'other*. – Bargains; Losses; After-Games; Retrievals.[1]

The rewards of a 'higher Place' might be high indeed, in terms both of political power (as Shaftesbury makes plain, the Court was still the real seat of government), and of the financial benefits which accompanied such power. During his four and a half years as Secretary of State the Earl of Nottingham received a total of nearly £37,000, and although the post must have necessitated considerable personal expense Nottingham's income was probably in excess of £26,000.[2] The Paymaster of the Forces drew a salary of £4,000 a year, 'but this was nothing to the enormous perquisites of the office, the commissions on foreign loans and the interest on balances reserved for the pay of the troops'.[3] Inevitably the courtier was ranked with the stock-jobber and the scrivener as a parasite on the economy. Lower down the political hierarchy the gains were proportionately smaller, yet still substantial enough to create hot-house conditions in which the basest cringing flourished, and where the rich and influential were plagued by dependents:

> Who starves by Nobles, or with Nobles eats?
> The Wretch that trusts them, and the Rogue that cheats.
> Is there a Lord, who knows a cheerful noon
> Without a Fiddler, Flatt'rer, or Buffoon?
> Whose table, Wit, or modest Merit share,
> Un-elbow'd by a Gamester, Pimp, or Play'r?
>
> (*To Bathurst* 237–42)

---

[1] Miscellany IV, ch. i, *Characteristicks*, vol. III, pp. 208–9.
[2] Habakkuk, 'Daniel Finch,' pp. 161–2.
[3] Mingay, *English Landed Society*, p. 74.

[ 97 ]

This is a far cry from the genuine hospitality and serenity that can still be found in the country, where men do not scramble for attention and rewards.

It is a far cry, too, from plain sincerity. Appearances are at their most deceptive in courts, where greed and opportunism are masked by the forms of good breeding. At levees and receptions 'Fop shews Fop superior complaisance',[1] and the abilities of the protean man come into their own: 'Such spirits are very proper in the Court, where we must comply and render our selves easie to conform to all kind of humours and manners, without being perceived to be guilty of constraint.'[2] The courtier is the perfectly adaptable man, but in the name of adaptability he has abandoned the self-respect and consistency of character that make for steadiness in personal relationships. He has allowed his integrity to be eroded by the prevailing currents of intrigue, acquisitiveness, and flattery: 'the Flatterer, who has no Principles in him, and leads not a Life properly his own, but forms and moulds it according to the various Humours, and Caprices of those he designs to bubble, is never one and the same Man, but a meer *Dapple* or *Trimmer*, who changes Shapes with his Company.'[3] Without strength of character the man of decorum tends at best to become a cipher. Worse, his politeness may be a cloak for indifference or subterfuge. Addison's equivocal behaviour during 1714 towards the rival translators of Homer, when he was giving his blessing simultaneously to the efforts of Pope and Thomas Tickell, must quickly have convinced the former that a man could be 'so obliging that he ne'er oblig'd'. Worst of all, good breeding may sharpen the edge of arrogance; Pope remarked to Swift that Bubb Dodington 'is so insupportably insolent in his civility to me . . . that I must affront him to be rid of it'.[4] It marks a crucial stage in the history of Sir Balaam when he 'marries, bows at Court, and

---

[1] *Dunciad* IV 138.
[2] S.C., *Art of Complaisance*, p. 164. Gay observes that the accomplished courtier outdoes Proteus: *Fables*, 1st series, no. xxxiii.
[3] Plutarch, 'How to know a Flatterer from a Friend', *Morals: Translated from the Greek, by Several Hands*, 5th ed. (1718), vol. II, p. 105.
[4] Letter of 6 January 1734, *Correspondence*, vol. III, p. 401.

grows polite', sinking deeper into the moral slime even as he believes himself to be rising on the social ladder.

In Court circles what passes for complaisance is in reality compliance and servile flattery. Financial and political ends are held to justify the most obsequious means. Elsewhere in society the need for 'politeness' can be made an excuse for intellectual timidity and shallowness, for erecting taboos round dangerous subjects, for never mentioning Hell to the fashionable congregation in Timon's Chapel. Addison and Steele sometimes write as if being 'put out of countenance', having one's feelings hurt in company, is the very worst of fates. Under such pressures as these good conversation may crumble into discourse 'too trivial to raise any Reflections which may put well bred Persons to the Trouble of Thinking';[1] well-bred persons will be content to hand round the fatuities assembled by Swift in his *Compleat Collection of Genteel and Ingenious Conversation*. Since a consensus of opinion held that it was better to err on the side of over-politeness than to risk being rude and blunt, the man who tries to speak his mind can be dismissed as a boor and conveniently ignored:

> To such extent good-nature now is spread,
> To be sincere is monstrously ill-bred.[2]

To many observers it seemed that the deviousness and hypocrisy of the Court were infiltrating the rest of society, driving sincerity before them. 'Nothing is thought beautiful, that is not painted,' declared Robert South in a sermon of 1676, and continued: 'so that, what between *French* fashions, and *Italian* dissimulations, the old, generous, *English* spirit . . . seems utterly lost and extinct; and we are degenerated into a mean, sharking, fallacious, undermining way of converse; there being a snare, and a trapan, almost in every word we hear, and every action we see. Men speak with designs of mischief, and therefore they speak in the dark.'[3] In his last and most

---

[1] *The Tatler*, no. 166.
[2] Robert Dodsley, 'On Good and Ill-Nature. To Mr. Pope', lines 15–16, in his *Trifles* (1745), p. 182.
[3] *Sermons Preached upon Several Occasions* (1737), vol. I, p. 323.

well-known sermon, preached on 29 July 1694, Archbishop Tillotson repeated South's lament in less vivid language:

> Amongst too many other instances of the great corruption and degeneracy of the age wherein we live, the great and general want of sincerity in conversation is none of the least. The world is grown so full of dissimulation and compliment, that mens words are hardly any signification of their thoughts; and if any man measure his words by his heart, and speak as he thinks . . . he can hardly escape the censure of rudeness and want of breeding. The old *English* plainness and sincerity, that generous integrity of nature and honesty of disposition, which always argues true greatness of mind, and is usually accompanied with undaunted courage and resolution, is in a great measure lost among us. . . .

For Tillotson sincerity is 'the solid foundation of all virtue, the heart and soul of all piety and goodness'.[1]

The satirist is bound to speak as he thinks, at the risk of being censured for 'rudeness and want of breeding'. To demand that Pope should be 'complaisant' to Peter Walter, to object to his rough handling of Francis Chartres, is laughably beside the point, though at the same time it makes a serious comment on the moral squeamishness of some of the poet's contemporaries. Not that all satirists are equally forthright. In the first Dialogue of the *Epilogue to the Satires* Pope's fictitious opponent, a man of the Court, taxes him with calling a crime a crime, and reminds him of the style which Horace had adopted:

> But *Horace*, Sir, was delicate, was nice;
> *Bubo* observes, he lash'd no sort of *Vice*:
> *Horace* would say, *Sir* Billy *serv'd the Crown*,
> Blunt *could do Bus'ness*, H[u]ggins *knew the Town*,
> In *Sappho* touch the *Failings of the Sex*,
> In rev'rend Bishops note some *small Neglects*. . . .
>
> (11–16)

What in Horace's hands would have appeared a compliment on Sir Billy's (Sir William Yonge's) devotion to duty would in reality have been a thrust at his time-serving and venality, Yonge's name being a

---

[1] John Tillotson, *Works*, ed. Thomas Birch (1752), vol. II, pp. 6–7.

byword for everything corrupt and contemptible. Sir John Blunt's most remarkable business successes were as a Director of the South Sea Company; Huggins, the cruel Warden of the Fleet Prison, '*knew the Town*' well enough to call numbers of fine gentlemen to testify to his good character when he was on trial for the murder of a prisoner. Horace is 'delicate' because his praise is purely ironical. The final couplet of this passage involves 'delicacy' of a slightly different kind, the Horatian trick of understatement whereby a gentle reference to failings and small neglects implies an abundance of graver faults. In the act of illustrating Horace's methods Pope's adversary shows himself a satirist, though he is very far from being worthy to keep satirical company with Pope. He endorses Court values and attitudes:

> Not twice a twelvemonth you appear in Print,
> And when it comes, the Court see nothing in't.

But he laughs nevertheless at the members of his own set, at Sappho and Sir Billy. Such is the treachery of the Court hanger-on, and for all his admiration of niceness and delicacy this man is emphatically, as the note to the first line of the poem describes him, an 'impertinent Censurer'. Pope may be echoing here a similar instance of self-contradiction in the taunt that had been levelled at him by Lord Hervey and Lady Mary Wortley Montagu:

> *Horace* can laugh, is delicate, is clear;
> You, only coarsely rail, or darkly sneer[1]

– a jibe that serves as prelude to the noble authors' own dark sneers. In any case, the impertinent Censurer has already revealed his personality by his chiding of the poet:

> You grow *correct* that once with Rapture writ,
> And are, besides, too *Moral* for a Wit.

The parenthetical 'besides' creates a provokingly insolent tone befitting the perverseness of judgment which equates Wit with immorality and flippancy. The adversary's character is such as to discredit any cause he supports, and the mere fact that this man

---

[1] *Verses Address'd to the Imitator of* . . . *Horace* (1733), lines 16-17.

praises Horatian delicacy makes us suspect that Pope is here calling
in question the moral propriety of applying this satirical technique
to the social and political scene in the year 1738. Our suspicions are
strengthened when the Censurer, with a witty adaptation of
Persius's famous lines, proceeds to sum up Horace's achievement:

> His sly, polite, insinuating stile
> Could please at Court, and make AUGUSTUS smile:
> An artful Manager, that crept between
> His Friend and Shame, and was a kind of *Screen.*

There is no merit in pleasing the English Court, and no possibility
of amusing the impervious George Augustus. More seriously,
'manager' is used here in its specialized sense of a Parliamentary
official whose duties include the presenting of articles of impeach-
ment. In such a context the adjective 'artful' is doubtfully complimentary, while 'Screen' is unequivocally contemptuous. For this
word, as Pope's own note observes, was a metaphor 'peculiarly
appropriated' to Sir Robert Walpole, having been freely applied to
his tactics in blocking investigations into the South Sea Bubble
disaster and various later scandals. Horace, unexpectedly, turns out
to be a kind of Walpole; to be Horatian is virtually to join the
enemy's camp. It is one thing to shield the victim of conversational
raillery from private discomfiture, quite another to protect one's
political ally from the shame of a public inquiry into his malpractices. The first part of the *Epilogue to the Satires* carries the
guarded subtitle 'A Dialogue Something like Horace'; the phrase
can be read as promising either a modest approximation to Horace's
manner or a poem in which Horace will be left morally behind.

Both parts of the *Epilogue* are concerned with the problem of
satirical outspokenness, with the difficulty of attacking 'Crimes that
scape, or triumph o'er the Law', because both are immediately concerned with the fate of satire. The Licensing Act of 1737 was seen
by the Opposition as a direct threat to the liberty of the press, so
that the satirist was being at the same time gagged by official censor-
ship and constrained by false notions of polite wit. Horatian delicacy,
with its indirectness and ironical understatements, is not a negligible

weapon, as Pope demonstrates in the first part of the *Epilogue*, both by putting so many brilliantly satirical lines into the Censurer's own mouth, and later, after his mock-recantation of satire, by wielding the weapon deftly himself. But it is a technique from which he officially dissociates himself, on the grounds that it lacks clear moral definition and is too subtly circuitous to meet the challenge of the times. Hence the gruff and manly tone with which the poet enters the poem. 'Go see Sir ROBERT' advises the Censurer, to which Pope responds:

> See Sir ROBERT! – hum –
> And never laugh – for all my life to come? . . .
> Would he oblige me? let me only find,
> He does not think me what he thinks mankind.
> Come, come, at all I laugh He laughs, no doubt,
> The only diff'rence is, I dare laugh out.

It is true that in his next 'speech' Pope abandons his no-nonsense manner, and offers to renounce satire, but this is a pretext to enable him to indulge in delicate satire of his own. His targets are the official organs of Court opinion ('No *Gazeteer* more innocent than I!'), and the vapid and effusive style that is the approved mode of Court expression, as in the tributes which were paid in 1737 to the virtues of the late Queen Caroline.[1] All this helps to focus the satirist's pressing concern with the problem of style. It also leads Pope's opponent to betray his malice. He points out that satire has a legitimate *raison d'être* – to attack great men who have fallen from power – and goes on to plead for immunity for two political Lords:

> But let all Satire in all Changes spare
> Immortal *S[elkir]k*, and grave *De [La Wa]re!*
> Silent and soft, as Saints remove to Heav'n,
> All Tyes dissolv'd, and ev'ry Sin forgiv'n,
> These, may some gentle, ministerial Wing
> Receive, and place for ever near a King!

---

[1] Lines 70 ff. Persius's first Satire laments that there is no 'Manly Greatness left in *Rome*' (Dryden's translation, line 206), since literature is being enfeebled by effeminate oratory and 'Such little Elegies as Nobles Write' (98). This Satire, like Pope's, is a dialogue between the poet and his 'Friend, or Monitor'; and the immediate context of the famous character of Horace is a discussion of the satirist's need to be outspoken, even 'fierce'.

There, where no Passion, Pride, or Shame transport,
Lull'd with the sweet *Nepenthe* of a Court;
There, where no Father's, Brother's, Friend's Disgrace
Once break their Rest, or stir them from their Place;
But past the Sense of human Miseries,
All Tears are wip'd for ever from all Eyes;
No Cheek is known to blush, no Heart to throb,
Save when they lose a Question, or a Job.

(91–104)

For sheer virtuosity this must rank as one of the finest examples in Pope of that 'delicate Satyr . . . which has the Face of Praise'.[1] 'Immortal' is the exact word for a statesman who has made himself indispensable to four monarchs. The tone of hushed reverence is beautifully sustained, from the sweeping gesture of the opening line down to the quotation from Isaiah which that line has already half-anticipated: 'and the Lord God will wipe away tears from off all faces.'[2] The reverence is then rapidly dissipated by the monosyllables of the last couplet, culminating in the stark ugliness of 'job'. In his *Dictionary* Dr Johnson defined 'job' in this sense as 'a low mean lucrative busy affair', and cited Pope's couplet in illustration.

This ingenious apotheosis of those who stand nearest the Throne provides the momentum for the poem's climax, as Pope takes up and elaborates the necessary connection between Vice and social and political 'Greatness':

*Vice* is undone, if she forgets her Birth,
And stoops from Angels to the Dregs of Earth:
But 'tis the *Fall* degrades her to a Whore;
Let *Greatness* own her, and she's mean no more:
Her Birth, her Beauty, Crowds and Courts confess,
Chaste Matrons praise her, and grave Bishops bless:
In golden Chains the willing World she draws,
And hers the Gospel is, and hers the Laws:
Mounts the Tribunal, lifts her scarlet head,
And sees pale Virtue carted in her stead! . . .
Hear her black Trumpet thro' the Land proclaim,
That "Not to be corrupted is the Shame."

---

[1] John Oldmixon, *An Essay on Criticism* (1728), p. 89.    [2] Isaiah xxv 8.

In Soldier, Churchman, Patriot, Man in Pow'r,
'Tis Av'rice all, Ambition is no more!
See, all our Nobles begging to be Slaves!
See, all our Fools aspiring to be Knaves!
The Wit of Cheats, the Courage of a Whore,
Are what ten thousand envy and adore.
All, all look up, with reverential Awe,
On Crimes that scape, or triumph o'er the Law:
While Truth, Worth, Wisdom, daily they decry –
"Nothing is Sacred now but Villany."

In degenerate times the satirist must be a plain dealer, so independent that he can denounce corruption wherever it breaks out,
whether in the Government or among the self-styled 'Patriots' of
the Opposition. Yet what is most remarkable about this concluding
passage, as Professor James Osborn has demonstrated, is that it is
simultaneously outspoken and oblique. Within the indignant assault
on general corruption is concealed a specific and very personal
attack on Walpole, for Vice Triumphant, the scarlet whore, is
identifiable as Molly Skerrett, long Walpole's mistress, who had
become his second wife in March 1738, two months before the poem
appeared.[1] Pope's italics, at the beginning of the passage, are more
sardonic even than usual: the fallen woman has been publicly owned
by the 'Great Man'.

It is a tribute to Walpole's ascendancy that this attack has to be
made so covertly. The passage contains therefore an element of
Horatian indirectness, but Pope accepts and employs this technique
only because he can assimilate it to a manner that would certainly
have struck his first readers as far more Juvenalian than Horatian.
It was one of the critical commonplaces of the age that Horace's
comic, jocose satire concerned itself with foibles, while Juvenal, the
tragic satirist, indignantly lashed the vicious and the criminal. As
early as 1732, in a prose letter prefixed to the third edition of the
*Epistle to Burlington*, Pope had contemplated a more tragic subject-

---

[1] J. M. Osborn, 'Pope, the Byzantine Empress, and Walpole's Whore', *Review of English
Studies*, new series, vol. VI (1955), pp. 372–82; reprinted in Mack, *Essential Articles*,
pp. 539–52.

matter: 'I will leave my Betters in the quiet Possession of their *Idols*, their *Groves*, and their *High-Places;* and change my Subject from their *Pride* to their *Meanness*, from their *Vanities* to their *Miseries*.'[1] And by 1738 it could be said of Pope, as the *Tatler* had said of Juvenal, that he 'attacks Vice as it passes by in Triumph, not [like Horace] as it breaks into Conversation. The Fall of Empire, Contempt of Glory, and a general Degeneracy of Manners, are before his Eyes in all his Writings.'[2] Dryden had been influential in establishing this contrast between the two Latin satirists, and, like Pope, Dryden at the end of his career had come to slight Horace for political reasons. In 1684 he could write that Horace's satires 'are incomparably beyond Juvenal's, if to laugh and rally is to be preferred to railing and declaiming.' In 1693, when he was hostile towards a Court that was largely indifferent towards him, he reversed his earlier estimate, and reproached Horace with being, among other things, a 'well-mannered Court slave, and a man who is often afraid of laughing in the right place'.[3]

In the *Epilogue to the Satires* Pope was consciously entering 'a sort of PROTEST against that insuperable corruption and depravity of manners, which he had been so unhappy as to live to see'.[4] And if the satirist does not enter a protest, no one else can be relied upon to do so. The appointed guardians of law and morality, the 'Watchmen of the Publick Weal', are inert. The Prelate, like a lazy ox, is 'slumb'ring in his Stall' and needs goading into action.[5] The cause of Virtue is served only by her 'Priestess Muse', the Muse of poetry, whose duty is both to cherish the good and to keep the vicious at bay. Though at the end of the second *Dialogue* Pope feels himself morally alone in his poetical ministration, drawing 'the last Pen for Freedom', there is no loss of confidence. Truth and Virtue will ultimately prevail over the flattering insincerities of the Court:

---

[1] Twickenham Edition, vol. III (ii), p. 132.
[2] *The Tatler*, no. 242.
[3] 'Preface to *Sylvae*', *Essays*, vol. II, p. 31; 'A Discourse concerning Satire', *Essays*, vol. II, p. 132 – see also pp. 134 and 139.
[4] *Dialogue II* note to line 255.
[5] *Dialogue II* 217-19.

Ye tinsel Insects! whom a Court maintains,
That counts your Beauties only by your Stains,
Spin all your Cobwebs o'er the Eye of Day!
The Muse's wing shall brush you all away:
All his Grace preaches, all his Lordship sings,
All that makes Saints of Queens, and Gods of Kings,
All, all but Truth, drops dead-born from the Press,
Like the last Gazette, or the last Address.

# CHAPTER SIX

# 'No Follower, but a Friend'

The future of satire and the Fall of Empire are urgent matters which leave little time for the formalities of good breeding. In the *Epilogue to the Satires* politeness has worn very thin, but is still just adequate to hold in check the hostility generated between the speakers:

> To *Cato*, *Virgil* pay'd one honest line;
> O let my Country's Friends illumin mine!
> – What are you thinking? *Fr*. Faith, the thought's no Sin,
> I think your Friends are out, and would be in.
>     *P*. If merely to come in, Sir, they go out,
> The way they take is strangely round about.
>
>                   (*Dialogue II* 120–5)

The chirping impertinence of 'I think your Friends are out, and would be in,' elicits from the poet a courteously dignified reply; what elements of good manners survive in this poetical exchange are entirely on Pope's side. To throw away in the cause of satire all social graces, all politeness, would be to sink to the level of Grubstreet. So although Pope is outspoken and independent, indeed because he is so, he has no qualms about proclaiming his friendship with high-born and well-bred politicians of whatever party:

> God knows, I praise a Courtier where I can.
> When I confess, there *is* who feels for Fame,
> And melts to Goodness, need I SCARBROW name? . . .
> How can I PULT'NEY, CHESTERFIELD forget,
> While *Roman* Spirit charms, and *Attic* Wit. . . .
> Names, which I long have lov'd, nor lov'd in vain,
> Rank'd with their Friends, not number'd with their Train;

And if yet higher the proud List should end,
Still let me say! No Follower, but a Friend.[1]

But there are limits to politeness, and as we have seen Pope is
increasingly concerned with showing where these limits must be set.
Forced to listen to the outpourings of the poetasters who besiege him
at Twickenham, the poet represents himself as being as courteous
under provocation as any gentleman could be. But he is, after all,
only human:

> Seiz'd and ty'd down to judge, how wretched I!
> Who can't be silent, and who will not lye;
> To laugh, were want of Goodness and of Grace,
> And to be grave, exceeds all Pow'r of Face.
> I sit with sad Civility, I read
> With honest anguish, and an aking head.
>
> (*To Arbuthnot* 33-8)

The poet suppresses his laughter, but cannot remain straight-faced;
his civility, counterbalanced as it is by his 'honest anguish', cannot
be other than 'sad'. The poet's door, it seems, has been hospitably
open to all comers; now in weary desperation he is forced to close it
in the faces of those who abuse his hospitality. This again is human
and understandable. Pope is being waylaid by the pirates and high-
waymen of letters, who stop his chariot and board his barge. His
privacy is impudently invaded by figures who glide ghost-like
through his sanctum, 'the Grotto of Freindship & Liberty'.[2] In
these extreme circumstances the poet's politeness takes its rightful
place as a minor element in his personality. It is more important
that in the first lines of the *Epistle* we should remark that he is kindly
towards his servant ('good *John*'), is hospitable, modest in avoiding
public acclaim, and a Church-goer. The civility of the true gentleman is seen to be firmly based on good nature and the Christian

---

[1] *Dialogue II* 63 ff. The Earl of Scarborough was firmly of the Court party, Pulteney and
Chesterfield two of Walpole's most eloquent opponents. In the penultimate line Pope
refers to his friendship with the Prince of Wales, who was at this time openly antagonistic
to the King and Court.
[2] Pope to Bathurst, 28 April 1741, *Correspondence*, vol. IV, p. 342.

religion. It is not an end in itself, and it is certainly not a mask for selfish greed.

In this *Epistle* Pope's delineation of his own character is subtle and unobtrusive. His ostensible purpose in the opening paragraphs is to present his besieged plight with dramatic force to the recipient of his verse-letter. Dr Arbuthnot, like Martha Blount, Lord Bathurst, and Lord Burlington, has a very positive role to play in the *Epistle* addressed to him. He is Pope's true friend, and the poem persuades us that the bond which exists between the two men is that genuine friendship which Robert South eulogized as 'the top, the flower, and crown of all temporal enjoyments'.[1] 'Familiar friends,' as Defoe observed, 'are wrote to in a familiar stile.'[2] Pope writes to Arbuthnot without forms and ceremonies; he evidently enjoys complete freedom of access. It is in effect a comment on the quality of their relationship, and a measure of Arbuthnot's sympathy, that Pope is able to unburden his heart at such length, making what Bacon in his essay 'Of Friendship' calls a 'kind of Ciuill Shrift or Confession'. And the closeness of the relationship is such that Arbuthnot can influence the course of the poem by his prudent advice. The prose 'Advertisement' prefacing the *Epistle* represents Pope as having spared the proper names of some of his victims at 'the Request of the learned and candid Friend to whom it is inscribed'. This giving and taking of advice is dramatized in the poem itself. As Pope begins to enumerate those who remain stubbornly unrepentant under his satiric attack Arbuthnot urgently interrupts:

> Does not one Table *Bavius* still admit?
> Still to one Bishop *Philips* seem a Wit?
> Still *Sapho* – "Hold! for God-sake – you'll offend:
> "No Names – be calm – learn Prudence of a Friend:
> "I too could write, and I am twice as tall,
> "But Foes like these!"
>
> (99–104)

Arbuthnot is concerned for his friend's safety, but too sensible to exaggerate the threat, so the anxious staccato of ' "Hold! for God-

---

[1] *Sermons*, vol. I, p. 29.  [2] *Compleat English Gentleman*, p. 132.

sake . . ." ' gives way to good-humour: 'I too could write, and I am twice as tall.' The suave assurance of this line emerges very clearly if we compare it with the alternative, and presumably earlier, reading: 'I too could write, and sure am twice as tall.' This is rhythmically flat and quite misses the playful emphasis of the final version, where the voice rises to the hyperbolical 'twice'. When we read the line we act out Arbuthnot's amusement; his smile plays round our lips. Pope's response is to assert that he suffers more from his flatterers than from such foes as Colley Cibber and Lady Mary Wortley Montagu. But in depicting these flatterers at work he does in fact refrain, as Arbuthnot has advised, from naming names. Instead of '*Colly*', '*Henley*', '*Sapho*', we now have:

> One dedicates, in high Heroic prose,
> And ridicules beyond a hundred foes;
> One from all *Grubstreet* will my fame defend,
> And, more abusive, calls himself my friend.
> This prints my Letters, that expects a Bribe,
> And others roar aloud, "Subscribe, subscribe".

Edmund Curll is of course immediately recognizable as the man who prints Pope's letters, but '*This* prints . . .' is more scathingly dismissive than even Curll's own name would have been. In this instance Pope drives home his personal thrust by the very act of complying with Arbuthnot's request.

Addison thought that 'there is no Subject of Morality which has been better handled and more exhausted' than that of friendship.[1] The important classical discussions of this topic, Plato's *Lysis*, the eighth and ninth books of Aristotle's *Nicomachean Ethics*, and Cicero's *de Amicitia*, certainly treat it as a 'Subject of Morality'. For they all emphasize that only good men can be true friends. Evil-minded people, being inconstant and unbalanced, faithful only to themselves, are unable to enter into lasting relationships even with their like. Friendship, therefore, as Aristotle declares at the opening of the eighth book of his *Ethics*, is itself a virtue, or at least implies and involves virtue. Pope was re-phrasing a traditional

---

[1] *The Spectator*, no. 68.

commonplace when, during his last illness, he observed: 'There is nothing that is meritorious but virtue and friendship, and indeed friendship itself is only a part of virtue.'[1] The *Epistle* implies the merits of the poet who pens it, and dramatizes the sympathy and humanity of the man who is being addressed; in addition the mere fact that the friendship between Pope and Arbuthnot appears to have continued undiminished throughout the long disease of the poet's life provides valuable indirect testimony to their moral characters. Since they are old friends, it follows that they must also be good men.

In the course of his *Spectator* paper Addison cites a verse from Ecclesiasticus: 'A faithful friend is the medicine of life' (vi 16). The comparison of a good friend to an able physician is a recurrent image in Plutarch's disquisition 'How to know a Flatterer from a Friend'.[2] It also runs through Bacon's essay, in which friendship is seen as preserving intellectual and emotional health, while Sir William Temple, at the conclusion of his essay 'Of Health and Long Life', reduces the metaphor to its literal terms: 'In all Diseases of Body or Mind, 'tis happy to have an able Physician for a Friend, or a discreet Friend for a Physician; which is so great a Blessing, that the Wise Man will have it to proceed only from God'; the Wise Man is the author of Ecclesiasticus, whom Temple goes on to quote.[3] Such precisely is the blessing which Pope enjoys in Dr Arbuthnot:

> Friend to my Life, (which did not you prolong,
> The World had wanted many an idle Song)
> What *Drop* or *Nostrum* can this Plague remove?
> Or which must end me, a Fool's Wrath or Love?
> A dire Dilemma! either way I'm sped,
> If Foes, they write, if Friends, they read me dead.

There is an unbridgeable gap between the man thus apostrophized and the parasites who are friends mercly to the poet's dinner table, his purse, or his literary prestige. It is one of the poem's delightful

---

[1] Spence, § 656.
[2] *Morals*, vol. II, pp. 98–151. Pope quotes at length from this piece, including one of the physician/friend comparisons, in a note to Book VI line 406 of his *Iliad* translation.
[3] *Works* (1720), vol. I, p. 289.

minor ironies that these men of rhyme seek Pope's advice as though he were their physician and friend. They consult him, however, not to be cured but rather to be preserved in their folly:

> All fly to *Twit'nam*, and in humble strain
> Apply to me, to keep them mad or vain.

The scribblers are a considerable nuisance, but being so blatantly selfish they can at least be easily disposed of. They play into the poet's hands ('Glad of a quarrel, strait I clap the door'), and reduce flattery to an absurdity:

> Say for my comfort, languishing in bed,
> "Just so immortal *Maro* held his head:"
> And when I die, be sure you let me know
> Great *Homer* dy'd three thousand years ago.

A much more insidious threat to the world of letters is posed by Atticus. He is all of a piece, a literary despot and one of those 'Prudes in friendship, who expect distance, awe and adoration'.[1]

> Willing to wound, and yet afraid to strike,
> Just hint a fault, and hesitate dislike;
> Alike reserv'd to blame, or to commend,
> A tim'rous foe, and a suspicious friend,
> Dreading ev'n fools, by Flatterers besieg'd,
> And so obliging that he ne'er oblig'd.

Atticus is not affable; there can be no intimacy with him. His reserve contrasts sharply both with Arbuthnot's frankness and concern, and with Bolingbroke's open-armed reception of Pope into the aristocracy of letters. The judicial tone of the Atticus portrait, its careful qualifications and antitheses, its *buts*, *ifs* and *yets*, suggest the man's frigid caution and emotional inhibitions. Men of spirit and promise are his potential rivals; like any petty tyrant he regards them 'with scornful, yet with jealous eyes,/And hate[s] for Arts that caus'd himself to rise'. Such attitudes are altogether incompatible with friendship, which by its very nature 'immediately banishes Envy under all

---

[1] Pope to Henry Cromwell, 30 December 1710, *Correspondence*, vol. I, p. 111. Pope was describing a type; he had not yet met Addison.

its Disguises.'[1] Being incapable of friendship Atticus is susceptible only to the flattery of foolish admirers.

With his suspicious fears Atticus is a travesty of the true friend. He is also, and it is a related point, a travesty of the true critic. In both aspects he had been prefigured in the *Essay on Criticism*, some four years before the Atticus lines were first sketched:

> *Now*, they who reach *Parnassus*' lofty Crown,
> Employ their Pains to spurn some others down;
> And while Self-Love each jealous Writer rules,
> *Contending Wits* become the *Sport of Fools*:
> But still the *Worst* with most Regret commend,
> For each *Ill Author* is as bad a Friend.
>
> (514–19)

In the *Essay on Criticism* Pope seems to have taken up a suggestion from the closing lines of Horace's *Ars Poetica*, where an analogy between the good critic and the good friend is hinted at. This analogy runs through the *Essay*, whether Pope is giving advice to contemporary judges of wit ('Be thou the *first* true Merit to befriend': 474), or commending their predecessors:

> Such late was *Walsh*, – the Muse's Judge and Friend,
> Who justly knew to blame or to commend;
> To Failings *mild*, but *zealous* for Desert. . . .[2]

Horace himself 'Will like a *Friend* familiarly convey/The *truest Notions* in the *easiest way*' (655–6). The small band of good critics occupies an honoured position equidistant from servile flatterers and from splenetic carpers. On one side are the bitter enemies of all wit but their own. On the other are the lackeys of literature:

> Of all this *Servile Herd* the worst is He
> That in *proud Dulness* joins with *Quality*,
> A constant Critick at the Great-man's Board,
> To *fetch and carry* Nonsense for my Lord.
>
> (414–17)

---

[1] Eustace Budgell, *Spectator* no. 385.
[2] Lines 729–31. The Twickenham Edition (vol. IV, p. 110) contrasts the behaviour of Walsh, the ideal critic, with that of Atticus, 'Alike reserv'd to blame, or to commend'.

The true judge of wit is generous-spirited but honest, neither servile nor malicious:

> Still pleas'd to *praise*, yet not afraid to *blame*,
> Averse alike to *Flatter*, or *Offend*.
>
> (742–3)

Such too is the character of the friend, who likewise stands midway between the extremes of fawning parasite and spiteful detractor. Such is Arbuthnot's character, as the *Epistle* creates it; he is not simply the poet's true friend, but the ideal friend, sympathetic, frank, sociable, unwavering in his constancy.[1] By addressing Arbuthnot as 'Friend to my Life' Pope at once establishes him in a central position between flatterers and foes, and sets him in opposition to both these extremes. Arbuthnot is on the side of life; Pope's false friends and enemies are equally selfish and equally bent on his destruction: 'If Foes, they write, if Friends, they read me dead'. This pattern of flatterer/friend/foe also underlies the passage I have discussed above in which Arbuthnot urges caution. Pope recites the names of his professed enemies; Arbuthnot's interruption introduces the voice of the real friend, and his exclamation ' "But Foes like these!" ' is then neatly turned by the poet:

> One Flatt'rer's worse than all;
> Of all mad Creatures, if the Learn'd are right,
> It is the Slaver kills, and not the Bite.[2]

In the *Essay on Criticism* the critic/friend analogy helps Pope to define and also to dignify the critic's function, by emphasizing the qualities of character which the critic must possess. In the *Epistle to Dr Arbuthnot* a more covert analogy, that of the satirist as friend, similarly enables him to exalt his own poetical function. For the satirist properly considered is a critic of his fellow-men who admonishes society only because, like a true friend, he has society's best interests at heart. He is not afraid to blame, though he is also pleased to praise when the opportunity presents itself. He is as un-

---

[1] Cicero, *de Amicitia* xviii 65.
[2] Lines 104–6. In lines 251 ff. Gay shares Arbuthnot's central position between the extremes of hostile and flattering Dunces.

willing to indulge in insincere flattery as he is to offend through irresponsible invective. Pope shows himself neither obsequious to the great, condoning the vices of the wealthy and powerful, nor a railing enemy of mankind. He is 'not proud, nor servile'. Unlike Bufo, and unlike Atticus, he has 'sought no homage from the Race that write'. Nor has he paid homage to the undeserving in fulsome dedications or complimentary verses. Such begging tricks earn nothing but scorn from a poet who feels secure in, even rather jaunty about, the financial independence he has gained through his highly successful translations:

> But (thanks to *Homer*) since I live and thrive,
> Indebted to no Prince or Peer alive. . . .
>
> *(Epistle II ii* 68–9)

Not without reason Pope is proud of having established himself as the first completely independent professional writer in England. The financial security which his pen has won, and which allows him to 'maintain a Poet's Dignity and Ease',[1] is the material foundation of his country gentleman's life at Twickenham. It is also an essential condition for writing unbiassed satire, particularly when that satire is directed against the prevailing corruption and place-hunting at Court. Boileau, Pope reminds us, was 'pension'd', and Dryden held the positions of Historiographer and Poet Laureate. Though we can appreciate the audacity of their achievements under these handicaps, Pope also means us to feel that their freedom of satirical speech must have suffered some curtailment. He himself can proceed to 'strip the Gilding off a Knave' because he is 'Un-plac'd, un-pension'd, no Man's Heir, or Slave'. Writing from a position of financial and moral strength he can write boldly:

> Yes, while I live, no rich or noble knave
> Shall walk the World, in credit, to his grave.[2]

The bolder the satirist, the more likely he is to be misrepresented. For their own peace of mind readers will try to dismiss his rebukes as the snarls of a misanthropist, or will refuse to acknowledge their general application and relish them instead as specific attacks on a

---

[1] *To Arbuthnot* 263.     [2] *To Fortescue* 111–20.

handful of acquaintances and public figures. 'The Truth of it is, Satyrists describe the Age, and Backbiters assign their Descriptions to private Men'.[1] Readers of this kind seek to degrade the satirist, to reduce him to the status of a lampooner, a man eager to offend, a foe to mankind. Such a status Pope loftily repudiates:

> Curst be the Verse, how well soe'er it flow,
> That tends to make one worthy Man my foe,
> Give Virtue scandal, Innocence a fear,
> Or from the soft-ey'd Virgin steal a tear!
> But he, who hurts a harmless neighbour's peace,
> Insults fal'n Worth, or Beauty in distress,
> Who loves a Lye, lame slander helps about,
> Who writes a Libel, or who copies out:
> That Fop whose pride affects a Patron's name,
> Yet absent, wounds an Author's honest fame;
> Who can your Merit selfishly approve,
> And show the Sense of it, without the Love;
> Who has the Vanity to call you Friend,
> Yet wants the Honour injur'd to defend;
> Who tells whate'er you think, whate'er you say,
> And, if he lye not, must at least betray:
> Who to the *Dean* and *silver Bell* can swear,
> And sees at *Cannons* what was never there:
> Who reads but with a Lust to mis-apply,
> Make Satire a Lampoon, and Fiction, Lye.
> A Lash like mine no honest man shall dread,
> But all such babling blockheads in his stead.
>
> (*To Arbuthnot* 283–304)

This passage ushers in Sporus. The formality of its construction, the dignified tone, as of a public prosecutor, are appropriate to its role, which is one of recapitulation and summing-up before the climax of evil is reached. Many threads are being drawn together. The 'Fop whose pride affects a Patron's name' is the epitome of Bufo, the proud and indifferent patron, and of 'prating *Balbus*' (275 ff.). Even that earlier and more innocuous flatterer, who 'more abusive, calls himself my friend', reappears in the line 'Who has the Vanity to call you Friend'. There is concentration too on another plane, for Pope

---

[1] *The Tatler*, no. 242. The point is enlarged upon by Addison in the *Spectator*, no. 568.

here unequivocally declares the *Epistle*'s allegiance to Horace. The poem has already alluded to Horace, by direct quotation (' "Keep your Piece nine years" '), by such fainter echoes as 'the Dog-star rages!' and 'read me dead', and by skilful use of the Horatian technique of gliding into dialogue and out again. Moreover Pope has shown himself perfectly at home in the Horatian styles, that of witty urbanity ('nay 'tis past a doubt,/All *Bedlam*, or *Parnassus*, is let out') and that of impassioned rhetoric: 'Who shames a Scribler? . . .' But it is within the long passage I have quoted that the *Epistle* comes closest to imitating Horace, for the account of the backbiter ('Who loves a Lye . . .') is an expanded version of part of the fourth Satire of the first Book:

> absentem qui rodit amicum,
> qui non defendit alio culpante, solutos
> qui captat risus hominum famamque dicacis,
> fingere qui non visa potest, commissa tacere
> qui nequit: hic niger est, hunc tu, Romane, caveto.[1]

This poem is Horace's apologia for satire, and these lines are its core, an answer to the charge that he is sadistic and malevolent. There is, Horace implies, a fundamental contrast between the man evil in his words and the essentially virtuous satirist.[2] Pope poses the satirist's difficulty even more acutely than does Horace, by raising the question of the malicious interpretation of realistic satirical detail. The episode of Timon's Villa had found a multitude of readers eager to equate that villa with the Duke of Chandos's palatial house of Cannons. At the same time Pope enlarges Horace's moral frame of reference. The 'babling blockhead' sins against Christian morality by contravening the injunction 'Love thy neighbour', and against chivalric ideals by

---

[1] Lines 81–5: 'The man who backbites an absent friend; who fails to defend him when another finds fault; the man who courts the loud laughter of others, and the reputation of a wit; who can invent what he never saw; who cannot keep a secret – that man is black of heart; of him beware, good Roman.'

[2] In Pope's first version of Horace's lines, published in the *London Evening Post*, 25 January 1732, and inscribed to Lord Hervey, this contrast is explicitly stated at the close: ' 'Tis not the *Sober Sat'rist* you should dread,/But such a *babling Coxcomb* in his Stead.' In the *Epistle* the sober satirist makes his appearance only after Sporus has been dealt with.

insulting 'fal'n Worth, or Beauty in distress'. In helping lame slander about he parodies genuine charity. Finally, the Fop's treachery strikes at the root of friendship: 'If thou hast opened thy mouth against thy friend, fear not; for there may be a reconciliation: except for upbraiding, or pride, or disclosing of secrets, or a treacherous wound: for for these things every friend will depart.'[1] The Fop is thus morally opposed to Arbuthnot, the true friend, and to Pope, for the responsible satirist, the antithesis of this blackguardly creature, is upright, discriminating, and moved by righteous indignation:

> Ask you what Provocation I have had?
> The strong Antipathy of Good to Bad.
> When Truth or Virtue an Affront endures,
> Th' Affront is mine, my Friend, and should be yours.
> Mine, as a Foe profess'd to false Pretence,
> Who think a Coxcomb's Honour like his Sense;
> Mine, as a Friend to ev'ry worthy mind;
> And mine as Man, who feel for all mankind.
>
> *(Dialogue II* 197–204)

The satirist is a friend to good men, to Truth and Virtue. And as a friend should be, he is a man of sensibility and compassion: 'For even satire is a form of sympathy.'[2]

The phrase 'all such babling blockheads' inadequately sums up the malicious and treacherous type-figure of the Fop. It does, however, prepare us for the merely contemptible aspect of Sporus, for Arbuthnot's prompt dismissal of him as insignificant and worthless, a 'Thing of silk', a 'Butterfly'. But such a response, as the poet proceeds to show, is inadequate; it takes account of Sporus's 'trifling Head' but ignores the more important fact of his 'corrupted Heart'. He is the embodiment of everything that has been brought together in the preceding passage, 'the Fop' made flesh and blood. He displays the foolish pride of a Bufo, the hypocritical civility of an Atticus:

---

[1] Ecclesiasticus xxii 22.

[2] D. H. Lawrence, *Lady Chatterley's Lover* (Harmondsworth, 1961), p. 104; Lawrence is here distinguishing true satire from personal gossip (that of Mrs Bolton), as Horace and Pope had done.

So well-bred Spaniels civilly delight
In mumbling of the Game they dare not bite.
Eternal Smiles his Emptiness betray,
As shallow streams run dimpling all the way.

Any secure personal relationship is denied to a puppet, an 'Amphibious Thing' who 'now trips a Lady, and now struts a Lord'. Sporus is therefore confined to those roles which lie on either side of true friendship. Just as he is physically a hermaphrodite, so morally he combines the activities of servile parasite and scurrilous detractor. He is a 'Flatt'rer at the Board', and, like the giddy, variable creatures of the first part of the *Epistle*, is 'never consonant to himself, nor properly his own Man . . . all his Passions, his Love and Hatred, his Joy and Sorrow, are borrowed and counterfeit.'[1] But he is also the Toad at the ear of Eve, spitting abroad his tales, lies, spite, smut, and blasphemies. As the incarnation of the desire to bring evil out of good, to betray, to misapply, to corrupt, Sporus is very properly identified as Satan, at once the Enemy and the False Friend of man.

No other Epistle of Pope's rises to such a statement of evil. The moral atmosphere of the poem has now to be cleansed, and Pope begins by asserting his own manliness and independence against the effeminacy and servility of Sporus, his own seriousness of purpose and commitment to virtue's cause against Lord Hervey's vicious flippancy. This passage ('Not proud, nor servile . . .') is as impersonal in manner and as deliberately shaped as the lines which introduce Sporus. Unlike those lines, however, this catalogue of the poet's moral successes is inert; the accumulation of pallid items does not compensate for a lack of strength and vitality in the verse. Even when the poet's father is presented as a type of virtue (382 ff.) the very thoroughness of the presentation seems a little heavy-handed. His mental and bodily health, his wisdom and serenity, and the 'Unspotted Names' of both parents, are set against the recurrent imagery of disease, madness, frenzy and dirt associated with Grubstreet; his innocence, honesty and humility against the backbiting, the lies, and the pride of Sporus. Pope's father was a stranger to

---

[1] Plutarch, 'How to know a Flatterer from a Friend', *Morals*, vol. II, p. 107.

courts; Sporus, the type of the corrupt courtier, is forever at the ear of Queen Caroline. More subtly, the poet's fervent prayer 'Oh grant me thus to live, and thus to die!' echoes his earlier wish, 'Oh let me live my own! and die so too!' (261), but marks an important step forward; the independence on which the poet has been priding himself is only a means to the kind of good life which Pope's father actually lived.

The last paragraph of this already long coda reveals Pope both as friend and son, tenderly caring for an aged mother, and praying for Heaven's blessing on Arbuthnot. Pope is now himself the physician, using 'lenient Arts' and smoothing the 'Bed of Death'. It is now his concern to 'explain the asking Eye', a phrase that in its restrained daring of expression captures all the poignancy of the sick-bed. Though Pope appears here primarily in his domestic capacity, the satirical poet is not forgotten. The writing of satire creates foes and friends, spins a web of personal relationships, as does no other form of literature. Having watched Pope, in his double role of private individual and public poet, conducting himself with exemplary and unfaltering rectitude through the complexities of these relationships, we can freely endorse the *Epistle*'s closing statement: 'Thus far was right, the rest belongs to Heav'n.'

# CHAPTER SEVEN

# Mammon

## I 'THE TRADING INTEREST'

The satirist combines the virtues of the faithful friend and the country gentleman. In his concern for others, his integrity, his modest way of life, and his hospitality, he is a standing rebuke to the Court, whose vices are concentrated in Sporus. Pope could be more straightforward and unwavering in his attitude to the Court than many country gentlemen of his time because he was financially more secure. Some of those who boasted of their political independence were perhaps rationalizing their inability to afford the costly attendance at Court which might ultimately win them a 'place'. For the average country gentleman was far from being well-to-do. I have referred above to the financial pressures which curtailed country hospitality;[1] unpaid local government work might also involve large expenses. Moreover, landowners were the most heavily taxed members of the community. When, in 1714, the legal rate of interest was reduced from six to five per cent, this measure was offered as a slight relief to the gentry: 'the heavy Burden of the late long and expensive War hath been chiefly born by the Owners of the Land of this Kingdom by reason whereof they have been necessitated to contract very large Debts and thereby and by the Abatement in the Value of their Lands are become greatly impoverished.'[2] In some cases this impoverishment was the delayed result of taxes and fines imposed on Royalist estates after the Civil War;[3] in others the debts could be laid squarely at the door of the gentleman's (or his heir's) irrespon-

---

[1] See pp. 78–9.   [2] *The Statutes of the Realm* (1810–28), vol. IX, p. 928.
[3] Habakkuk, 'The English Land Market', pp. 158–9.

sibility. Defoe, with the practical education of a Dissenting Academy behind him, and with a well-developed sense of the value of book-keeping, castigates those landowners who are too proud to audit their own accounts or to take the letting of their farms and properties into their own hands.[1] A thoughtless young man, newly come into a modest inheritance, might squander it in high living. Thomas Smith of Shaw House, Wiltshire, records in his Diary the dramatic con-clusion of a business visit to London: 'At two this Morning was call'd up, where at my coming down Staires I found Mr Webb, Nephew to him of Farley of the same Name, in an extream necessi-tous Condition, having spent his whole Substance and is in want of all Necessarys of Life perfectly, not being now above 6 or 7 and twenty, a great Example of a profligate base Temper, he now coming in a begging Manner: but could have but little time with him ye Coach being ready.' On his return to Wiltshire, however, Thomas Smith duly reported the young man's plight to his uncle.[2] Quite apart from the perils of London the need to maintain a 'figure' in local society, and to keep abreast of one's neighbours with a fine house and equip-age, could involve ruinous expenditure. Defoe commented that 'every gentleman seems to be willing to liv[e] as gay as he can.'[3]

'Our Gentry,' wrote Steele, 'are, generally speaking, in debt; and many Families have put it into a kind of Method of being so from Generation to Generation.'[4] In such precarious circumstances a single financial setback, or a sequence of small misfortunes, might force the family to sell a part or the whole of its estate. When an estate was hedged about, as many were, by protective legal devices, a private Act of Parliament was necessary before the owner or his trustees could offer land for sale. From the evidence supplied by these Acts it appears that the land market was at its most active be-tween 1688 and 1714, when no fewer than 244 Acts were passed;[5]

---

[1] *Compleat English Gentleman*, pp. 244–5.
[2] J. A. Neale, *Charters and Records of Neales of Berkeley, Yate and Corsham* (Warrington, 1907), pp. 194–5.
[3] *Compleat English Gentleman*, p. 104.
[4] *The Spectator*, no. 82.
[5] Habakkuk, 'The English Land Market', p. 156. In the much longer period from 1714 to 1770 only 219 Acts are recorded.

many of these specified that the sale was designed to meet debts, or, less frequently, to raise portions for daughters. There were two main groups of purchasers who moved into the vacuum left by the impoverished gentlemen: first, the large and well-established landed proprietors, whose incomes, from farm-rents, timber, mining-rights and so on, were substantial enough to support the burden of taxation and even the occasional bout of extravagance. In Bedfordshire and Northamptonshire the already large and efficiently run estates of the Earls of Halifax and Kent, and of the Dukes of Grafton and Bedford, grew even larger.[1] The very size of these properties demanded a degree of organization – an estate office and well-kept accounts – that the smaller landowner was unable or unwilling to contrive. With these large landowners may be included the 'new men' who came suddenly into wealth and prominence after a few years of profitable Government service, like the Duke of Chandos, or as the result of a more than usually successful legal practice, like Pope's friend Lord Bathurst, an inveterate snapper-up of properties who bought energertically in the home counties besides enlarging his estate at Cirencester. Professor Habakkuk has argued that these Government servants and lawyers, though their fortunes were spectacularly made, represented like the landowners the stable and conservative elements in society; they were in any case not numerous. So the movement of property into the hands of this first group of purchasers, since it tended to consolidate the *status quo*, passed with relatively little comment.

Those buyers who attracted more attention, because they were often felt to be disturbing the social structure, were a second group, men newly enriched from the proceeds of manufacturing or (most commonly) of trade. When tradesmen retire from business 'with immense wealth, not less than two or three hundred thousand pound, nay with half a million in their pockets',[2] they feel justified in laying out some of their wealth in grander things than balance-sheets. The metamorphosis of the merchant into the country gentleman was no new phenomenon. The process was familiar enough in the sixteenth

---

[1] H. J. Habakkuk, 'English Landownership, 1680–1740', *Economic History Review*, vol. X (1940), p. 5. I am indebted to this article for much of the present paragraph.
[2] Defoe, *Compleat English Gentleman*, p. 266.

and seventeenth centuries; many of the substantial squires of the Civil War period were of merchant stock. And at the end of the seventeenth century land was still a good financial investment, yielding a relatively small but very secure return. 'For money is a disposable commodity, and in the passage doth easily stick to the hands of those who have the power to transmit it. But Land is an apparent visible Estate, which the Law hath so provided for, that it cannot be diverted, or conceal'd.'[1] The traditional view of the land as man's real mainstay and nourisher was still influential: 'Land . . . is most valuable of all Things, because it gives all Things.'[2] Most important, landownership conferred social prestige and political influence. The London shipbuilder Sir Henry Johnson bought the manor of Aldeburgh; with it came seats in Parliament for himself and his brother, a merchant in the East India trade.[3] A less ambitious businessman would be content to buy, or to build, a neat house convenient enough for him to travel daily into the City. Others had houses further afield, their week-end and summer residences. Defoe noted with approval that the new 'handsom large Houses' to be seen in Essex and Surrey were usually 'Citizen's *Country-Houses*, whither they retire from the hurries of Business, and from getting Money, to draw their Breath in a clear Air'.[4]

This movement of property involved a continuous reshaping of the structure of rural society, especially in the home counties, and demanded a mutual accommodating of needs and interests on the part of tradesmen and landowners. There were, inevitably, business contacts between the landed producers of grain and wool and the merchants who handled these commodities for export. Addison

---

[1] Caleb Trenchfield, *A Cap of Gray Hairs, for a Green Head* (1671), p. 123.
[2] Vanderlint, *Money Answers All Things* (1734), p. 114. Professor Habakkuk quotes a cruder expression of this sentiment by, of all people, Peter Walter: 'I live on Bread and Butter and milk porridge; and it must be land that contains the cows for this, whereas none of the stock companies have a single cow': 'The English Land Market,' p. 170.
[3] Robert Walcott, *English Politics in the Early Eighteenth Century* (Oxford, 1956), pp. 27, 162 and 164.
[4] *Tour*, ed. Cole, vol. I, pp. 6 and 168–9. The merchants of Bristol, Liverpool and Hull, and industrialists in wool-manufacturing and mining areas were also buying estates conveniently near their offices: L. B. Namier, *England in the Age of the American Revolution*, 2nd ed. (1961), p. 11.

argues that trade has 'made our Landed Estates infinitely more Valuable than they were formerly'.[1] Other connections were tacked together by that kind of arranged match, immortalized by Hogarth, in which the merchant's daughter marries a pedigree, and the beau is united to a strong-box. Swift reported such a marriage to Stella in September 1711: 'Lord Raby, who is earl of Strafford, is on Thursday to marry . . . the daughter of Sir H. Johnson [the politician-shipbuilder] in the city; he has threescore thousand pounds with her, ready money; besides the rest at the father's death.'[2] Sir William Temple remarked, in 1685, 'I think I remember, within less than Fifty Years, the first Noble Families that Married into the City for down-right Money.'[3] Successful marriages certainly played an important part in creating the family fortunes of the Earls of Ashburnham and the Dukes of Bedford and Newcastle; the biggest landlords naturally attracted the wealthiest heiresses, and the great estates became even greater.[4] The merchant's family, for its part, gained an entrée into polite society: Sir Balaam's daughter 'flaunts a Viscount's tawdry wife'.

In these ways the line of demarcation between the landed and trading 'interests' was blurred. Addison's point that trade enhanced the value of land would have seemed self-evident to many large proprietors. But then Addison was aiming to soothe the smaller landowners, who were jealous of their acres and their independence, hostile towards the usurping *nouveaux-riches*, and unreasoningly antagonistic to commerce. In a later number of the *Spectator* Steele took up Addison's argument, and brought this hostility into the open: 'There is scarce any thing more common than Animosities between Parties that cannot subsist but by their Agreement. . . . And this is always the Case of the landed and trading Interest of *Great Britain*; the Trader is fed by the Product of the Land, and the landed Man cannot be cloathed but by the Skill of the Trader; and yet those Interests are ever jarring.' The remainder of the essay is devoted to the verbal contest between the representatives of these interests, Sir

---

[1] *The Spectator*, no. 69.     [2] *Journal to Stella*, ed. Williams, vol. I, p. 351.
[3] 'Of Popular Discontents', *Works*, vol. I, p. 268.
[4] Mingay, *English Landed Society*, pp. 76 and 78.

Roger de Coverley and Sir Andrew Freeport, the self-made man. Sir Andrew, enjoying a long and triumphant last word, alludes rather unchivalrously to the way in which the Coverley fortunes were once rescued by the intervention of a generous merchant, and concludes: "'Tis the Misfortune of many other Gentlemen to turn out of the Seats of their Ancestors, to make Way for such new Masters as have been more exact in their Accompts than themselves; and certainly he deserves the Estate a great deal better who has got it by his Industry, than he who has lost it by his Negligence.'[1] In areas of the country where social mobility had been restricted during the seventeenth century, and where rapid profits were now beginning to be made, the displacement of the gentry was sudden and thorough. The old Catholic families of Northumberland were almost entirely supplanted by mine-owners and coal-shippers: 'Before 1745, the new men were completely in the saddle.'[2] But it was the appearance of 'new Masters' in the home counties which attracted most comment. Defoe reported on reliable hearsay that less than a fifth of the 'antient families' of Kent and Essex had survived, the estates of the remainder having been bought by merchants and tradesmen.[3]

The newcomers were regarded, as they had been in the sixteenth century, with suspicion and disfavour. They were condemned as disruptive influences, brash upstarts who naturally wished to conceal or repudiate their lowly origins – the prospering Sir Balaam 'leaves the dull Cits' for the fashionable end of town.

> And there's your green Nobility,
> On Citizens so witty,
> Whose Fortune and Gentility,
> Arose from LONDON's City.[4]

---

[1] *The Spectator*, no. 174; Sir Andrew is alluding to matters mentioned in no. 109. Steele had previously dramatized this jarring of interests in the quarrel between the merchant Peter Plumb and the impoverished gentleman Thomas Gules (*The Tatler*, no. 256); and he was to return to the subject in *The Conscious Lovers* (1722).

[2] Edward Hughes, *North Country Life in the Eighteenth Century: The North-East, 1700–1750* (1952), p. xviii; see also pp. 1–13.

[3] *Compleat English Gentleman*, p. 263.

[4] Henry Carey, 'The Beau Monde', stanza xiv, *Poems on Several Occasions*, 3rd ed. (1729), p. 225.

One of the easiest ways of keeping the new men in their social place was to point out that wealth is no substitute for aristocratic breeding, that the social climber is still tainted with the manners of the trades-man. 'For let a Man get never so much Money to buy an *Estate*, he cannot purchase one Grain of GENTILITY with it . . . for put him into what Circumstance you please, he will discover himself one Time or other in Point of Behaviour, to be of a mean Extract, Awk-ward, Ungenteel and Ungenerous, a *Gentleman* at second Hand only, or a vain-glorious *Upstart*: For *you cannot make a silken Purse of a Sow's Ear*.'[1]

If the successful merchant or financier could not purchase gen-tility he might at least hope to purchase a title. 'Sir John Enville', formerly plain Jack Anvil, describes how he has made a 'very great Fortune' thanks to his 'very happy Genius for getting Money'; consequently, 'for these my good Services I was Knighted in the thirty fifth Year of my Age.'[2] Some citations in the Honours Lists required no satirical highlighting. In June 1720, shortly before the collapse of the South Sea Bubble, John Blunt, the driving force be-hind the enterprise, received a baronetcy 'for his extraordinary ser-vices in raising public credit to a height not known before'.[3] Balaam inevitably becomes Sir Balaam after being enriched by the death of his father and a lucky ship-wreck; and we can assume that Sir Job, his lightweight counterpart, is such another City Knight:

> Sir Job sail'd forth, the evening bright and still,
> "No place on earth (he cry'd) like Greenwich hill!"
> Up starts a Palace, lo! th'obedient base
> Slopes at its foot, the woods its sides embrace,
> The silver Thames reflects its marble face.
> Now let some whimzy, or that Dev'l within
> Which guides all those who know not what they mean
> But give the Knight (or give his Lady) spleen;

---

[1] Nathan Bailey, *An Universal Etymological English Dictionary*, 4th ed. (1728), s.v. 'Gentleman'.

[2] Addison, *Spectator* no. 299. 'Enville' is usually identified as the ironmaster Sir Ambrose Crawley (formerly Crowley).

[3] John Carswell, *The South Sea Bubble* (1960), p. 157.

"Away, away! take all your scaffolds down,
"For Snug's the word: My dear! we'll live in Town."[1]

Of the attributes of his Biblical namesake Sir Job, who is the equivalent of Horace's 'Dives', has only prosperity. He is defenceless against a Devil who tempts not with sore boils but with the spleen. Immodestly he chooses to build nothing less than a Palace, and that on a conveniently conspicuous site (we are perhaps meant to see social presumption in his building so near the Queen's House at Greenwich). The word-play in 'up starts' makes the swift rise of the building symbolize the career of its owner, just as the delightfully humanized Palace expresses his vanity ('The silver Thames reflects its marble face') and his snobbish pride: 'th'obedient base/Slopes at its foot'. Men like Sir Job are without taste, self-knowledge, or a sense of responsibility; yet they are respected members of a community that honours riches. 'A Man of Wealth is dubb'd a Man of worth' – but 'worth', as so often in Pope, is a wry pun.[2]

When Bacon enumerated the 'ways to enrich' he declared that 'the *Improuement of the Ground*, is the most Naturall Obtaining of *Riches*; For it is our Great Mothers Blessing, the Earths.'[3] A century later its place has been usurped, at least in Mr Spectator's opinion: 'I regard trade . . . as the most natural and likely Method of making a Man's Fortune; having observed, since my being a Spectator in the World, greater Estates got about *Change*, than at *Whitehall* or *St. James*'s. I believe I may also add, that the first Acquisitions are generally attended with more Satisfaction, and as good a Conscience.'[4] For the merchant to have had as 'good a Conscience' as the courtier would have seemed to Pope, and to many of his contemporaries, a very doubtful compliment, if not simply an ironical joke. It was rather more frequently asserted that the consciences of tradesmen, large and small alike, were far from good. The epitaph of Sir George Mertins, a Lord Mayor of London who died in 1727, is evidently pointing to a rare distinction when it claims that 'In Trade, he was without Extortion'.[5] It was plausible to assume that cheating and ex-

---

[1] *To Bolingbroke (Epistle I i)* 138–47.   [2] *To Murray (Epistle I vi)* 81.
[3] 'Of Riches.'   [4] Budgell, *Spectator* no. 283.
[5] John Hackett, *Select and Remarkable Epitaphs* (1757), vol. I, p. 186.

[ 129 ]

tortion were the rule, if only because legal machinery to deal with such matters was inadequate and cumbersome (like the restrictions on corn-engrossers) or simply non-existent; obtaining money by false pretences became an indictable offence only in 1757.[1] It was left to churchmen, essayists, and satirists to expose the ways of the con-fidence-trickster, the fraudulent projector, and the over-reaching shopkeeper, so that in the absence of official curbs and checks the malpractices of tradesmen became a satirical commonplace. In *The Beggar's Opera* Lockit takes it for granted that 'honest Tradesmen' are ready to cheat one another.[2] Robert Gould asks rhetorically, 'what's a *Tradesman* but a *licens'd Thief*?', and denounces the 'secret Trading Villain' as more evil than an assassin.[3] More slyly, Pope makes an oblique criticism of the merchant in the course of inform-ing us, with full mock-heroic elaboration, that it is now three o'clock in the afternoon:

> The hungry Judges soon the Sentence sign,
> And Wretches hang that Jury-men may Dine;
> The Merchant from th'*Exchange* returns in Peace,
> And the long Labours of the *Toilette* cease.
>
> (*Rape of the Lock* III 21–4)

The merchant has had a successful day's transactions on the Stock Exchange. The phrase 'in Peace', however, suggests not only his self-satisfaction but also his immunity from the molestation and pro-secution that have pursued the condemned wretches. The merchant's dubious activities are condoned by society.

Not that Pope was blind to the importance of trade for Britain's economy. In *Windsor-Forest* he celebrates the glories of a maritime nation by adapting the terms that Virgil had used to praise agricul-tural Italy under the rule of Augustus:

> Let *India* boast her Plants, nor envy we
> The weeping Amber or the balmy Tree,

---

[1] Carswell, *South Sea Bubble*, p. 14.

[2] Act III scene ii. Cf. 'I grant my bargains well were made,/But all men over-reach in trade': Gay, *Fables*, 1st series, no. xxvii, lines 9–10.

[3] 'The Corruption of the Times by Money' (1693), *Works*, vol. II, p. 296; and 'A Satyr against Man', *Works*, vol. II, p. 158.

> While by our Oaks the precious Loads are born,
> And Realms commanded which those Trees adorn.[1]

A peaceful and prosperous Britain is necessarily a commercial Britain. At the end of the *Epistle to Burlington* the catalogue of public works which are to be inaugurated by that [nobleman includes harbour developments and improvements in inland communications. Without a firm basis of mercantile activity the economy could not support Burlington's architectural enterprises; buildings and trade rise and fall together. But Pope did not forget that trade, however much it may be glorified as an abstraction, is ultimately the sum of the negotiations of individual shopkeepers, merchants and governments, negotiations which seemed to him, as they had to Elizabethan moralists, susceptible to ethical judgment. The career of Sir Balaam is based from first to last on perverted standards of morality. Near the beginning of the tale Pope comments that Balaam's 'word would pass for more than he was worth'; the later affair of the diamond reveals that Pope is not thinking only of Balaam's ability to obtain financial credit:

> Asleep and naked as an Indian lay,
> An honest factor stole a Gem away:
> He pledg'd it to the knight; the knight had wit,
> So kept the Diamond, and the rogue was bit.

In the business world there is no honour among thieves.

When he describes the factor as 'honest' Pope is deliberately turning against the mercantile community one of its favourite terms of praise. The term was ready-made for the ironist, and the verb 'stole' exposes at a single stroke the meaninglessness of the stock epithet. Pope himself is very far from using *honest* glibly; on the contrary, his handling of the word is careful and somewhat old-fashioned. In the seventeenth century honesty was usually synonymous with virtue or moral rectitude. It could still accurately render the Latin *honestum* (as in Thomas Cockman's very popular translation of Cicero's *de Officiis*, first published in 1699), while the 'honest man' was the precise equivalent of the classical *vir bonus*. Robert Gould invites us to

---

[1] Lines 29–32; the Twickenham Edition notes the parallel with *Georgics* II 136 ff.

[ 131 ]

Search thro' the Nation, find me if you can,
That Prodigy, a Truely Honest Man.[1]

And in 1708 the lexicographer John Kersey defined *honest* simply as 'Good, Vertuous, Just'.[2] But the frequent use of the word in the context of trade and business, emphasizing one particular kind of virtuous behaviour, helped to restrict its meaning, so that the sense 'dealing fairly, not lying, cheating or stealing' was coming in the early eighteenth century to be established as the dominant one. Jeremy Collier, spokesman of the bourgeoisie, seems unaware of any meaning of the noun *honesty* other than that of 'clear Dealing'.[3] Pope, however, resists this semantic tendency. He clings to the older and wider sense, as when he declares that 'An honest Man's the noblest work of God',[4] or when at the end of '1740' he expresses the pious hope that the Prince of Wales will rescue his country's low fortunes, so that

Europe's just balance and our own may stand,
And one man's honesty redeem the land.

Pope's usage is an implied rebuke to the values of commercialism; being truly honest involves far more than what passes under that name in the business world. More important, his conservative attitude towards the word's meaning is consistent with, indeed is part of, his conservative attitude towards moral standards. Throughout his poetry a traditional and comprehensive morality is being brought to bear on an age whose moral principles are steadily diminishing. In the *Epistle to Arbuthnot* three occurrences of *honest*, all with the wide meaning, cluster round the portrait of Sporus. Two of them ('an Author's honest fame,' and 'A Lash like mine no honest man shall dread') remind us of values which the modern foppish courtier has forgotten, but which it is essential to invoke. The third specifically contrasts the evil Sporus with the poet's father, who was 'By Nature honest, by Experience wise'. But Pope's father is dead, and honesty itself is in danger of dying out with those who practise it.

---

[1] 'A Satyr against Man', *Works*, vol. II, p. 162.
[2] *Dictionarium Anglo-Britannicum: or, a General English Dictionary.*
[3] 'Of Honesty', *Essays upon Several Moral Subjects*, Part IV, 2nd ed. (1725), pp. 31–93.
[4] *Essay on Man* IV 248.

This modest Stone what few vain Marbles can
May truly say, here lies an honest Man.

So begins Pope's commemorative Epitaph on his friend and colleague
Elijah Fenton. Here, regret for Fenton, and for declining honesty,
is fittingly expressed through literary reminiscence, an imitation
of Crashaw's 'Epitaph upon Mr Ashton':

> The modest front of this small floore,
> Beleeve me, Reader, can say more
> Than many a braver Marble can,
> *Here lyes a truly honest man.*

The ethical chaos engendered by Court and City compels good
men to be as elusive and retiring as wild game:

> To find an honest man, I beat about,
> And love him, court him, praise him, in or out.
> *(Dialogue II* 102–3)

Were it not for the satirist, reminding us of traditional values, seeking out the few surviving exemplars of virtue and sounding their
praises, the precious moral links with the past would be broken, the
ideal of the *vir bonus* would be forgotten, and honesty would perish.


## II THE MONEYED MEN

Pope, imitating Horace, condemns the merchant for being absurdly
motivated by selfish fears:

> To either India see the Merchant fly,
> Scar'd at the spectre of pale Poverty!
> See him, with pains of body, pangs of soul,
> Burn through the Tropic, freeze beneath the Pole![1]

The merchant pursues riches because he feels himself pursued by
poverty. Such a satirical attitude sets Pope apart equally from the
Whig standpoint of the *Spectator* and from the remarkably similar
views advanced in the *Craftsman*, the journal of the Tory Opposition
during the early 1730s. Addison regarded the merchant as a public

---

[1] *To Bolingbroke* 69–72.

hero: 'there are not more useful Members in a Commonwealth than Merchants. They knit Mankind together in a mutual Intercourse of good Offices, distribute the Gifts of Nature, find Work for the Poor, add Wealth to the Rich, and Magnificence to the Great.'[1] His eulogistic essay was reprinted in the *Craftsman* as the climax of a campaign on behalf of the merchant's rights and interests.[2] Spanish attacks on British shipping, particularly the affair of Captain Jenkins' ear, gave the Opposition powerful arguments against an ineffective administration, and an opportunity to woo the trading interest to its side. The indispensable merchant is enthroned in antithesis to the parasitic courtier, and Addison's arguments are embellished with the watchwords of the Opposition: 'As *Commerce* is the Thing, which renders every Country rich and consequently powerful, so the *Merchant*, in this View, may be said to be the most useful Member of the Society, in which He lives. . . . Under whatever Government He lives, the Merchant may be truely said to be an independent Man. He must always be an Enemy to *arbitrary Power*, and his *Industry* will ever set Him above the Temptation of *Corruption*. It is *Liberty*, which makes *Trade* flourish.'[3] The merchant must be persuaded to demonstrate his independence by joining forces with the Opposition, the party of the old-established landed gentry. And that party, for its own purposes, is therefore as eager as Addison ever was to deplore the 'invidious Distinction of the *landed* and *trading Interest*'.[4]

In seeking to abolish one distinction the *Craftsman* found it expedient to uphold another, that which Cicero had made between *mercatores* and *negotiatores* – the former a company of estimable and innocent men, the latter 'a vile Race of *Usurers*, a Sort of *Money-Scriveners*, who prey'd on the Necessities of Mankind, and were always held in the utmost Contempt'. In London, unhappily, the introduction of '*money'd Companies*' has transformed 'many an *honest*, *generous*, *industrious Merchant* into a *little*, *pitiful*, *pilfering*

---

[1] *The Spectator*, no. 69.
[2] No. 352 (31 March 1732).
[3] *The Craftsman*, no. 329 (21 October 1732); quotations are from the collected edition, 14 vols., 1731–7.
[4] *The Craftsman*, no. 350.

*Stock-jobber*.[1] It was in this third 'interest', that of the moneyed men, that the Opposition party located its true enemies. Into this base category fell financiers and Company Directors, scriveners, usurers and stock-jobbers, all the 'leeches who fill themselves continually with the blood of the nation, and never cease to suck it'.[2] To see these moneyed men as a clearly-defined and cohesive group is to see them through the eyes of Tory politicians and Tory satirists. The outstandingly successful financiers were those in whom self-interest predominated, men who were 'alike in nothing but one Lust of Gold';[3] they required no spokesman, no partisan journal to expound their policies. Yet there were alliances between these individualists, and there were coteries which formed around the nuclei of the large financial Companies such as the Sword Blade, and the Bank of England. The foundation of the Bank in 1694 had rescued the Government from acute monetary difficulties. In return for a loan of above a million pounds the Bank secured for itself important financial privileges and a measure of political influence. These privileges were strengthened by the 'engrafted stock' dealings of 1697, which established the Bank's supremacy over rival institutions and were reputed to have made a personal profit of £50,000 for its Director, Sir Gilbert Heathcote. According to Lord Bolingbroke this new practice of loans by private individuals to the State prepared the way for a host of evils: 'Thus the method of funding and the trade of stock-jobbing began. Thus were great companies created, the pretended servants, but in many respects the real masters of every administration.'[4] The Opposition might protest that 'the landed men are the true owners of our political vessel: the moneyed men, as such, are no more than passengers in it';[5] but the passengers were not so easily cowed. During Walpole's Ministry a hundred M.P.s held Bank stock, of whom a third normally voted with the Opposition.

[1] *The Craftsman*, no. 329.
[2] Henry St John, Viscount Bolingbroke, 'Some Reflections on the Present State of the Nation', *Works*, ed. David Mallet (1754), vol. III, p. 163.
[3] Pope, *To Bolingbroke* 124.
[4] 'Reflections', *Works*, vol. III, p. 151.
[5] Ibid., p. 174.

Whenever the Bank's privileges were threatened the Tory minority among these stockholders united solidly with the rest, and in 1737 this powerful lobby helped to defeat Sir John Barnard's proposals to reduce both the Bank's holding of the National Debt and the interest upon it.[1]

The political influence of the Bank was none the less potent for being kept discreetly in the background; the *pretended* servants were real masters. It was the idea of a secret power behind the Throne, or the Speaker's Chair, which so alarmed the Opposition. Addison's rapturous account of the 'just and regular Oeconomy' which characterizes all the operations of the Bank, and his description of the radiant figure of Public Credit,[2] are challenged by Bolingbroke's attack on 'the funds'. The establishment of Public Credit has given rise, in his view, to a 'whole mystery of iniquity', while 'the main springs that turn, or may turn, the artificial wheel of credit, and make the paper estates that are fastened to it, rise or fall, lurk behind the veil of the treasury'.[3] Trade has the merit of dealing in solid material goods, whereas high finance is unreal, an intangible 'mystery' which is viewed by turns with amazement and suspicion. Its abstract nature and secretive habits are brought together in the *Epistle to Bathurst* (lines 35–78), where Pope contemplates the benefits arising from the recent creation of 'paper-credit', that arbitrary process by which the status that belongs to pieces of gold is conferred on scraps of paper. The gold standard, though itself arbitrary, has at least proved convenient for gamblers, as Pope shows by considering the drawbacks of a simpler economic system, appropriate only to primitive heroic times, in which wealth is measured by incommodious possessions:

> His Grace will game: to White's a Bull be led,
> With spurning heels and with a butting head.
> To White's be carried, as to ancient games,
> Fair Coursers, Vases, and alluring Dames.

---

[1] Norman Hunt, 'The Russia Company and the Bank of England', *The Listener*, vol. LXIV (1960), p. 782.

[2] *The Spectator*, no. 3.

[3] 'A Dissertation upon Parties', Letter xix (first published as *Craftsman* no. 443), *Works*, vol. II, p. 245.

As an instrument of bribery and corruption, however, gold has its own serious limitations:

> Once, we confess, beneath the Patriot's cloak,
> From the crack'd bag the dropping Guinea spoke,
> And gingling down the back-stairs, told the crew,
> "Old Cato is as great a Rogue as you."
> Blest paper-credit! last and best supply!
> That lends Corruption lighter wings to fly!
> Gold imp'd by thee, can compass hardest things,
> Can pocket States, can fetch or carry Kings;
> A single leaf shall waft an Army o'er,
> Or ship off Senates to a distant Shore;
> A leaf, like Sibyl's, scatter to and fro
> Our fates and fortunes, as the winds shall blow:
> Pregnant with thousands flits the Scrap unseen,
> And silent sells a King, or buys a Queen.

This passage is itself 'pregnant' with verbs suggesting furtive activity ('pocket', 'flits') and the total commercialization of politics ('fetch or carry', 'ship off'); both lines of suggestion converge in the starkly uncompromising final verse, where monarchs are silently bought and sold. The *Epistle* forces our attention onto the insidious and pervasive influence of money. It also insists on the affinities between all immoral ways of gain. The transition from gambling at White's to financial corruption on an international scale anticipates the end of the *Epistle*; Balaam's wife 'falls to play' (the verb implies both greedy appetite and moral lapse), he accepts a bribe from France to redeem his fortunes, and is doomed. Again, since the successful gambler, like the usurer, is engaged in making his money breed, it is only to be expected that the unscrupulous Francis Chartres, 'after a hundred tricks at the gaming-tables', should take 'to lending of money at exorbitant interest and on great penalties, accumulating premium, interest, and capital into a new capital, and seizing to a minute when the payments became due'.[1] 'So money upon money increases, copulates, and multiplies, and guineas beget guineas in *sæcula sæculorum*.'[2]

---

[1] Pope's note on *Epistle to Bathurst* 20.
[2] Pope to Broome, 14 July 1723, *Correspondence*, vol. II, p. 182.

The desire to enrich oneself with the minimum effort and the maximum speed was encouraged and exploited by the Government's use of public lotteries to raise funds. To satisfy the gambling fever private lotteries were set up on the Government pattern. 'Wagering was not only a fashionable amusement, it was also an important interest amongst all classes, and it entered to a considerable extent into many business transactions.'[1] During the speculative boom which culminated in the South Sea Bubble crisis over two hundred insurance companies were floated in London alone; they offered, among other things, insurance on births and marriages. Traditionally, the rapid acquisition of wealth was condemned as unnatural and diabolical. 'When *Riches* come from the Deuill,' said Bacon, 'they come vpon Speed.' Satan appropriately makes his final conquest of Sir Balaam in a shower of unearned income, at which point the merchant degenerates into the moneyed man:

> The Tempter saw his time; the work he ply'd;
> Stocks and Subscriptions pour on ev'ry side,
> 'Till all the Dæmon makes his full descent,
> In one abundant show'r of Cent. per Cent.,
> Sinks deep within him, and possesses whole,
> Then dubs Director, and secures his soul.

A representative moneyed man was Sir Robert Clayton (1629–1707), a London scrivener who was employed in estate negotiations by eminent landowners throughout the kingdom. He was a trustee of George Villiers, the second Duke of Buckingham, and was rumoured to have 'swallowed' much of the Duke's property.[2] The political importance of wealth is suggested by his making a personal loan of £30,000 to William III to pay off the troops. Naturally Clayton was a Director of the Bank of England, and a Lord Mayor of London. As a more than representatively successful moneyed man he appealed to Defoe's admiration for private enterprise. In *Roxana* Clayton

---

[1] W. R. Scott, *The Constitution and Finance of English, Scottish and Irish Joint-Stock Companies to 1720* (Cambridge, 1910–12), vol. I, p. 383.
[2] D. C. Coleman, 'London Scriveners and the Estate Market in the Later Seventeenth Century', *Economic History Review*, 2nd series, vol. IV (1952), p. 227.

appears in the capacity of unpaid financial adviser to the heroine, arranging a 'substantial safe Mortgage for 14000 Pound', and making her money breed. In proposing that Roxana should marry some eminent merchant he becomes a propagandist for the trading interest, a more reputable sector of the community, and the one nearest to Defoe's own heart: 'Sir *Robert* said, and I found it to be true, that a true-bred Merchant is the best Gentleman in the Nation; that in Knowledge, in Manners, in Judgment of things, the Merchant out-did many of the Nobility . . . that a Merchant in flush Business, and a capital Stock, is able to spend more Money than a Gentleman of 5000 *l.* a Year Estate. . . . That an Estate is a Pond; but that a Trade was a Spring.'[1] The real-life Sir Robert, like other moneyed men, considered it no bad thing to invest in landed estates, and so to acquire direct political influence. Among the properties in Surrey bought by himself and his scrivening partner was the manor of Bletchingly, which brought with it a seat in Parliament. This estate had been sold to discharge Lord Peterborough's debts, neatly proving the fictional Sir Robert's point that 'the Gentlemen . . . ay, and the Nobility too, are, almost all of them, Borrowers, and all in necessitous Circumstances.'[2]

The scrivener combined the functions of estate-agent, broker, money-lender, and solicitor, and operated with a freedom unknown to his modern counterparts. He was well placed to snap up bargains for himself that came along in the way of business for others, and could often assist a needy gentleman by buying some of his property. The scrivener in Congreve's *Love for Love* is a 'Mr Trapland'. The apparently harmless clerk who 'pens a Stanza when he should *engross*',[3] is a scrivener in embryo; the engrossing, or preparing, of legal documents will lead to the engrossing of riches. Such a man, if the itch of verse had not claimed him, might have risen to be another John Blunt, who was, Pope informs us with evident distaste, 'originally a scrivener'.[4] Or he might have become a second Peter Walter,

---

[1] *Roxana, the Fortunate Mistress*, ed. Jane H. Jack (1964), pp. 164 and 170.
[2] Ibid., p. 167.
[3] *Epistle to Arbuthnot* 18.
[4] Note to *Epistle to Bathurst* 135.

obsessed with 'this *per Cent.* and that *per Year*'.[1] Yet for all his sordid materialism Walter enjoys the confidence and respect of his noble clients:

> His *Office* keeps your Parchment-Fates entire,
> He starves with cold to save them from the Fire;
> For you, he walks the streets thro' rain or dust,
> For not in Chariots Peter puts his trust;
> For you he sweats and labours at the Laws,
> Takes God to witness he affects your Cause,
> And lyes to every Lord in every thing,
> Like a King's Favourite – or like a King.
>
> *(Donne II* 71–8)

The cold formality of 'affects your Cause', and the rhythm of the two lines beginning 'For you . . .' skilfully suggest Peter's fawning insincerities. With its echo of the Psalmist's injunction 'Put not your trust in princes',[2] Pope's line about chariots implies not only that Peter regards a coach as so much wasteful expenditure, but also that he puts no faith in the lordly owners of fine chariots. Trust, in these negotiations, is an entirely one-sided affair, and such that Walter rose to become 'steward to the Duke of Newcastle, and other noblemen and gentlemen';[3] at his death in 1746 he was said to be worth £300,000. Some of this wealth was in landed property which, like other scriveners, he had acquired slowly and stealthily:

> In shillings and in pence at first they deal,
> And steal so little, few perceive they steal;
> Till like the Sea, they compass all the land,
> From Scots to Wight, from Mount to Dover strand. . . .
> Piecemeal they win this Acre first, then that,
> Glean on, and gather up the whole Estate:
> Then strongly fencing ill-got wealth by law,
> Indentures, Cov'nants, Articles they draw. . . .
>
> *(Donne II* 83 ff.)

What makes the scrivener so formidable in Pope's eyes is that his

---

[1] *Donne II* 56.
[2] Psalm cxlvi 3.
[3] John Hutchins, *The History and Antiquities of the County of Dorset*, 3rd ed. (1861–73), vol. III, p. 671.

intimate knowledge of the land market is supported by access to credit facilities, and backed by legal expertise. Unrestrained by moral scruples, such powerful moneyed men will purchase both property and souls. John Blunt's accumulation of wealth is impelled by the very loftiest of motives:

> No mean Court-badge, great Scriv'ner! fir'd thy brain,
> Nor lordly Luxury, nor City Gain:
> No, 'twas thy righteous end, asham'd to see
> Senates degen'rate, Patriots disagree,
> And nobly wishing Party-rage to cease,
> To buy both sides, and give thy Country peace.
>
> *(To Bathurst* 147–52)

### III THE USE OF RICHES

Since Peter Walter is a social upstart, it follows that he is insolent and ungenteel in behaviour:

> No young Divine, new-benefic'd, can be
> More pert, more proud, more positive than he.
>
> *(Donne II* 51–2)

The new men who were invading the land-market were, as we have seen, frequently reproached with lacking both the breeding and the sense of responsibility to be found in the true landowner: 'To avoid Confusion, it is to be noted, that a Peasant with a great Estate is but an Incumbent, and that he must be a Gentleman to be a Landlord.'[1] Sir Gilbert Heathcote and other large-acred men have no conception of rural economics, no idea of using their possessions:

> Yet these are Wights, who fondly call their own
> Half that the Dev'l o'erlooks from Lincoln Town.[2]

The envious restlessness of the 'new men' prevents them from enjoying their property; one estate is merely the stepping-stone to

---

[1] Steele, *Tatler* no. 169.

[2] *Epistle II ii* 244–5. Discontented people were said to look at those they envied in the same way 'as the Devil look'd over *Lincoln*': Swift, *Polite Conversation*, in *Prose Works*, vol. IV, p. 160; see also Twickenham Edition, vol. IV, p. 340.

[ 141 ]

another. Such preoccupation with present gain is completely at odds with the country gentleman's peace of mind, his sense of permanence. Secure and unhurried in the present, he is untroubled about the future. Instead of greedily amassing wealth he takes delight, like Lord Bathurst, in planting trees, a pursuit which has 'something in it like Creation', and which expresses 'the Love which we ought to have for our Country, and the Regard which we ought to bear to our Posterity'.[1] Unlike the moneyed man the country gentleman is not bounded by merely selfish considerations. Pope strikes the proper attitude in a letter to Ralph Allen:

> I am pleasd to think my Trees will afford Shade & Fruit to Others, when I shall want them no more. And it is no sort of grief to me, that those others will not be Things of my own poor Body, but it is enough they are Creatures of the same Species, and made by the same hand that made me.[2]

Pope's solemn tone betrays an uneasiness which the brave front tries to conceal. A few weeks earlier, writing to William Fortescue at his Devonshire country house, he had more frankly and more poignantly presented the facts of his situation:

> It gives me pleasure to reflect that you are now at your own Home, and in a Condition of Life which may encourage you to beautify and im- prove that which may be the Receptacle of your Age, & the End of all your Labors. You can cast a Glympse at Posterity, in your Daughter, & please yourself in the thought of Childrens Children enjoying it: I see nothing but Mrs Vernon [the lessor of his Villa], or a Sugar-baker, to succeed to my Plantations.[3]

Pope was a man without posterity and without property, for under laws passed during William III's reign Roman Catholics were pre- vented from purchasing or even inheriting land. These statutes were not rigidly enforced, but Pope felt himself legally committed to the condition of a perpetual tenant. Moreover, many of his Twickenham neighbours (for social not religious reasons) were also leaseholders,

---

[1] Addison, *Spectator* no. 583.
[2] 6 November 1736, *Correspondence*, vol. IV, pp. 40–41.
[3] 21 September 1736, *Correspondence*, vol. IV, p. 34.

occupying fashionable houses there for a season or two, while in Middlesex as a whole properties were changing hands so frequently during the seventeenth and early eighteenth centuries that 'no dominating gentry had time to take root and form a county interest'; 'local life was much less under the leadership of landed proprietors than in almost any other county, and it was fragmentary in consequence.'[1] Even while he appreciated the sense of stability conferred by the land and its associated way of life, Pope admitted the fluidity of property. His own circumstances, together with local conditions, led him to emphasize that the value of land, as of wealth, lies not in its being owned but in its being used. The conclusion of *To Bethel* (published in 1734) expresses much the same sentiments as the letter to Fortescue, but keeps melancholy at bay by having Swift raise the delicate matter of the poet's posterity, and by countering his regrets with a humorous double rhyme:

> "Pray heav'n it last! (cries Swift) as you go on;
> "I wish to God this house had been your own:
> "Pity! to build, without a son or wife:
> "Why, you'll enjoy it only all your life." –
> Well, if the Use be mine, can it concern one
> Whether the Name belong to Pope or Vernon?
> What's *Property*? dear Swift! you see it alter
> From you to me, from me to Peter Walter . . .
> At best, it falls to some ungracious Son
> Who cries, my father's damn'd, and all's my own.
> Shades, that to Bacon could retreat afford,
> Become the portion of a booby Lord;
> And Hemsley once proud Buckingham's delight,
> Slides to a Scriv'ner or a City Knight.
> Let Lands and Houses have what Lords they will,
> Let Us be fix'd, and our own Masters still.

The penultimate couplet refers to the sale of the Yorkshire estate of Helmsley by the trustees of the Duke of Buckingham. It was bought for £90,000 by Sir Charles Duncombe, a London banker, on his retirement in 1695; John Evelyn reported that Duncombe had

---

[1] Michael Robbins, *Middlesex* (1953), pp. 25 and 120.

nearly as much again in ready money.[1] The verb 'slides' defines both the slippery nature of property in general and the degrading effect of this particular purchase; the contemptuous 'or' shows that Pope is indifferent to the identity of the new owner, but also makes the usual jibe that the wealthy scrivener will undoubtedly receive a knighthood.

Pope's imitation of Horace's second Epistle of the second Book, published three years later than *To Bethel*, is a plea for a settled and contented mind. It, too, treats at some length the question of property, since the owning of land may well be thought to ensure mental tranquillity. As in the *Epistle to Burlington* the idea of 'Use' is all-important, and, again as in that poem, 'Use' is closely linked to the aim of 'following Nature'. For to follow Nature is to live up to one's capacity, to realize the full potential of one's possessions and one's personality. And when Time begins to sap our energies it becomes more urgent for us to exploit what still remains firm. The conclusion of *Epistle II ii* advises us to make at least a dignified exit:

> Learn to live well, or fairly make your Will;
> You've play'd, and lov'd, and eat, and drank your fill:
> Walk sober off; before a sprightlier Age
> Comes titt'ring on, and shoves you from the stage:
> Leave such to trifle with more grace and ease,
> Whom Folly pleases, and whose Follies please.

As man is steward of his body, an actor on God's stage, so is he steward of his property, whether he calls himself tenant or owner. Property, one of the eighteenth century's most cherished idols, is as uncertain as life, and its very uncertainty obliges us to utilize it sensibly while we can. In this *Epistle*, as in *To Bethel*, a discussion of the true 'Use' of an estate (lines 230 ff.) leads to a consideration of the instability, in terms of mere ownership, of all estates:

> The Laws of God, as well as of the Land,
> Abhor, a *Perpetuity* should stand:
> Estates have wings, and hang in Fortune's pow'r
> Loose on the point of ev'ry wav'ring Hour;

---

[1] *Dictionary of National Biography; Victoria County History of Yorkshire, North Riding,* vol. I (1914), p. 492.

Ready, by force, or of your own accord,
By sale, at least by death, to change their Lord.

That casual-seeming phrase 'at least by death' deliberately introduces
a new and sombre note. For death makes a final mockery of all vast
possessions, even those of Lord Bathurst, that exemplary planter
and improver of the soil:

> Man? and for ever? Wretch! what wou'dst thou have?
> Heir urges Heir, like Wave impelling Wave:
> All vast Possessions (just the same the case
> Whether you call them Villa, Park, or Chace)
> Alas, my BATHURST! what will they avail?
> Join Cotswold Hills to Saperton's fair Dale,
> Let rising Granaries and Temples here,
> There mingled Farms and Pyramids appear,
> Link Towns to Towns with Avenues of Oak,
> Enclose whole Downs in Walls, 'tis all a joke!
> Inexorable Death shall level all,
> And Trees, and Stones, and Farms, and Farmer fall.

Ownership of land may encourage a man to face the future calmly
and securely; but it may also induce a complacent self-satisfaction
that needs to be jolted by a memento mori. Again, the creation of a
large estate (provided it is created by a responsible individual) may
seem beneficial for society because it is a process of consolidating,
unifying, and ordering; yet the accumulation of 'vast Possessions',
whether they be land or gold, must in the end be unflatteringly
labelled covetousness. Already, in his comment that 'Estates have
wings' (line 248), Pope has quietly given to landed property the
proverbial attributes of riches: 'Wilt thou set thine eyes upon that
which is not? for riches certainly make themselves wings; they fly
away as an eagle toward heaven.'[1] Now he echoes Isaiah: 'Woe unto
them that join house to house, that lay field to field, till there be no
place, that they may be placed alone in the midst of the earth!'[2]
Archbishop Tillotson quoted this verse in a sermon against covetousness, and linked it to the parable of the rich man who was 'continually

---

[1] Proverbs xxiii 5. Pope also echoes this verse in To Bathurst 171–2.     [2] Isaiah v 8.

increasing his estate and enlarging his barns, to make more room still for his fruits, that he might *lay up goods in store for many years*. The parable' (Tillotson continues) 'does not so much as intimate any indirect and unjust ways of gain, which this man used to increase his estate; but condemns his insatiable desire and thirst after more; so that even *this* alone is *covetousness*, and a great fault, though it were attended with no other; because it is unreasonable, and without end.'[1] In short, the useful splendour represented by Bathurst's granaries and farms bears an ineradicable taint of avarice. Pope, as usual, has the best of both worlds. He shares many of the assumptions and values of the landed gentry yet is himself immune, in his five modest and rented acres at Twickenham, from the temptations of conspicuous waste, and from the subtler temptations of Bathurst's agricultural magnificence.

Robert South, like Tillotson, preached against covetousness, using as his text the same verse from St Luke's Gospel: 'And he said unto them, Take heed, and beware of covetousness: for a man's life consisteth not in the abundance of the things which he possesseth.'[2] Both divines frame a very wide definition of covetousness, so as to include men's 'anxious, carking *care* about the things of this world', their '*rapacity in getting*', and that 'tenaciousness in keeping' which shuts up the gates of charity. They both recognize that covetousness can present itself to us in the guise of prudent parsimony, of making ample provision for our children, or of securing for ourselves the honour and good repute that in a materialistic age riches are thought to bestow:

> But to the world, no bugbear is so great,
> As want of figure, and a small Estate.[3]

---

[1] *Works* (1752), vol. II, p. 225. This parable (St Luke xii 16–21) is expounded by Isaac Barrow in a sermon on 'The Consideration of our Latter End', *Works*, ed. John Tillotson (1716), vol. III, p. 120–2.

[2] Luke xii 15, introducing the parable of the rich man. South preached two consecutive sermons on this text (*Sermons*, vol. IV, pp. 391–473), and Tillotson, closely following South's arguments and the disposition of his material, a sequence of four (*Works*, vol. II, pp. 222–44).

[3] Pope, *To Bolingbroke* 67–8.

Finally, covetousness may beguile us 'under the specious pretence of industry in our callings', a warning which is particularly interesting in coming from Tillotson, with his Puritan background and middle-class sympathies. Sir Balaam, frugal and sober, 'constant at Church, and Change', charitable only with farthings, cannot help but prosper; the materially-minded will often obtain their material rewards. Bishop Butler, preaching 'Upon the Character of Balaam', sees him as a type of the materialist, the man who prostitutes himself for gain. Balaam 'wanted to do what he knew to be very wicked, and contrary to the express command of God; he had inward checks and restraints, which he could not entirely get over; he therefore casts about for ways to reconcile this wickedness with his duty'. So Pope's hero salves his conscience after the affair of the diamond:

> Some scruple rose, but thus he eas'd his thought,
> "I'll now give six-pence where I gave a groat,
> "Where once I went to church, I'll now go twice –
> "And am so clear too of all other vice."

This hollow sanctimonious boast is immediately followed by 'The Tempter saw his time . . .', and by Balaam's sudden affluence; wickedness and its rewards are reconciled with duty. Butler goes on to argue that the materialist is by definition the supremely unreasonable man: 'there is no account to be given in the way of reason, of men's so strong attachments to the present world: our hopes and fears and pursuits are in degrees beyond all proportion to the known value of the things they respect. This may be said without taking into consideration religion and a future state; and when these are considered,the disproportion is infinitely heightened.'[1] It is virtually as a homiletic *exemplum* that the tale of Sir Balaam is used to conclude the *Epistle to Bathurst*. When Pope has posed the 'knotty point' as to whether misers and prodigals meet their reward in this world or the next, the tale, offered ostensibly as a relief from such an abstruse problem, demonstrates that they receive their due rewards in both.

---

[1] Joseph Butler, *Works*, ed. J. H. Bernard (1900), vol. I, pp. 95–8. This sermon was first published in 1726, six years before the *Epistle to Bathurst*.

[ 147 ]

Lord Bathurst himself is very obviously neither miser nor prodigal. He has so successfully avoided the pitfalls of extremes, illustrated in Cotta and his son, that Pope can appeal to him to instruct us by his aristocratic example:

> The Sense to value Riches, with the Art
> T'enjoy them, and the Virtue to impart,
> Not meanly, nor ambitiously pursu'd,
> Not sunk by sloth, nor rais'd by servitude;
> To balance Fortune by a just expence,
> Join with Oeconomy, Magnificence;
> With Splendor, Charity; with Plenty, Health;
> O teach us, BATHURST! yet unspoil'd by wealth!
> That secret rare, between th'extremes to move
> Of mad Good-nature, and of mean Self-love.
> To Want or Worth well-weigh'd, be Bounty giv'n,
> And ease, or emulate, the care of Heav'n.
> Whose measure full o'erflows on human race
> Mend Fortune's fault, and justify her grace.
>
> (219–32)

The *Epistle to Bathurst* was originally entitled *Of the Use of Riches*, and the nobleman would seem to have taken to heart the words of Isaac Barrow: 'Riches are Χρήματα, things whose nature consists in usefulness . . . it is the art and skill to use affluence of things wisely and nobly, which makes it wealth.'[1] The verse-structure of the passage insists on the wisdom of moderation and balance. As Pope observed to Spence, 'the middle is the point for virtue',[2] including, it would seem, 'the Virtue to impart'. Since we have just witnessed the misguided patriotic fervours of the younger Cotta, we may not be inclined to demand of Bathurst a more vigorous imparting of his possessions, lest he too incur the charge of being madly good-natured. There is, besides, a strong classical and Christian tradition that charity must be discriminating: 'To Want or Worth

---

1 'The Duty and Reward of Bounty to the Poor', *Works*, vol. I, p. 325. There are several small verbal parallels between this sermon and the *Epistle to Bathurst*. Pope owned a set of Barrow's sermons; see his letter to Jacob Tonson, 3 September 1721, *Correspondence*, vol. II, p. 81.
2 Spence, § 297.

*well-weigh'd*, be Bounty giv'n.' 'Charity misplaced, as it is in truth and reality no charity in itself, so it is hardly any in us, when we squander it so imprudently, as to pass by a certain and real object, and give it those of whom we are not certain that they are true objects of charity.'[1] Isaac Barrow emphasizes that the charitable man does not fling away his goods as if he loathed or despised them, 'but fairly and softly, with good consideration he disposeth of them here and there, as reason and need do require'.[2] Conversely, the Timon who appears in the *Epistle to Murray* (*Epistle I vi*) is childish and arbitrary:

> His Wealth brave Timon gloriously confounds;
> Ask'd for a groat, he gives a hundred pounds.
>
> (85–6)

Worst of all, a benefactress like Narcissa, who 'made a Widow happy, for a whim',[3] actually insults her beneficiary.

With his careful charity the nobleman is performing Heaven's part: 'And ease, or emulate, the care of Heav'n'. Yet even as Pope sets such wealthy aristocrats as Bathurst on the side of the angels he is ingeniously undermining the foundations of their charity.

> Whose measure full o'erflows on human race
> Mend Fortune's fault, and justify her grace.

According to this definition charity is wealth that overflows from a full 'measure'; there is no question of voluntarily pouring it out. The couplet echoes the prudential doctrine of such divines as Samuel Clarke, who declares that the Church asks us to be 'charitable out of the Superfluities of our plenty and abundance; not to lay down our *lives*, or leave even the *comfortable Enjoyments* of life, but only to forsake the unreasonable and unfruitful Pleasures of Sin, the Madness and Follies of Profuseness. . . .'[4] Christianity no longer requires men to sell all they have and give to the poor. Though

---

[1] Tillotson, *Works*, vol. II, p. 597.
[2] *Works*, vol. I, p. 304.
[3] *To a Lady* 58.
[4] *Works* (1738), vol. I, p. 212; quoted in Leslie Stephen, *History of English Thought in the Eighteenth Century*, 3rd ed. (1902), vol. II, p. 340.

Fortune is to be blamed for scanting the needy, the religious implications of the phrase 'justify her grace' suggest that in making the rich man rich Fortune is an agent of what other churchmen, including Tillotson and Butler, would have considered a divinely-arranged social and economic plan: 'For, as Solomon expresses it in brief, and with much force, "the rich ruleth over the poor".' And this their general intercourse, with the superiority on one hand, and dependence on the other, are in no sort accidental, but arise necessarily from a settled providential disposition of things, for their common good.'[1]

Pope concludes his account of the aristocratic use of riches with a flourish of images and antitheses:

> Wealth in the gross is death, but life diffus'd,
> As Poison heals, in just proportion us'd:
> In heaps, like Ambergrise, a stink it lies,
> But well-dispers'd, is Incense to the Skies.
>
> (*To Bathurst* 233–6)

The second couplet is a wittily pointed and decorous version of a popular maxim: 'Money, like dung, does no good till it is spread.'[2] The antithesis of *stink* and *incense* completes the pattern set up in the preceding couplet with *death* and *life*, *poison* and *heals*. The effect of these sheer oppositions is to imply that the rich may be prompted by negative, even basically selfish considerations, that their charity may be a matter rather of getting rid of noxious wealth than of generous giving. Yet the final 'well-dispers'd' does something to counteract these implications, since it can be taken to mean both a wide and a sensible distributing of wealth. Pope is treading circumspectly; he refrains from easy judgments, and adopts a subtly qualified attitude towards the bounty of the well-to-do, comparable

---

[1] Butler, *Works*, vol. I, p. 219. Cf. Tillotson, *Works*, vol. II, pp. 244 and 598; and Barrow, *Works*, vol. I, pp. 319–20. At the conclusion of *Spectator* no. 219 Addison hopes that 'those who are in meaner Posts of Life' will 'by a just Deference and Submission to their Superiors make them happy in those Blessings with which Providence has thought fit to distinguish them'.

[2] Morris P. Tilley, *A Dictionary of the Proverbs in England in the Sixteenth and Seventeenth Centuries* (Ann Arbor, 1950), M 1071, citing Thomas Fuller's *Gnomologia* (1732).

with his later attitude in *Epistle II ii* towards Bathurst's 'vast Possessions'.

Pope's epithet 'well-dispers'd' also echoes, though faintly, the Psalmist's praise of the virtuous man: 'He hath dispersed, he hath given to the poor; his righteousness endureth for ever.'[1] Isaac Barrow took this verse as the text for his sermon on 'Bounty to the Poor'. The bountiful man is there comprehensively defined as one who not only gives what he has, but also does what he can, for the welfare, health and peace of mind of his neighbours; he is a man who truly loves his neighbour as himself. This definition points unmistakably to the real hero of the *Epistle to Bathurst*, the Man of Ross. He is the physician and magistrate of his community, the friend of the poor and hungry:

> Is any sick? the MAN of ROSS relieves,
> Prescribes, attends, the med'cine makes, and gives.
> Is there a variance? enter but his door,
> Balk'd are the Courts, and contest is no more.
> Despairing Quacks with curses fled the place,
> And vile Attornies, now an useless race.

'Such is true charity,' which 'will render a man a general benefactor, in all matters . . . will make him a bountiful dispenser of his goods to the poor, a comforter of the afflicted, a visiter of the sick, an instructer of the ignorant, an adviser of the doubtful, a protector of the oppressed, an hospitable entertainer of strangers, a reconciler of differences, an intercessor for offenders, an advocate of those who need defence, a succourer of all that want help.'[2] 'Fortune', by which Pope means both the general distribution of wealth and any particular affluence, whether acquired or inherited, made three appearances in the thirty lines devoted to Lord Bathurst and his fellow-noblemen; it has no place here. The emphasis is all on the activity and energy of John Kyrle, the Man of Ross, and on the fact that he performs these miracles of charity on an income of 'five hundred pounds a year'. The beneficence of Lord Oxford and Lord

---

[1] Psalm cxii 9.
[2] Barrow, 'The Nature, Properties and Acts of Charity', *Works*, vol. I, pp. 260–1.

Bathurst need involve them in no hardship; their 'Fortunes' are necessary preconditions of their Bounty:

> Who copies Your's, or OXFORD'S better part,
> To ease th'oppress'd, and raise the sinking heart?
> Where-e'er he shines, oh Fortune, gild the scene,
> And Angels guard him in the golden Mean!
>
> (243–6)

In comparison with John Kyrle they are human and imperfect, whereas the Man of Ross, as Professor Wasserman has pointed out, is in part Moses ('From the dry rock who bade the waters flow?'), and in part Christ, dividing the 'weekly bread'.[1] He is a reproach to 'Grandeur' and 'proud Courts'; he is an implicit rebuke to the cautious prudence of many an eighteenth-century churchman, and he withstands the onset of Mammon, who 'of all the competitors and antagonists of God, invading God's right, and usurping his place, is . . . the most dangerous, and desperately repugnant'.[2]

---

[1] Earl R. Wasserman, *Pope's 'Epistle to Bathurst'*: *A Critical Reading, With an Edition of the Manuscripts* (Baltimore, 1960), p. 42.
[2] Barrow, *Works*, vol. I, p. 317.

# CHAPTER EIGHT

# 'The Stoic's Pride'

'Man is *mundi utriusque nexus, the bond of both worlds,* as *Scaliger* calls him, in whom the world of bodies, and the world of spirits do meet, and unite; for in respect to his body, he is related to this visible world, and is of the earth; but in respect of his soul, he is allied to heaven, and descended from above.'[1] The claims of these two worlds are imperious, and difficult to reconcile. On the one side are ranged reason, intellect, the soul; on the other, instinct, passion, and the senses. Man's position, on this 'isthmus of a middle state', presents a formidable challenge to his powers, a challenge which needs to be recognized and met. In practice, however, instead of being self-aware and decisive man is too often simply alarmed by his pre-cariousness or paralysed by bewilderment:

> In doubt to deem himself a God, or Beast;
> In doubt his Mind or Body to prefer.
>
> (*Essay on Man* II 8–9)

Pope's point is that such deeming and preferring, such erecting of simple choices between alternatives, is a misguided and wasteful activity. Whether he refuses the claims of body in the interests of mind, or champions the senses against the intellect, man denies his own special potentialities, his own uniqueness as bond or nexus.

Indeed, by the very act of making such a choice man falls into sin. If he deems himself a beast, if he 'prefers' his body, he finds himself caught in a web of evil, entangled in avarice, lechery,

---

[1] Tillotson, *Works*, vol. II, p. 552. Cf. Addison's final paragraph in *Spectator* no. 519.

gluttony, wrath and sloth. These are the sins which imprison man in what Tillotson calls the 'world of bodies', and being all of them sins of the flesh they are commonly found in one another's company. Swift represents them, in brutal combination, as the Yahoos. Pope shows them to be closely associated as agents of corruption in contemporary society:

> Alike in nothing but one Lust of Gold,
> Just half the land would buy, and half be sold:
> Their Country's wealth our mightier Misers drain,
> Or cross, to plunder Provinces, the Main:
> The rest, some farm the Poor-box, some the Pews;
> Some keep Assemblies, and wou'd keep the Stews;
> Some with fat Bucks on childless Dotards fawn;
> Some win rich Widows by their Chine and Brawn;
> While with the silent growth of ten per Cent,
> In Dirt and darkness hundreds stink content.[1]

Pope's major target in this energetic denunciation is the love of money, and the power of avarice to corrupt the soul. But the love of money, the root of all the evils that relate to man's appetites, throws up strong shoots of sensuality. The line about 'rich Widows' appears at first to be an innocent re-creation, in contemporary terms, of Horace's 'Crustis & *Pomis*, Viduas venentur avaras' (75), referring to widow-hunters who woo with presents of cakes and fruit; chine and brawn were common gifts in the early eighteenth century, especially at Christmas. Pope's words, however, yield a more covert meaning. There are puns here on *brawn* as human muscle, and on *chine* as back or back-bone, which unite to make an (admittedly fairly stock) jibe at the sensuality of widows, their haste to remarry, and their preference for 'strong-backed', virile men.[2] This satirical side-blow has been lightly anticipated in the ambiguous motives of those who 'wou'd keep the Stews'. As in Jonson's *Volpone*, the 'Lust of Gold' is inextricably intertwined with the lusts of the flesh.

---

[1] *Epistle I i (To Bolingbroke)* 124–33.
[2] The same jibe occurs in Pope's version of Donne's second Satire: 'when rank Widows purchase luscious nights' (87), a line which has no counterpart in Donne. Cf. the 'letter' printed in *Spectator* no. 561: 'I am a tall, broad-shouldered, impudent, black Fellow, and, as I thought, every way qualified for a rich Widow. . . .'

Pope had already gone out of his way to emphasize this close relationship in the opening lines of *Sober Advice from Horace* (1734), a free imitation of the second Satire of the first Book. Horace begins with four brief character sketches: the prodigal Tigellius, contrasted with the miser who refuses to help a starving friend; a spendthrift who squanders his fortune to gratify his gluttony, and the wealthy, extortionate, self-tormenting Fufidius. Horace contrives these pairings in order to demonstrate that fools, in avoiding one vice, fly to the opposite extreme (line 24). Pope forsakes both the arrangement and the sex of Horace's examples, and although he reaches the similar conclusion that 'Women and Fools are always in Extreme' (28), he has arrived there by considering cases in which Horace's extremes are fused in one and the same person. Pope's four women are all prodigal of their bodies *and* financially grasping; the third, as in Horace, is a glutton into the bargain:

> "Treat on, treat on," is her eternal Note,
> And Lands and Tenements go down her Throat.
>
> (13–14)

The first three look pale beside Fufidia (yet another alias for Lady Mary Wortley Montagu), who 'thrives in Money, Land, and Stocks', and exacts twice the legal rate of interest from her debtors:

> For Int'rest, ten *per Cent.* her constant Rate is;
> Her Body? hopeful Heirs may have it *gratis.*
> She turns her very Sister to a Job,
> And, in the Happy Minute, picks your Fob:
> Yet starves herself, so little her own Friend,
> And thirsts and hungers only at one End:
> A Self-Tormentor, worse than (in the Play)
> The Wretch, whose Av'rice drove his *Son* away.

Lust, however it manifests itself, destroys man's essential humanity. Fufidia is a self-tormentor; Balaam's wealth, like Volpone's, is dearer to him than all human ties. Yet when man deems himself a god, giving the preference to mind over body, he is equally guilty of denying his nature. Those who scorn the limitations of the human condition, who 'quit their sphere, and rush into the skies',[1] are in fact rushing to embrace the sin of pride. Pascal put the dilemma most forcefully: 'What then is to be the Fate of Man! shall he be equal to GOD? or shall he not be superiour to the Beasts? . . . What Religion shall instruct us to correct at once our Pride, and our Concupiscence?'[2] What Pascal's translator calls 'concupiscence' is thus an equal and opposite tendency to pride, and in Pope's satirical view each of these evil powers seems to have its favoured area of operation. Covetousness is rampant in the City, while pride flourishes among the 'huffing, braggart, puft *Nobility*' at Court,[3] and among scholars, pedants, and scribblers. Cornelius, the father of Martinus Scriblerus, majestically demands: 'Is not Man the Lord of the Universe?'[4] The Grubstreet hacks pride themselves on prostituting what slender talents they possess: William Arnall 'writ for hire, and valued himself upon it'.[5] In most cases these hacks have strayed into a literary career from humble but useful vocations, induced to neglect their real gifts 'thro' self conceit of greater abilities'.[6] Their Laureate is the pert and incorrigible Cibber. But because man's unique position makes him a prey to both pride and concupiscence, these vices can never be compartmentalized. The corridors of Court power are buzzing with sexual as well as political intrigue. Sir Balaam grows presumptuous over his gains:

> Behold Sir Balaam, now a man of spirit,
> Ascribes his gettings to his parts and merit,
> What late he call'd a Blessing, now was Wit,
> And God's good Providence, a lucky Hit.

Timon's chapel tempts its congregation to physical sloth, while its painted ceiling provides mild pornographic thrills; but the essential attribute of the villa and its owner is stated at the outset: 'So proud, so grand. . . .' And when Pope offers his ironical advice to Murray,

---

[1] *Essay on Man* I 124.
[2] *Thoughts on Religion*, trans. Basil Kennet (1704), p. 35.
[3] *Donne* IV 201.
[4] *Memoirs of Scriblerus*, ch. ii, ed. Kerby-Miller, p. 100.
[5] Note to *Dunciad* II 315.
[6] *The Dunciad*, 'Martinus Scriblerus, of the Poem', Twickenham Edition, vol. V, p. 50.

Advance thy golden Mountain to the skies;
On the broad base of fifty thousand rise,[1]

the 'Mountain' represents both the heaps of the miser and the hills piled up by the Giants in their hubristic attempt to scale Olympus. Man's behaviour continually disrupts the order and harmony of the universe. The oscillations of his personality, 'this hour a slave, the next a deity',[2] are endlessly self-thwarting. Pope explores this predicament most fully in the *Essay on Man*, though he returns to the problem in a later poem, also addressed to Lord Bolingbroke and in some ways an addendum to the *Essay*, *The First Epistle of the First Book of Horace Imitated* (1738). The denunciation of the 'Lust of Gold' forms the climax of the central section of this *Epistle*, a section describing the obsessive pursuit of riches by the entire nation, with the Court and City at its head. Before making his survey of rampant greed Horace advertises the moral remedies for all the passions which may enslave and unsettle the human heart. In doing so he compiles a list of vices which corresponds closely to that of the Seven Deadly Sins:

> Fervet Avaritia, miseroque Cupidine pectus?
> Sunt *verba* & *voces*, quibus hunc lenire dolorem
> Possis, & magnam morbi deponere partem.
> Laudis amore tumes? sunt certa *piacula*, quæ te
> *Ter* pure lecto poterunt recreare libello.
> Invidus, iracundus, iners, vinosus, *Amator*,
> Nemo adeo *ferus* est ut non mitescere possit,
> Si modo culturæ patientem commodet aurem.[3]

Pope keeps close to Horace and the traditional Sins, with one significant departure:

---

[1] *Epistle I vi* (*To Murray*) 73–4.
[2] *Essay on Man* I 68.
[3] Lines 33–40: 'Is your bosom fevered with avarice and sordid covetousness? There are spells and sayings [the precepts of philosophy] whereby you may soothe the pain and cast much of the malady aside. Are you swelling with ambition? There are fixed charms which can fashion you anew, if with cleansing rites you read the booklet thrice. The slave to envy, anger, sloth, wine, lewdness – no one is so savage that he cannot be tamed, if only he lend to treatment a patient ear.' The relationship between Horace's catalogue and the Deadly Sins is discussed in Morton W. Bloomfield, *The Seven Deadly Sins* (East Lansing, Michigan, 1952), pp. 37, 45–6, and 72.

Say, does thy blood rebel, thy bosom move
With wretched Av'rice, or as wretched Love?
Know, there are Words, and Spells, which can controll
(Between the Fits) this Fever of the soul:
Know, there are Rhymes, which (fresh and fresh apply'd)
Will cure the arrant'st Puppy of his Pride.
Be furious, envious, slothful, mad or drunk,
Slave to a Wife or Vassal to a Punk,
A Switz, a High-dutch, or a Low-dutch Bear –
All that we ask is but a patient Ear.

(55–64)

In view of the deflating conclusion of the Epistle, Horace's claims for the power of the word are exaggerated, and are meant to seem so. Characteristically, Pope relies on parentheses to create a lightly ironic tone which will serve as the equivalent of Horace's transparent hyperboles. 'Between the Fits' and 'fresh and fresh apply'd' are a more explicit, and more explicitly good-humoured, admission that the fever of the soul must after all be pronounced incurable. The fit will recur, no matter what moral wisdom is preached in the interim. Complete control is unattainable; it is impossible to uproot passion from the heart of man. The impossibility is highlighted by Pope's unexpected inclusion of Love in the list of passions to be subdued.[1] The reader has scarcely time to repudiate the suggestion that his blood rebels with unworthy Avarice before he is trapped into admitting the universal sway of a more tender feeling.

He is not, however, altogether unprepared for the appearance of this feeling. Horace's wry simile 'Ut nox longa quibus mentitur amica'[2] has already been refined into 'Long as the Night to her whose love's away' (36). This alteration becomes the more striking when we consider Dacier's eulogy of the original: 'Rien n'est plus fort que cette comparaison tirée du vice, & employée pour la vertu.'[3]

---

[1] Horace's 'Avaritia' and 'Cupidine', followed as they are by the singular 'hunc dolorem', presumably both refer to the one vice of covetousness: see Bloomfield, *Seven Deadly Sins*, p. 46.

[2] Line 20: 'As the night seems long for one whose mistress proves false. . . .'

[3] *Œuvres d'Horace en latin et en françois*, ed. André Dacier, 3rd ed. (Paris, 1709), vol. VIII, p. 48. Dacier quotes Satire I v 82–4 to show that Horace knew from personal experience the misery of waiting for a mistress.

Pope, who was very probably aware of this comment, has deliberately muted Horace's audacity, for by making the sufferer a woman he at least allows the possibility of an innocently romantic situation. Again, at the beginning of the poem Horace's 'Nunc itaque, & Versus & cætera ludicra pono'[1] is modified to:

> Farewell then Verse, and Love, and ev'ry Toy,
> The rhymes and rattles of the Man or Boy.
>
> (17–18)

This, although flippant, is not at all coy. Horace's 'cætera ludicra', his amorous adventures, have become the more candid 'Love, and ev'ry Toy'. Moreover, Pope's valediction has an ironic flavour missing from the Latin. Horace may not be entirely serious about giving up his other playthings, but he is genuinely turning from lyrical to epistolary verse. For almost ten years he has been working on the first three Books of Odes, and this Epistle is in part an announcement of the themes that he proposes to deal with, the attitudes he proposes to adopt, in the new genre. Pope's farewell to Verse can scarcely be taken at its face value when it is followed by nearly two hundred assured and polished lines of the same kind of moral poetry that he has been producing for the last seven years. We appreciate that it is retracted even as it is uttered, and that its evident irony spills over on to 'Love, and ev'ry Toy'. The rhymes and rattles are not so easily surrendered, the power of Love is not so airily dismissed. For the satirist is no paragon. Though he is numbered among Reason's friends, he makes no false boast of being always and entirely reasonable:

> A Voice there is, that whispers in my ear,
> ('Tis Reason's voice, which sometimes one can hear)
> "Friend Pope! be prudent, let your Muse take breath. . . ."
>
> (11–13)

He admits that his method of acquiring wisdom is haphazardly eclectic, and not even fully under his control:

---

[1] Line 10: 'So now I lay aside my verses and all other toys.'

As drives the storm, at any door I knock,
And house with Montagne now, or now with Lock.

(25-6)

So that even while the first paragraphs of the *Epistle* argue the need for moral discipline and effort, the human imperfections that obstruct moral progress are not forgotten. Habits and desires persist, Reason cannot always make herself heard, and Love may keep us wretched, for all the poetical advice we receive. The *Epistle* demonstrates that men are emphatically not their own masters. Most of them are too obsessed by their lusts to be restrained by satire, and like Sir Job (lines 138-47) they are so changeable in their obsessions that satire is for ever trying to hit a moving target. The poet himself, as he finally confesses to Lord Bolingbroke, is as 'incoherent' as the rest:

When (each Opinion with the next at strife,
One ebb and flow of follies all my Life)
I plant, root up, I build, and then confound,
Turn round to square, and square again to round;
You never change one muscle of your face,
You think this Madness but a common case,
Nor once to Chanc'ry, nor to Hales apply;
Yet hang your lip, to see a Seam awry!
Careless how ill I with myself agree;
Kind to my dress, my figure, not to Me.
Is this my Guide, Philosopher, and Friend?
This, He who loves me, and who ought to mend?
Who ought to make me (what he can, or none,)
That Man divine whom Wisdom calls her own,
Great without Title, without Fortune bless'd,
Rich ev'n when plunder'd, honour'd while oppress'd,
Lov'd without youth, and follow'd without power,
At home tho' exil'd, free, tho' in the Tower.
In short, that reas'ning, high, immortal Thing,
Just less than Jove, and much above a King,
Nay half in Heav'n - except (what's mighty odd)
A Fit of Vapours clouds this Demi-god.

This is a delicately controlled piece of raillery, displaying the skill which Pope flatteringly pretends to have learnt from Bolingbroke himself:

Form'd by thy converse, happily to steer
From grave to gay, from lively to severe.
(*Essay on Man* IV 379–80)

The rebuking of Bolingbroke for his indifference ('Careless how ill
I with myself agree') is quickly softened by the poet's quoting his
own generous tribute, at the conclusion of the *Essay on Man*, to
'my guide, philosopher, and friend', while the succeeding couplet
brings the even more handsome compliment that Bolingbroke is the
poet's only hope of salvation: 'what he can, or none'. The balanced,
dignified lines which follow, and which have Bolingbroke's political
career principally though not exclusively in view, are in their turn
undercut by the playfulness of the close. The last three lines, hover-
ing on the edge of a pictorial image, suggest a being uncomfortably
suspended between earth and heaven, his head literally in the clouds.
Fleeing from the world of bodies, a world dominated by the Lust of
Gold, the demi-god abandons his humanity in order to become what
is simply a contradiction in terms, a 'Man divine'.

This heroic personage, aptly described as a 'Thing', is recognizably a Stoic figure, and to prick his dignity by reminding
him of his human vulnerability, of his kinship to the whimsical Sir
Job, is a traditional device of anti-Stoic satire. Stoicism expects too
much of ordinary human nature, and is therefore a form of presumption. It encourages the individual to quit his sphere, to get at
least half-way to Heaven, to usurp a position he was never intended
to enjoy. One way of humbling the Stoic's pride in his superiority
to Fortune's blows is to remind him of the irresistible and mundane
torment which he may suffer from an aching tooth:

> For there was never yet philosopher,
> That could endure the tooth-ach patiently;
> However they have writ the stile of Gods,
> And made a pish at chance and sufferance.[1]

In his edition of Shakespeare, Pope gave this speech his marginal
commas of approbation. He also admired the dramatic exchange

---

[1] *Much Ado about Nothing* V i 35–8.

between Brutus and Cassius which constitutes the turning-point of the famous quarrel scene in *Julius Cæsar*:

> BRU. O *Cassius*, I am sick of many griefs.
> CAS. Of your philosophy you make no use,
>      If you give place to accidental evils.
> BRU. No man bears sorrow better – *Portia*'s dead.
> CAS. Ha! *Portia* –
> BRU. She is dead!
> CAS. How scap'd I killing, when I crost you so?

(IV iii 144–50)

Cassius's admission that it is in the nature of men to grieve over 'accidental evils' makes very forcibly another traditional argument against the vanity of Stoicism, an argument of more weight than the toothache. Stoic doctrines promise secure foundations for a steadfast life; in fact they ask us to pay dearly for a stability that turns out to be illusory. In seeking to convince man that he is not a slave, Stoicism mistakenly tries to prove him a deity. Its opponents therefore urge the impracticability and unnaturalness of its programme, and remind man of the inescapable claims of his human nature:

> . . . there are some evils and calamities of human life, that are too heavy and serious to be jested withal, and require the greatest consideration, and a very great degree of patience to support us under them . . . as the loss of friends and dearest relations; as the loss of an only son. . . . These certainly are some of the greatest evils of this world, and hardest to be born. For men may pretend what they will to philosophy, and contempt of the world, and of the perishing comforts and enjoyments of it; to the extirpation of their passions, and an insensibility of these things, which the weaker and undisciplin'd part of mankind keep such a wailing and lamentation about: But when all is done, nature hath framed us as we are, and hath planted in our nature strong inclinations and affections to our friends and relations; and these affections are as naturally moved upon such occasions, and pluck every string of our hearts as violently, as extreme hunger and thirst do gnaw upon our stomachs.[1]

Any attempt to stifle the passions, to achieve the high calm of

---

[1] Tillotson, *Works*, vol. II, p. 98.

Stoical 'apathy', is doomed to failure. Man has 'too much weakness for the Stoic's pride'.[1]

In the Preface to his translation of Epictetus George Stanhope declares that Stoicism sets up a false god, 'an imaginary Perfection, which few ever did, and none ought to attain to.'[2] Such a declaration, with its implied corollary that Christianity takes a more realistic view of sinning human nature, is necessary in such a context because Epictetus, one of the most austere and high-minded of the pagan Stoics, was commonly regarded as the most 'Christian' among them. He opposed the current Stoic doctrine of the lawfulness of suicide; he declared that a man should be willing to lay down his life for his friend. Though Christianity has absorbed some of the teachings of Epictetus, Marcus Aurelius, and Seneca, it remains, as Stanhope was concerned to emphasize, fundamentally distinct from their self-sufficient philosophy. The approval we give the Stoics (Stanhope speaks of Epictetus's 'admirable Instructions') must always be counterpoised by a recollection of their shortcomings: 'wherein soever those Systems of Morality differ from the Christian, they are manifestly inferiour to them.'[3]

This seems to be Pope's strategy in the *Sixth Epistle of the First Book of Horace Imitated* (*To Murray*), published a few weeks before the *Epistle to Bolingbroke*. In its opening lines Pope actually reinforces Horace's advocacy of the Stoic ideal of serenity and imperturbability in the face of material temptations:

> *Nil Admirari*, prope res est una, Numici!
> Solaque, quæ possit facere & servare beatum.[4]

> "Not to Admire, is all the Art I know,
> "To make men happy, and to keep them so."

Not only is Horace's qualifying *prope* silently omitted; Pope also proceeds to underline the validity of this doctrine:

---

[1] *Essay on Man* II 6.
[2] *Epictetus his Morals*, 4th ed. (1721), sig. A6ʳ.
[3] Ibid., sigs. A4ʳ and A6ʳ.
[4] ' "Marvel at nothing" – that is perhaps the one and only thing, Numicius, that can make a man happy and keep him so.'

Plain Truth, dear MURRAY, needs no flow'rs of speech,
So take it in the very words of *Creech*.

Pope's opening quotation from Thomas Creech is both a back-handed compliment to his predecessor, and a considered indication of his own moral conservatism. The translation of Horace by 'painful *Creech*', as Prior not unjustly called him,[1] appeared in 1684. His verb 'admire' accurately renders the Latin 'admirari' because it carries what seems to have been its predominant late seventeenth-century meaning, that of wondering amazement, even stupefaction. In this sense *admiration* was proverbially 'the daughter of ignorance' and a mark of folly: 'For Fools *Admire*, but Men of Sense *Approve*'.[2] Naturally the Stoics were the determined foes of such irrational behaviour, seeing it as a violent response to crude stimuli, a surrender of self-control. According to Stoic doctrine the wise and virtuous man should be as unruffled as he appears at the conclusion of Juvenal's tenth Satire (the translation is Dryden's):

> Serene and Manly, harden'd to sustain
> The load of Life, and Exercis'd in Pain;
> Guiltless of Hate, and Proof against Desire;
> That all things weighs, and nothing can admire.

By 1738, when Pope's *Epistle to Murray* was published, *admiration* was losing its sense of mere amazement, and reverting to that of pleased approbation: 'we wonder at any thing which is strange, tho' we properly only admire what has some extraordinary perfection.'[3] Constable's careful phrasing ('we properly only admire') shows that he regards the semantic change as still in progress; Pope, since he clings to the pejorative sense of the verb, would appear to have regarded it as a change for the worse, depriving the satirist of a valuable weapon. Men will go on 'admiring' in the old way, but the satirist will have no convenient and classically sanctioned term with

---

[1] 'A Satyr on the modern Translators', line 111, *Works*, vol. I, p. 22.
[2] Pope, *Essay on Criticism* 391; cf. line 340: 'Her *Voice* is all these tuneful Fools admire'. Earlier in the poem Pope notes that the Greek critics 'taught the World, *with Reason* to Admire': line 101.
[3] John Constable, *Reflections upon Accuracy of Style* (1731), p. 2.

which to censure their conduct. Already the values of sincerity and hospitality have been discarded as obsolescent, and the meaning of honesty is shrinking. Now rash and hysterical behaviour, the folly of the unthinking, is widely condoned:

> But art thou one, whom new opinions sway,
> One, who believes as Tindal leads the way,
> Who Virtue and a Church alike disowns,
> Thinks that but words, and this but brick and stones?
> Fly then, on all the wings of wild desire!
> Admire whate'er the maddest can admire.
> Is Wealth thy passion? Hence! from Pole to Pole,
> Where winds can carry, or where waves can roll,
> For Indian spices, for Peruvian gold,
> Prevent the greedy, and out-bid the bold. . . .
>
> (63–72)

In this *Epistle* Pope has created a remarkably plain (and intermittently Creech-like) style as the vehicle for his 'Plain Truth'. The 'flow'rs of speech' are few and unobtrusive, as befits an austere theme. The wit is subdued – with one brilliant exception:

> Rack'd with Sciatics, martyr'd with the Stone,
> Will any mortal let himself alone?
>
> (54–5)

The first line of this couplet exactly fulfils Horace's demand that the poet should revitalize the medium of ordinary speech by his skilful ordering of words.[1] The seriously witty allusion to the death of St Stephen ('martyr'd with the Stone') revives the faded metaphor in 'rack'd', and implies standards of Christian fortitude by the side of which the counsel *nil admirari* seems pleasantly undemanding. The Stoic is merely negative in his refusal to admire; the Christian martyr, though a passive sufferer, is actively bearing witness. His heroism is kept before us by the assurance that, in contrast with physical torments,

> The case is easier in the Mind's disease;
> There, all Men may be cur'd, whene'er they please.

---

[1] 'notum si callida verbum/reddiderit iunctura novum': *Ars Poetica* 47–8; 'you will express yourself most happily, if a skilful setting makes a familiar word new.'

This short paragraph closes with the *Epistle*'s most important positive statement, a brief and simple tribute to Henry Hyde, Viscount Cornbury:

> Would ye be blest? despise low Joys, low Gains; ⎫
> Disdain whatever CORNBURY disdains; ⎬
> Be Virtuous, and be happy for your pains. ⎭

'For your pains' is a further example of a cliché rejuvenated by its context, and like 'blest' and 'Joys' it harks back to the earlier 'martyr'd'. Stoic disdain and the Stoic commandment 'Be Virtuous', though they are given their due, are subsumed under the more strenuous discipline of Christian fortitude.

Admiration and pride have a common parent, namely ignorance. For admiration implies 'our ignorance of other things; *pride*, our ignorance of ourselves'.[1] The danger of Stoicism is that in combating the first kind of ignorance it promotes the second. Its attractiveness, to which Pope was by no means insensitive, lies in its determination to oppose the world's 'mad trade' for gold, 'or Popularity, or Stars and Strings'.[2] It advocates temperance and the ability to live on little with a cheerful heart; it strives to calm man's inherent restlessness. 'Who pants for glory finds but short repose', while those who have tasted glory still 'hate to rest, and dread to be alone'.[3] Virtue is achieved and sustained by unremitting effort, yet it is a 'contented thing',[4] and the only thing that is so. Although Pope, like Horace before him, scorned the extreme Stoic position and its attendant absurdities, he could, with an eclecticism worthy of Horace, extract the sweetness from this philosophy. In commending feminine 'good humour' he is commending a gentle and appealing version of Stoic equanimity. Belinda has exulted excessively in her victory at the card-table, and been excessively disturbed by the rape of her lock; like other 'thoughtless Mortals' she is 'too soon dejected, and too

---

[1] Pope, *Works*, vol. III, p. 295 – part of Warburton's comment on Pope's 'Fanes, which admiring Gods with pride survey': 'To Mr Addison', line 9.
[2] *To Murray* 13–14.
[3] *Epistle II i* 300; *Epistle to a Lady* 228.
[4] *Dialogue I* 140.

soon elate!'[1] Clarissa, though her words fall on deaf ears, offers the necessary corrective:

> What then remains, but well our Pow'r to use,
> And keep good Humour still whate'er we lose?
> And trust me, Dear! good Humour can prevail,
> When Airs, and Flights, and Screams, and Scolding fail.

(V 29–32)

'Good Humour' may well be a more valuable asset than Stoic calm. It is not concerned to insulate the individual consciousness, and it is not stubbornly proud. Though it makes for personal stability, it is also socially influential; it 'prevails' on others. So Martha Blount, unlike her merely dazzling contemporaries, is able 'to raise the Thought and touch the Heart'.[2] Measured by the narrow scale of women's activities in the eighteenth century, the operations of 'temper' and 'humour' assume something of heroic proportions:

> Oh! blest with Temper, whose unclouded ray
> Can make to morrow chearful as to day;
> She, who can love a Sister's charms, or hear
> Sighs for a Daughter with unwounded ear;
> She, who ne'er answers till a Husband cools,
> Or, if she rules him, never shows she rules,
> Charms by accepting, by submitting sways,
> Yet has her humour most, when she obeys;
> Lets Fops or Fortune fly which way they will;
> Disdains all loss of Tickets, or Codille;
> Spleen, Vapours, or Small-pox, above them all,
> And Mistress of herself, tho' China fall.

(To a Lady 257–68)

---

[1] Rape of the Lock III 101–2.   [2] To a Lady 250.

# CHAPTER NINE

# Discords and Harmonies

The citizens of ancient Athens, according to Bishop Sprat, were 'men of hot, earnest, and hasty minds'.[1] Perceiving the dangers to which their temperaments exposed them, they wisely urged upon one another the need for self-knowledge and moderation, while some upheld the value of Stoic 'apathy' and serenity. For very similar reasons the most articulate of Bishop Sprat's contemporaries advocated the disciplining of passion and imagination, and espoused some of the tenets of Stoicism, not only because the shadow of the Civil War still hung darkly over them, but also because they recognized that they and their fellow-countrymen were all too easily swayed by their hot and hasty dispositions. Sir William Temple was 'apt to be warme in disputes & expostulations, wch made him hate the first, & avoy'd the other'.[2] Matthew Prior recalls that the Earl of Dorset 'was naturally very subject to Passion', but adds that 'the short Gust was soon over, and served only to set off the Charms of his Temper, when more Compos'd.'[3] At a time when libels and lampoons were weapons freely drawn in self-defence, Pope's unwillingness to retaliate upon his enemies ('Full ten years slander'd, did he once reply?') seems so exceptional as to be positively virtuous. 'If a Man has any Talent in Writing, it shews a good Mind to forbear answering Calumnies and Reproaches in the same Spirit of Bitterness with which they are offered: But when a Man has been

---

[1] Thomas Sprat, *The History of the Royal Society of London* (1667), p. 7.
[2] Lady Giffard, 'The Character of S^r W. Temple', in *The Early Essays and Romances of Sir William Temple*, ed. G. C. Moore Smith (Oxford, 1930), p. 28.
[3] *Works*, vol. I, p. 253.

at some pains in making suitable returns to an Enemy, and has the Instruments of Revenge [invectives and satires] in his Hands, to let drop his Wrath, and stifle his Resentments, seems to have something in it Great and Heroical. There is a particular Merit in such a way of forgiving an Enemy. . . .'[1] It is a measure of what the age expects of human nature that the renunciation of revenge can be exalted into an act of forgiveness, and that Pope can follow Horace in proposing, as a test of true wisdom, the question 'Can'st thou endure a Foe, forgive a Friend?'[2]

In public and in private, in high and low life, feelings were so quickly roused, and so freely expressed, that any form of self-discipline became a valued proof of good breeding and good sense. Even to refrain from physical violence, when provoked, was a matter for comment and congratulation. A French courtesy-writer describes how a gentleman 'found himself abus'd by a Person of much inferior Quality; he had a Cane in his Hand, and at his first Commotion was tempted to strike the Man who had thus fail'd in Respect: He entred his Chamber to let his Passion cool before he would finish the Affair that occasion'd his Disorder. A Person of less Temper would have reek'd [sic] his Spleen, by caning the senseless Coxcomb; but I am persuaded a Man of Honour is much asham'd of himself when he considers in cool Blood, what Violences his Anger has led him to.'[3] A case tried before Lord Chief Justice Holt at the Old Bailey in 1704 demonstrates that a person of less temper and politeness might well have wreaked his spleen even more violently. It shows, too, that the law was far from assuming that men could perform miracles of self-control.

> There being an affray in the streets, one Stedman, a foot-soldier, ran hastily towards the combatants. A woman seeing him run in that manner cried out, "You will not murder the man, will you?" Stedman replied, "What is that to you, you – ?" The woman thereupon gave

---

[1] Addison, *Spectator* no. 355.
[2] *Epistle II ii* 317.
[3] J. B. Morvan de Bellegarde, *Reflexions upon the Politeness of Manners*, 2nd ed. (1710), p. 134. There is no reason to think that English readers would not also have admired this 'fine Instance of Moderation'.

him a box on the ear, and Stedman struck her on the breast with the pommel of his sword. The woman then fled, and Stedman pursuing her stabbed her in the back. Holt was at first of opinion that this was murder, *a single box on the ear from a woman not being sufficient provocation to kill in this manner, after he had given her a blow in return for the box on the ear*. And it was proposed to have the matter found special.[1] But if afterwards appearing in the progress of the trial that the woman struck the soldier in the face with an iron patten, and drew a great deal of blood, it was held clearly to be no more than manslaughter. The smart of the man's wound and the effusion of blood might possibly keep his indignation boiling to the moment of the fact.[2]

Daily life in London and the larger towns was lived in a context of affrays and riots. The lawlessness of the time is caught in several of Hogarth's prints and paintings, as well as in numerous accounts of watchmen assaulted, travellers molested, and property damaged. The First Earl of Bristol recorded in his Diary that on 7 June 1716 'several drunken officers of ye Guards with thier [sic] servants attacked my coach, (dear wife being in it very big with child) my self & servants in ye strand.'[3] The most spectacular terrorist activities were those of the 'Mohock' gangs who thrust themselves into public notice early in 1712, when political tension was already dangerously high: 'they take Care to drink themselves to a Pitch, that is, beyond the Possibility of attending to any Motions of Reason or Humanity; then make a general Sally, and attack all that are so unfortunate as to walk the Streets thro' which they patroll. Some are knock'd down, others stabb'd, others cut and carbonado'd.'[4] Many of these disturbances, especially the spasmodic riots of apprentices, reflected the economic uncertainties and confusions of the time. A financial crisis or rumour of crisis, a failure of crops, a sudden rise in unemployment, were good grounds for demonstrations and unrest.

---

[1] I.e. that a special verdict of homicide in self-defence should be returned; the offender would then be pardoned, and would merely forfeit some of his property.

[2] From Foster's *Crown Cases*, quoted in C. K. Allen, *Legal Duties and Other Essays in Jurisprudence* (Oxford, 1931), p. 82; italics in the original.

[3] Hervey, *Diary*, p. 63; the officers subsequently apologized and were forgiven.

[4] Steele, *Spectator* no. 324. The Tory Government systematically, but falsely, blamed this eruption of violence on the Whigs: *Spectator*, ed. Bond, vol. III, pp. 186–7.

These economic vicissitudes affected the lives of all, but were felt most acutely and responded to most readily by those who composed the London 'Mob' – 'the Dregs of the Creation' in Lady Chudleigh's scornful phrase.[1] 'The angry Buzz of a Multitude is one of the bloodiest Noises in the World';[2] and the multitude was not slow to vent its rage against a stern government measure, an unpopular public figure, or a minority group. Peter Briggins, a Quaker merchant living in Bartholomew Close, refers frequently in his Diary to the mob's being 'very rude'. When his neighbours declined to set candles in their windows to celebrate the Peace of Utrecht their windows were promptly smashed. Yet such violence is of little moment by comparison with Briggins's laconic entry for 17 November 1715, when the ferment caused by the Jacobite Rising had reached its climax: 'Ye Mob very mobish in ye City & 4 or 5 shot dead.'[3]

At such a time the havoc of the Civil War must have been recalled with more than usual solemnity, and the need for order and control asserted with more than usual vigour. 'Our late Rebellion', its causes and effects, provided the theme of many a sermon and pamphlet. Robert South declared that 'the great long rebellion . . . cannot be too frequently, too severely, and too bitterly, upon all publick occasions, ripp'd up and reflected upon. All the pulpits in the king's dominions ought to ring of it, as long as there is a man alive who lived when the villany was committed.'[4] Thomas Sherwill, preaching on the anniversary of Queen Anne's Accession, emphasizes that only the Monarchy and the Established Church can furnish a steadfast defence against the Satanic forces of anarchy, masquerading as Puritan individualists:

'Tis true indeed, that about the middle of the last Century, there were found amongst us wicked Men, Sons of *Belial*, fearing neither God, nor the King, who, out of a pretence of establishing a more pure Religion,

---

[1] Mary Chudleigh, *Essays upon Several Subjects in Prose and Verse* (1710), p. 117.
[2] George Savile, Marquess of Halifax, 'Political Thoughts and Reflections', in *Complete Works*, ed. Walter Raleigh (Oxford, 1912), p. 219.
[3] *The Eliot Papers*, ed. Eliot Howard, no. II (Gloucester, 1894), p. 63.
[4] *Sermons*, vol. VI, pp. 80-1.

[ 171 ]

*transform'd* themselves like him, whose Agents they were, into *Angels of Light*, and overthrew all that was Good or Sacred.

Then was it that Monarchy lay bleeding . . . and blessed times, without doubt, they were; when *every man*, there being *no King in* our *Israel, did that which was right in his own eyes;* times of great Disorder and Confusion, unsetled and tumultuous . . . the Nation never found rest or quiet, till Church and State were again fix'd upon their proper and respective Basis's, Episcopacy and Monarchy.[1]

Sherwill's claim is unfounded, for the Restoration signally failed to restore rest and quiet. During the alarms of the Popish Plot and the Exclusion Bill civil strife seemed imminent, and the cry went up that 'forty-one is come again.' This period of crisis was swiftly followed by Monmouth's rebellion in 1685, and that in its turn by the Revolution of 1688, when Mary Woodforde, the wife of a Prebendary of Winchester, lamented that since William's landing 'we have the sound of wars and desolation in our Land, and Soldiers continually passing up and down which keeps us in continual expectations of a Battle'. She went on to pray that the new King and Queen might be 'a blessing to this unsettled Land'.[2]

Pope, with greater historical realism than Sherwill, and with a strong Tory prejudice against the Revolution Settlement and William III, dates the true establishment of rest and quiet from the Peace of Utrecht, signed in 1713. He begs George Granville, the poet and politician to whom *Windsor-Forest* is dedicated, to chronicle the recent past in lofty verse:

> Make sacred *Charles*'s Tomb for ever known,
> (Obscure the Place, and uninscrib'd the Stone)
> Oh Fact accurst! What Tears has *Albion* shed,
> Heav'ns! what new Wounds, and how her old have bled?

---

[1] *Monarchy attended with High Birth the Best Establishment. A Sermon Preach'd before the University of Cambridge* (Cambridge, 1709), pp. 11–12.

[2] *Woodforde Papers and Diaries*, ed. D. H. Woodforde (1932), pp. 19 and 21. Mary Woodforde had already condemned Monmouth's rising as 'horrid treason' (p. 13). She was perturbed by insubordination in any quarter: '*March* 6 [1687]. This evening I had the cutting news that my second boy was in rebellion at the College at Winton [Winchester], where he and all his Companions resolved not to make any verses, and being called to be whipped for it several of them refused to be punished, mine amongst the rest' (p. 15).

> She saw her Sons with purple Deaths expire,
> Her sacred Domes involv'd in rolling Fiie,
> A dreadful Series of Intestine Wars,
> Inglorious Triumphs, and dishonest Scars.
> At length great *ANNA* said – Let Discord cease!
> She said, the World obey'd, and all was *Peace*!
> (*Windsor-Forest* 319–28)

But Pope was no more a political prophet than was Sherwill. Queen Anne died only a year after *Windsor-Forest* was published, and left the crucial problem of the Succession still unsolved. The first years of the next reign scarcely seemed to promise peace and a settled state of things, for they witnessed the political storms of the Bolingbroke and Harley impeachments, the 1715 Rising, and the beginnings of the speculative fever that was to culminate in the South Sea Bubble disaster. That fever itself was both cause and symptom of disquietude. During the late seventeenth and early eighteenth centuries men's uncertainties seem increasingly to have sought an outlet in financial speculation, lotteries, and games of chance. In 1711 the Government turned these tendencies to public account by imposing a duty on the sale of playing-cards and dice. At the end of nine years the revenue from this source had trebled, having made a spectacular leap at the time of the first Jacobite Rising, and another when the Bubble affair came to a head.[1]

As late as 1729 an anonymous 'Gentleman of the Middle-Temple' was desiring his readers to remember that 'the most arbitrary and tyrannical Prince that ever was, even a *Nero* or *Caligula*, never destroyed either so many Lives or Estates of his Subjects in the Course of his whole Reign, as have been devoured in the Space of a very few Years by a Civil War, the Truth of which this poor Nation too sadly experienc'd in the Time of the Grand Rebellion.'[2] This writer invokes the events of the 1640s in order to discredit the non-conformists of his own day, for like Thomas Sherwill he is thoroughly representative in laying responsibility for the Grand

---

[1] T. S. Ashton, *Economic Fluctuations in England 1700–1800* (Oxford, 1959), pp. 177–8 and 193.
[2] *The Young Gentleman's New-Year's Gift: or, Advice to a Nephew* (1729), pp. 20–1.

Rebellion entirely on the furious fanaticism and 'Enthusiasm' of
the Puritans. The 'enthusiast' is his own moral arbiter; he does that
which is 'right in his own eyes.' Politically he is a subversive element
in the state. Socially he is to be pitied as an unfortunate eccentric.
'There is not,' says Addison, 'a more melancholy Object than a Man
who has his Head turned with Religious Enthusiasm.'[1] Examining
this madness more closely, Addison finds that it arises from 'in-
discreet Fervours of Devotion, or too intense an Application of the
Mind to its mistaken Duties.' The remedy is plain: 'since Devotion
it self (which one would be apt to think could not be too warm) may
disorder the Mind, unless its Heats are tempered with Caution and
Prudence, we should be particularly careful to keep our Reason as
cool as possible, and to guard our selves in all Parts of Life against
the Influence of Passion, Imagination, and Constitution.' These
disturbing forces deprive a man of self-possession, which he cannot
afford to lose, even in what may seem the best of causes. So Pope's
plea for equanimity and moderation inevitably leads him to upbraid
the folly of the Puritan Saints:

> Whether we joy or grieve, the same the curse,
> Surpriz'd at better, or surpriz'd at worse.
> Thus good, or bad, to one extreme betray
> Th'unbalanc'd Mind, and snatch the Man away;
> For Vertue's self may too much Zeal be had;
> The worst of Madmen is a Saint run mad.
>
> (*To Murray* 22–7)

The context of this passage is Pope's censure of 'admiration', or
what Richard Flecknoe disparagingly called 'the drunkenness of the
understanding';[2] and seventeenth-century religious enthusiasm had
been one of its most extreme manifestations. The fact that for some
fifty years after the Restoration the word *admiration* more commonly
denoted foolish amazement than pleased approval can be attributed
to the distaste with which 'enthusiastic' behaviour was regarded, and
to the widespread need to treat it with the contempt it seemed to

---

[1] *The Spectator*, no. 201.
[2] Quoted in Constable, *Reflections upon Accuracy of Style*, p. 160.

deserve. The enthusiast brings himself into disrepute by his emotional raptures and flaunted convictions. Unlike the Christian martyr, who is invoked later in Pope's *Epistle to Murray*, the enthusiast merely 'fancies himself inspired with the Divine Spirit'.[1]

The Stoic is (or appears to be) the converse of the Enthusiast. He is guarded in his behaviour, and he restrains his feelings, whether of mirth or sorrow. To the Augustans, therefore, Stoicism was doubly attractive, as a personal safeguard against the blows and buffets of a violent age, and as a reproach to the fanaticism which had precipitated the gravest crisis in recent history. The energy with which the extreme Stoic position was repeatedly attacked by churchmen and satirists is a tribute to the spell it cast over the age. Roger L'Estrange's translation of Seneca's *Morals* was first published in 1678 and reached its tenth edition in 1711; a copy of it reposes in the 'Lady's Library' wittily catalogued by Addison in the thirty-seventh number of the *Spectator*. This fashionable neo-Stoicism reveals little of the classical emphasis on being sternly virtuous, little of the noble idealism that informs Epictetus's discussion of friendship. The delights, not the demands, of friendship now occupy the centre of attention, for one of the merits of a steadfast friendship is its superiority to the turbulence of being in love.

> From love, from angry love's inclement reign
> I pass awhile to friendship's equal skies.

So Shenstone announces at the beginning of his fifth 'Elegy'.[2] Tranquillity of mind, what the age liked to call 'Ease', is the ideal condition, and to achieve it all friction must be carefully eliminated. The social composure of the well-bred man, who is never 'out of countenance', never flamboyant or eccentric in his behaviour, finds its counterpart in the mental composure of the Stoic.

---

[1] Bailey, *English Dictionary*, 4th ed. (1728).
[2] The eighteenth-century exaltation of the lasting joys of friendship consciously follows Cicero (as in *de Amicitia* v 17), and Horace (as in Satire I v 44). It also directly reflects the fact that many of the English Augustans never married (like Horace), or married very late.

In short, the stringencies of classical Stoicism have now been
sufficiently diluted with Epicureanism to be both practicable and
palatable. Lady Mary Chudleigh's modest ambition in life is to
achieve 'a pleasing Serenity, a delightful Calmness of Soul, and . . .
a Chearfulness of Temper'. As she remarks elsewhere, the way to be
truly easy, so that no accidents can 'ruffle and disturb our Thoughts,
is to retire into our selves, to live upon our own Stock'.[1] We must
neither expose ourselves too much to life, nor expect to much from
it. Men will therefore choose to speak ironically, adopting a stance
of detached superiority and masking their deepest feelings. Circumspection is the rule. The fear of mismanaging an argument, says
Budgell, 'has made some approve the Socratical way of Reasoning,
where while you scarce affirm any thing, you can hardly be caught
in an Absurdity'.[2] For to be caught in an absurdity is to be vulnerable to that cruellest of torments, ridicule, which destroys self-
esteem and personal ease: 'there is scarce a Punishment which can
be heavier than that of being laughed at.'[3]

The 'retiring into ourselves' which Lady Chudleigh recommends
is facilitated by first retiring into the country. There a man can
create a haven of calm in his own garden, and fulfil Epicurus's
dictum: 'Live concealed'. In a small seventeenth-century formal
garden, with its alley-walks, fountains and summer-houses, one may
achieve the Epicurean ideal of happiness, a contented 'Indifference
to the common Enjoyments and Accidents of Life . . . Tranquillity of Mind, and Indolence of Body'.[4] Here then is a temptation to the country gentleman to withdraw yet further into himself
and relax his ties with the local community, ties of 'house-keeping'
and alms-giving, his legal and traditional responsibilities. It is more
undemanding to live in indolence of body, upon our own stock, to
achieve an innocent but essentially self-centred existence. The
'happy man' of the Restoration period is commonly conceived as
a placid, detached spectator of bustle, even of imminent chaos, in

---

[1] *Essays*, p. 75; Preface to *Poems on Several Occasions* (1703), sig. A6ʳ.
[2] *The Spectator*, no. 197.
[3] Halifax, 'Advice to a Daughter', in *Works*, p. 38.
[4] Temple, 'Upon the Gardens of Epicurus', *Works* (1720), vol. I, pp. 173–4.

the world outside.[1] The anarchy of woods and hills beyond the boundary wall of the estate symbolizes the political turmoil from which the retired gentleman is now happily remote.

The pleasures of a retired life are extolled throughout Cowley's 'Essays in Verse and Prose,' and Cowley constantly enhances them by contemplating the storms which rage in the great world outside. In troubled times it is wise to act the part of the bush that stands safe while lightning shatters the oaks. So Cowley's favourite adjective is 'little', with all its cosy, protective associations:

> Blest be the man (and blest he is) whom e're
> (Plac'd far out of the roads of Hope or Fear)
> A little Field, and little Garden feeds.

'I confess, I love Littleness almost in all things. A little convenient Estate, a little chearful House, a little Company, and a very little Feast, and if I were ever to fall in love again (which is a great Passion, and therefore, I hope, I have done with it) it would be, I think, with Prettiness, rather than with Majestical Beauty.'[2] John Pomfret's poem *The Choice* (1700) continues where Cowley leaves off. William III is now on the throne, the horror of the Civil War is beginning to recede, and the ideal residence need no longer remain aloof from the activities of men:

> Near some fair Town, I'd have a private Seat,
> Built Uniform, not Little, nor too Great. . . .
> I'd have a Clear, and Competent Estate,
> That I might Live Gentilely, but not Great.[3]

The country gentleman's social obligations begin to reassert themselves; Pomfret will dispense hospitality to the poor, and entertain his neighbours. But the Epicurean ideals are not pushed into the background. The poet looks forwards to the prospect of having two intimate friends living close by, and hopes to enjoy from time to

---

[1] See Maren-Sofie Røstvig, *The Happy Man : Studies in the Metamorphoses of a Classical Ideal*, vol. I, 2nd ed. (Oslo, 1962), ch. v.
[2] 'Of Agriculture' and 'Of Greatness', *Essays*, pp. 419 and 429.
[3] Lines 5–6 and 33–4. Quotations from Pomfret in this chapter are taken from his *Poems on Several Occasions*, 3rd ed. (1710).

time the company of 'some Obliging, Modest Fair'; he would not,
however, wish to go so far as to marry her:

> If Heav'n a Date of many Years wou'd give,
> Thus I'd in Pleasure, Ease, and Plenty live.
> And as I near approach'd the Verge of Life,
> Some kind Relation, (for I'd have no Wife)
> Shou'd take upon him all my Wordly Care,
> While I did for a better State prepare.
> Then I'd not be with any Trouble vex'd;
> Nor have the Ev'ning of my days perplex'd.

Pomfret's poem is an unashamed and prosaic day-dream.

Clearly, a 'Competent Estate' denoted nothing austere. Cowley
thinks in terms of an income of five hundred pounds a year, and 'a
convenient brick house, with decent Wainscot, and pretty Forest-
work hangings'.[1] 'Competent' might even be stretched to include an
elegant and compact Palladian villa, the eighteenth-century
equivalent of the classical *villa urbana*. The Palladian villa was a
genteel luxury: it was emphatically not a machine for living in.
Colonel Fane's Mereworth Castle, designed by Colen Campbell,
was at first occupied for only a few weeks each year, 'in order to
entertain fashionable parties from Tunbridge Wells'; when Fane
took up permanent residence pavilion blocks had to be added to
provide bedrooms for the staff and to accommodate stables and a
brew-house.[2] Lord Burlington's Chiswick House was sited only fifty
feet away from the Jacobean family mansion, and had therefore no
need of kitchen and servants' quarters; it was wholly and ornately
devoted to the gratification of Lord Burlington and his choicest
friends. The villa is Pomfret's wish fulfilled. It is a 'private Seat'; it
has 'a little Vault . . . stor'd/With the Best Wines', and a study
lined with the best authors; it is a perfect setting for conversation.
And it has the added advantage of proclaiming the impeccable taste
of its owner, since it is a concentrate of Palladio, Vitruvius, and
Inigo Jones.

---

[1] 'Of Greatness', *Essays*, pp. 431–2.
[2] Christopher Hussey, *English Country Houses: Early Georgian*, pp. 58–9 and 64.

The early eighteenth-century villa is a delightful retreat, but (not being a self-contained country house or *villa rustica*) only a temporary retreat. For convenience, therefore, it should be situated within easy reach of London; for salubriousness, on the smoke-free Western side of the capital, preferably in the Thames valley: 'From *Richmond* to *London*, the River sides are full of Villages, and those Villages so full of Beautiful Buildings, Charming Gardens, and rich Habitations of Gentlemen of Quality, that nothing in the World can imitate it. . . .'[1] Here the best people retired when their public careers, or the London season, came to an end. Pope, at Chiswick and later at Twickenham, lived in the most select of neighbourhoods. When he writes to John Caryll, apologizing for not having visited him earlier and rather tactlessly listing all the visits he has paid instead, his evident pride in being received into polite society is touching in its ingenuousness:

> I have been indispensably obliged to pass some days at almost every house along the Thames; half my acquaintance being upon the breaking up of the Parliament become my neighbours. After some attendance on my Lord Burlington, I have been at the Duke of Shrewsbury's, Duke of Argyle's, Lady Rochester's, Lord Percival's, Mr Stonor's, Lord Winchelsea's, Sir Godfrey Kneller's (who has made me a fine present of a picture) and Dutchess Hamilton's. All these have indispensable claims to me, under penalty of the imputation of direct rudeness, living within 2 hours sail of Chiswick. Then am I obliged to pass some days between my Lord Bathurst's, and three or four more on Windsor side.[2]

From Twickenham Pope can travel to London by land or water, yet is remote enough from the great world to be able to cultivate his garden (provided no men of rhyme interrupt), and to converse peaceably with his friends over a bottle of wine. Pope has thus achieved the 'mixt State' which he eulogized in a contribution to the *Spectator* in 1712. Addressing an imaginary correspondent he writes: 'I find you shift the Scene of your Life from the Town to the Country, and enjoy that mixt State which wise Men both delight in, and

---

[1] Defoe, *Tour*, vol. I, p. 165; cf. p. 392.
[2] 6 August 1717, *Correspondence*, vol. I, pp. 417–18.

are qualified for. Methinks most of the Philosophers and Moralists have run too much into Extremes in praising entirely either Solitude or publick Life; in the former Men generally grow useless by too much Rest, and in the latter are destroy'd by too much Precipitation.'[1] Some years earlier Pope had written a youthful Ode in unreserved praise of solitude; now the ideal of a secluded existence is giving way to a characteristically Augustan compromise between a life of retirement and contemplation, and one of public activity. The London 'season' was a device to secure this compromise for the privileged, who could enjoy metropolitan winters of political activity, visits and entertainments, and rural summers on country estates. The career of Sir William Temple set a nobler example, alternating between public service on diplomatic missions and private retirement spent in study and gardening. 'A Philosophical Mind resolves to live according to the Convenience and Rules of Nature, and endeavours to enjoy at once all the Varieties of an active Life, and all the Quiet & Peace of a Retir'd Solitude.'[2] When, in *To Fortescue*, Pope describes his life at Twickenham he is careful to remind us of the earlier and more strenuous days of the 'best Companions' who grace his retreat. Bolingbroke's parliamentary oratory is now reduced to domestic proportions:

> There *St. John* mingles with my friendly Bowl,
> The Feast of Reason and the Flow of Soul:

while Lord Peterborough's military talents are put to peaceful uses:

> And He, whose Lightning pierc'd th' *Iberian* Lines,
> Now, forms my Quincunx, and now ranks my Vines,
> Or tames the Genius of the stubborn Plain,
> Almost as quickly, as he conquer'd *Spain*.[3]

The poet himself is actively hospitable even in retirement; he is also energetically promoting the cause of Virtue through his writings.

---

[1] *The Spectator*, no. 406.
[2] The Diary of Anthony Hammond, British Museum Add. MS. 22584, fol. 29ʳ. The entry is dated January 1717.
[3] Lines 125 ff. I am indebted for this point to Thomas E. Maresca, 'Pope's Defense of Satire', *E L H*, vol. XXXI (1964), pp. 382–3.

In his 'Retir'd Solitude' the gentleman will take delight in his library and his collections. Evelyn advised his grandson about the proper care of his 'Cabinets of Medalls, Intaglios, Coynes, Seales, modern Coines, &c.', and of his 'Cabinet of natural Curiositys' containing 'shells, chrystals, stones, sparrs, natural and Artificial, collected casualy, usefull to Natural philosophy & contemplation of the work of God'.[1] Pope's grotto, decorated with geological specimens contributed by his friends and correspondents, was, among other things, a small museum. Connoisseurs like Matthew Prior collected bronzes and jewels, coins and medals, prints, drawings, paintings and sculptures. Private collecting on this scale is a self-indulgent and self-centred occupation, one which assorts naturally with the Epicurean ideal of retiring into oneself. The zeal with which it was pursued in the Restoration and early eighteenth century suggests that it helped to satisfy a desire for the security of tangible things, a need for material assurances in an uncertain world. The Augustans show a marked preference for the real, the certain, the substantial and the useful over the immaterial, the debatable, the elusive and the theoretical. Trade is more respectable than the mysteries of high finance and political arithmetic. Lockean political theory is deeply committed to the sanctity of property, Lockean psychology to the reports of the senses. Pope claimed that 'the rule laid down in the beginning of the *Essay on Man* of reasoning only from what we know is certainly a right one, and will go a great way toward destroying all the school metaphysics.'[2] For metaphysical speculation is both frustrating and fruitless:

> The mind, in Metaphysics at a loss,
> May wander in a wilderness of Moss.
> (*Dunciad* IV 449–50)

In contrast, experimental science – the 'new Philosophy' – takes its stand on matters of fact, on carefully checked and recorded observations. 'Our Reasoning Faculty as well as Fancy, does but Dream, when it is not guided by sensible Objects. We shall compound where

---

[1] *Memoires for my Grand-son*, ed. Geoffrey Keynes (Oxford, 1926), pp. 54–5.
[2] Spence, § 303.

Nature has divided, and divide where Nature has compounded, and create nothing but either Deformed Monsters, or at best pretty but impossible Mermaids.'[1] Cowley here, like Bacon before him, has his eye on the creations of the Schoolmen. For want of proper foundations they produced, even at their most constructive, merely systems of cobwebs. But too often their intellectual operations were corrosive, for they indulged in a 'humor of disputing, which Breaks the force of things by the subtilty of words.'[2] The distinctive merits of the Royal Society, as its first historian so clearly saw, were that it allowed 'things' their full importance; that it was constructive and practical – 'it is better to *do*, than to *talk* well';[3] and that it relied upon collaborative effort. For its members it was a real, and for the public at large a symbolic antidote to the turmoils of the mid-seventeenth century, when the 'humor of disputing' had run unchecked, and men had delighted in being individualists:

> The contemplation of [Nature], draws our minds off from past, or present misfortunes, and makes them conquerers over things, in the greatest publick unhappiness: while the consideration of *Men*, and *humane affairs*, may affect us, with a thousand various disquiets; *that* never separates us into mortal Factions; *that* gives us room to differ, without animosity; and permits us, to raise contrary imaginations upon it, without any danger of a *Civil War*. . . .
>
> For the *Royal Society* had its beginning in the wonderful pacifick year, 1660. . . . And I shall here joyn my solemn wishes, that as it began in that time, when our Country was freed from confusion, and slavery: So it may, in its progress, redeem the minds of Men, from obscurity, uncertainty, and bondage.[4]

The 'new philosophy', neo-Stoicism, the ideal of the 'Retir'd Gardener', even the concern with manners and breeding, are all to some degree protective measures, defences against fears and uncertainties. It is difficult to reconstruct the emotional climate of an

---

[1] Cowley, *A Proposition for the Advancement of Experimental Philosophy* (1661), in *Essays*, p. 247.
[2] Sprat, *History of the Royal Society*, p. 332.
[3] Sprat, p. 132.
[4] Sprat, pp. 56 and 58; see also pp. 426–7.

age in which public order lies under a constant threat. The gloomy prognostications of that age may come to appear unwarrantably pessimistic (a criticism that has been levelled at Pope's *Epilogue to the Satires*), if not unintentionally absurd: a 'very wise and great citizen' announced to the Duchess of Marlborough 'that it was plain that England would entirely be ruined but just the time he could not say'.[1] Yet the very number of the defences, and of their advocates, indicates that men's fears were real and pressing.

Some of these bulwarks may have seemed flimsy at the time, and one of them, neo-Stoicism, was severely handled both by the satirists and by those churchmen who regarded it as a weak but alluring rival to religious faith. Certainly the Church itself promised much more substantial safeguards against disorder within and without, against the temptations of pride and concupiscence, and against Hell's dire agents of political anarchy. Towards the end of his first *Letter concerning Toleration* Locke declares that Christianity 'carries the greatest opposition to Covetousness, Ambition, Discord, Contention, and all manner of inordinate Desires; and is the most modest and peaceable Religion that ever was.'[2] In context, however, this tribute sounds a trifle hollow, for one of the side-effects of the *Letter* is to hinder the 'opposition' from functioning efficiently. Locke's intellectual energy, in this as in his later work, is directed towards pinpointing problems and clarifying issues. Confusion must be swept away, true must be disentangled from false, and firm lines drawn between powers and faculties that are commonly and erroneously believed to be related or even inseparable.[3] In the *Letter* Locke argues that the provinces of the magistrate and of the Church have no territory in common. The magistrate, or civil authority, has power over the things of this world, over property but not over souls; he can punish by fine, confiscation, imprisonment, and death.

---

[1] G. S. Thomson, *Letters of a Grandmother*, pp. 158–9. See also Spence, § 601.
[2] *A Letter concerning Toleration*, trans. William Popple (1689), p. 55.
[3] For example, in Book IV ch. xviii of the *Essay Concerning Humane Understanding* Locke treats 'Of Faith and Reason, and their distinct Provinces'. Similarly, 'these two Powers, Political and Paternal, are so perfectly distinct and separate, and built upon so different Foundations, and given to so different Ends. . . .': *Two Treatises of Government*, 2nd ed. (1694), p. 217.

[ 183 ]

Conversely, the only penalty which the Church can impose is that of excommunication, the banishing of a soul. From this it follows that 'nothing ought, nor can be transacted in this Society [the Church], relating to the Possession of Civil and Worldly Goods'; ecclesiastical authority 'neither has any Jurisdiction in things Civil, nor any manner of Power of Compulsion, nor any thing at all to do with Riches and Revenues'.[1] This is an important step in Locke's plea for toleration, because he is concerned only with toleration towards Dissenters (atheists and Roman Catholics remain outside the pale), because the stronghold of Dissent is the City of London, and because the commercial transactions of the City are essential to the prosperity of the nation as a whole. The Established Church is not only being asked to tolerate the doctrines and forms of worship of the Dissenters; it is also being persuaded to relinquish its right to speak out on matters of gain, and on questions of 'Riches and Revenues'. The business dealings of the Dissenters must pass without clerical comment. In the cause of religious toleration Locke seeks to deprive the Church of its traditional role as spokesman of that essentially moral economic theory which insisted on fair dealings and 'reasonable gain', and was firmly opposed to usury.

Elizabethan opponents of this economic morality were vociferous in their demands that the activities of merchants should not be overseen by interfering clerics. Locke can be more moderate because by the end of the seventeenth century churchmen are less disposed to interfere. They strive to be rational and impartial, to see a problem from every side. And they have become more resigned to economic realities. Robert South, debating the legality of usury, arrives at no clear verdict. His inclination to censure all such transactions is qualified by his perception that censure would be in vain; self-interest 'is the grand wheel and spring that moves the whole universe. Let Christ and Truth say what they will, if interest will have it, gain must be godliness.'[2] But Jeremy Collier is decisively of the merchants' party. '*Trade*,' says his mouthpiece 'Alphius', 'subsists upon Credit, and sets up with *Crutches*.' Since England's material well-

---

[1] *Letter*, pp. 13 and 53.      [2] *Sermons*, vol. I, pp. 98–9.

being increasingly depends upon trade and the ability to raise financial support for new ventures, the movement of credit must not be encumbered by moral restraints and prohibitions. 'Bishops and Councils have no Authority to bind Property, and determine the Condition of Estates'; they have absolutely no power 'to determine Civil Affairs' such as usury, which is 'altogether a civil Question'. This argument, which was also Locke's, constitutes in Alphius's eyes a large part of the case for 'lawful Usury'.[1] Commercial and financial misdemeanours may be proved criminal; they can no longer be held to be sinful.

What little remains of effective communication between Church and counting-house is a one-way affair. Religion is infiltrated by the values of materialism. Isaac Barrow, preaching on 'The Duty and Reward of Bounty to the Poor' before the Lord Mayor and Aldermen of London, makes some remarkable, not to say damaging, concessions to the business interests of his congregation:

> The way to gain abundantly is, you know well, to trade boldly. . . . 'Tis so likewise in the evangelical negotiations; if we put out much upon score of conscience or charity, we shall be sure to profit much. Liberality is the most beneficial traffick that can be; it is bringing our wares to the best market; it is letting out our money into the best hands; we thereby lend our money to God, who repays with vast usury; an hundred to one is the rate he allows at present, and above a hundred millions to one he will render hereafter; so that if you will be merchants this way, you shall be sure to thrive, you cannot fail to grow rich most easily and speedily.[2]

God is not only the Supreme Architect, but also the Supreme Financier. So Swift was left to regret, with fine irony, that a restoration of '*real* Christianity; such as used in primitive Times . . . to have an Influence upon Mens Belief and Actions,' would 'ruin Trade' and 'turn our Courts, Exchanges and Shops into Desarts.'[3]

The Church was the more willing to restrain its moral energies

---

[1] 'Of Usury', in *Essays upon Several Moral Subjects*, Part III, 3rd ed. (1720), pp. 186 and 211-12.
[2] *Works*, vol. I, p. 328.
[3] 'An Argument against Abolishing Christianity', *Prose Works*, vol. II, p. 27.

because it was mindful of its fate during the Cromwellian inter-regnum. Its very existence could once again be jeopardized if men failed to hold a middle course between violent extremes. The task of holding such a course would be much simplified if the less zealous among the Dissenters could be absorbed into the rest of society, while for its own part the Church itself eschews anything which might savour of fanaticism. Radical comment on social morality has now no place in its concerns, so that its condemnation of covetous-ness lacks the pressure and immediacy of Pope's attacks on avarice. Churchmen preach charity, but acquiesce in the assumptions that society will always be divisible into superiors, equals, and inferiors, and that to enjoy an 'easy competence' is a worthy ideal. The stability of the existing social system might well be damaged, as Swift saw, by a sudden infusion of apostolic rigour and austerity. It will never be shaken by those who live in undisturbed tranquillity:

> Men of a middle condition, are indeed doubly happy. First, that, with the poor, they are not the objects of *pity;* nor, 2. With the rich and great, the mark of *envy.* . . . The honest country gentleman, and the thriving tradesman, or country farmer, have all the real benefits of nature, and the blessings of plenty, that the highest and richest grandees can pretend to . . . they have no ill-got places to lose; they are neither libelled nor undermined, but, without invading any man's right, sit safe and warm in a moderate fortune of their own. . . . And he who is not contented with such a condition, must seek his happiness (if ever he have any) in another world, for providence itself can provide no better for him in this.[1]

The Church recognized its kinship with men of a middle con-dition, since it constituted a *via media* between the extremes of 'Popery' and 'Fanaticism'. To avoid these extremes it may also be necessary to avoid any imputation of being over-serious and devout; one must not be thought to be enthusiastic. 'In this *polite* age of ours, we have so *liv'd away* the spirit of devotion, that many seem afraid even to be suspected of it.'[2] Christian apologists therefore insist that religion is quite compatible with, indeed actually promotes, 'cheer-

---

[1] South, *Sermons*, vol. V, pp. 426–7.
[2] William Law, *A Serious Call to a Devout and Holy Life* (1729), p. 482.

fulness': 'In a word, the true Spirit of Religion cheers, as well as composes, the Soul; it banishes indeed all Levity of Behaviour, all vicious and dissolute Mirth, but in exchange fills the Mind with a perpetual Serenity, uninterrupted Chearfulness, and an habitual Inclination to please others, as well as to be pleased in it self.'[1] Addison here concedes a little to the Puritan temper by renouncing dissoluteness and levity. The gentleman is no rake or libertine, but he has no taint of Puritan moroseness either. Addison's essay begins with the anecdote of the sombre Head of an Oxford College who terrified a young candidate for admission by asking 'how he abounded in Grace', and concluded the interview by demanding '*Whether he was prepared for Death*?' Puritan melancholy, at best amusingly eccentric, at worst embarrassing and disturbing, must yield to ease and cheerfulness: 'It has been a great Artifice of the Devil, to possess the Minds of inconsidering Men with an Opinion, that Religion is a soure, morose, ill-natur'd Thing; that 'tis an Enemy to every thing which is pleasant and chearful; and that whoever engages in the Practice of it, must, from that Instant, renounce all the Pleasures and Enjoyments of Life.'[2] The new religion does away with sourness and severity. And from the same motives the new architecture banishes dim religious light from churches, and gloom from private houses: 'one would think the People of former Ages, were afraid of Light, and good Air. . . . Whereas the Genius of our Times is altogether for light *Stair-cases*, fine *Sash-windows*, and lofty *Ceilings*.'[3]

As William Law clearly perceived, social life had annexed the life of the spirit. The habitual inclination to please others as well as to be pleased in oneself, which Addison considers a particular gift of religion, is the hall-mark of the polite gentleman. Its other gifts, 'perpetual Serenity' and 'uninterrupted Chearfulness', are simply the state of mind of an eighteenth-century disciple of Epicurus.

---

[1] Addison, *Spectator* no. 494; see also nos. 381 and 387.
[2] William Melmoth, *The Great Importance of a Religious Life Consider'd* (1711), p. 8.
[3] Neve, *City and Countrey Purchaser*, p. 71. Large and dimly-lit churches were also associated with the other undesirable religious 'extreme', Catholicism: see G. W. O. Addleshaw and F. Etchells, *The Architectural Setting of Anglican Worship* (1948), pp. 61–2 and 249–50.

Law himself reminded the age that 'as all virtue is founded in *truth*, so humility is founded in a *true* and *just* sense of our *weakness*, *misery*, and *sin*.'[1] But Law's earnest intensity was exceptional, hence Dr Johnson's eager response to his serious call. The age could readily acknowledge the need for intellectual humility, for an awareness of man's weakness and the limitations of his faculties, but found it more difficult to see the relevance of humility of soul. It tended to equate humility with modesty, and to recommend it on the grounds that it helps to lubricate the wheels of society: humility 'keeps us reserv'd and silent, modest and respectful, attentive to what is said, and willing to be instructed, makes us easie in Conversation, not apt to be passionate, dogmatical, or imposing.'[2] The polite gentleman will be diffident in conversation with his superiors. Before his inferiors he will behave with a modest condescension that will involve no sacrifice of his self-respect. It is only an apparent paradox that a man can take pride in humility of this undemanding kind. Pope boasts that he is 'So humble, he has knock'd at *Tibbald*'s door';[3] the poet has fallen into one of the moral clichés of the time in order to make easy fun of Theobald's social and intellectual status.

Humility, mortification, praying for one's enemies, are more exacting than Addisonian cheerfulness. And they are more unpalatable antidotes to human pride than is the classical doctrine of self-knowledge, which Christian teaching has absorbed and passed beyond. 'Enthusiasts' clearly lack self-knowledge. They confuse their illusions with reality; they believe themselves inspired, and give way to imaginary raptures. Their 'admiration' is as unthinking as the intellectual arrogance of contemporary scientists:

> Go, wond'rous creature! mount where Science guides,
> Go, measure earth, weigh air, and state the tides;
> Instruct the planets in what orbs to run,
> Correct old Time, and regulate the Sun.

> (*Essay on Man* II 19–22)

The scientists fall into the sin of 'reas'ning Pride' because they refuse

---

[1] *Serious Call*, p. 295.    [2] Lady Mary Chudleigh, *Essays*, p. 31.
[3] *Epistle to Arbuthnot* 372.

to recognize man's shortcomings. Pope offers them sensible advice: 'Trace Science then, with Modesty thy guide'; 'Know then thyself, presume not God to scan.'[1] In his warm advocacy of self-knowledge Pope is sometimes more classical than his sources. Thus in the *Epistle to Bolingbroke* he imparts a clear sense of purpose to Horace's programme of moral reform:

> Sic mihi tarda fluunt *ingrataque* tempora, quæ spem
> Consiliumque *morantur* agendi gnaviter *id*, quod
> Æque *pauperibus* prodest, *locupletibus* æque
> Æque neglectum *pueris, senibusque* nocebit.[2]

The point of this lies in its deliberate vagueness and magisterial vacuity. It is part of Horace's parody of Stoicism, and its pretentiousness will be finally dissipated at the end of the Epistle. Pope, with the addition of a single phrase, makes the lines wholly serious:

> So slow th'unprofitable Moments roll,
> That lock up all the Functions of my soul;
> *That keep me from Myself;* and still delay
> Life's instant business to a future day. . . .[3]

The philosopher-poet now sets a clear target before his eyes; the 'instant business' of life is to acquire self-awareness and understanding. Earlier, in *Windsor-Forest*, Pope had similarly modified Lucan's account of the Stoic principles of Cato:

> Hi mores, haec duri inmota Catonis
> Secta fuit, servare modum finemque tenere
> Naturamque sequi patriaeque inpendere vitam. . . .[4]

Pope's happy man, retired from active politics, wanders

---

1 *Essay on Man* II 43 and 1.
2 Epistle I i 23–6: 'so slow and thankless flow for me the hours which defer my hope and purpose of setting myself vigorously to that task which profits alike the poor, alike the rich, but, if neglected, will be harmful alike to young and to old.'
3 Lines 39–42; my italics.
4 *Pharsalia* II 380–2: 'Such was the character, such the inflexible rule of austere Cato – to observe moderation and hold fast to the limit, to follow nature, to give his life for his country. . . .'

thoughtful in the silent Wood,
Attends the Duties of the Wise and Good,
T'observe a Mean, be to himself a Friend,
To follow Nature, and regard his End.

(249–52)

The Stoic ideal of laying down one's life for one's country is re-
placed by a less rigorous rule, and one whose tendency is to restrain
the Stoic's pride, since 'Being to himself a Friend' presumably includes the kind of self-knowledge that prevents a man from foolishly
straying beyond his sphere.

Pope's re-writing of Lucan in this passage has created a further
dimension of classical reference. 'T'observe a Mean, be to himself
a Friend' now echoes both of those maxims which Sir William Temple called 'the Golden Sentences at *Delphos*; Know thy self. Nothing
too much.'[1] Of these sentences the second was to be expounded by
Horace and Plutarch, Montaigne and Boileau, to name only the most
prominent among Pope's literary ancestors. In his insistence on
moderation he is their true heir. At about the time he was completing
*Windsor-Forest* he made his first version of Donne's second Satire, a
poem which ends by lamenting the displacement of the older, socially responsible gentry and by celebrating the Horatian ideal of the
golden mean:

Where are those Troops of Poor that throng'd before
The good old Landlords hospitable Door?
Well, I cou'd wish that still in Richmens Homes
Some Beasts were kill'd, tho' not whole Hecatombs:
That both Extreams were banisht from their Halls,
*Carthusian* Fasts, and fulsom *Bacchanalls*:
And all mankind wou'd that blest Mean observe
In which none 'ere cou'd surfeit, none could starve.[2]

Twenty years later the 'Design' prefixed to the *Essay on Man*
claims, with quiet pride, that the poem steers 'betwixt the extremes
of doctrines seemingly opposite'. The *Essay* was originally planned

---

[1] 'Heads, Designed for an Essay upon the Different Conditions of Life and Fortune',
*Works*, vol. I, p. 306.
[2] Lines 119–26. This early MS version was first printed in the Twickenham Edition,
vol. IV, pp. 132 ff.

as the first part of an '*Opus Magnum*' which would present a 'system of Ethics in the Horatian way'; its remaining sections were to be concerned with 'moderation, or "The Use of Things". '[1]

In his pious wish that mankind will observe the 'blest Mean' Pope is emphatically a man of his time. Moderation is instinctively exalted into a guiding principle by an age which has recently witnessed the unloosing of anarchy, and sees all disturbances, national and individual, as ugly manifestations of excess and extremism. The eighteenth century was fittingly ushered in by Pomfret's *Choice*, for in making his choice Pomfret carefully treads a middle course. His country retreat will be 'not Little, nor too Great'; the friends he entertains must be 'exactly Free/From loose Behaviour, or Formality'; the neighbouring 'Modest Fair' must neither 'seem Reserv'd, nor talk too much', and Pomfret would enjoy her company, as he would his wine, 'seldom, and with Moderation'. Thus men's desires are politely shackled. His poem is so soothingly (and appropriately) mediocre that it could not fail to be popular. It went through four editions within a year, and Dr Johnson thought that 'perhaps no composition in our language has been oftener perused'.[2]

In another poem, 'To his Friend, inclin'd to Marry,' Pomfret advises against choosing a wife either 'from too exalted, or too mean a State':

> Who moves within the middle Region, shares
> The least Disquiets, and the smallest Cares.
> Let her have Wit, but let that Wit be free
> From Affectation, Pride, and Pedantry:
> For the effect of Woman's Wit is such,
> Too little is as dangerous, as too much.[3]

'Dangerous', which seems a portentous adjective to use in such a domestic context, reveals Pomfret's anxiety about conflict and 'Disquiets' in any sphere of human activity. For the dark background of all this preoccupation with the mean is the turbulence of the seventeenth century,

---

[1] Pope to Swift, 28 November 1729, *Correspondence*, vol. III, p. 81; Spence, § 299.
[2] *Lives of the Poets*, vol. I, p. 302.
[3] *Poems*, p. 119.

When proud Rebellions wou'd unhinge a State,
And wild Disorders in a Land create.[1]

One of the most substantial defences against a repetition of such political chaos is what the age likes to call 'our Happy Constitution', 'happy' because the liberty of the subject and the power of the Crown are nicely adjusted and reconciled. Such a delicate balance of forces is possible only in a limited, or as Locke significantly described it, a 'moderated' monarchy.[2] The Constitution enshrined the same kind of moderation that was to be observed in the temperate English climate and the temperate English religion. Indeed the Constitution even deserved the epithet 'blessed', which Halifax bestowed upon it, since it reflected the attributes of God himself. Halifax concludes his *Character of a Trimmer* with an eloquent assertion:

That our Climate is a *Trimmer*, between that part of the World where men are Roasted, and the other where they are Frozen; That our Church is a *Trimmer* between the Phrenzy of Platonick Visions, and the Lethargick Ignorance of Popish Dreams; That our Laws are Trimmers, between the Excess of unbounded Power, and the Extravagance of Liberty not enough restrained; That true Virtue hath ever been thought a *Trimmer*, and to have its dwelling in the middle between the two Extreams; That even God Almighty himself is divided between his two great Attributes, his Mercy and his Justice.[3]

Moderation, however, is not by itself sufficient to ensure social stability. 'It is necessary, in the present Constitution of things, that Order and Distinction should be kept up in the World.'[4] The Augustan mind delights to construct hierarchies, whether among the literary 'kinds' or among the classes of society, but its delight is, basically, a need to create order out of imminent chaos. Shortly after the Restoration a reactionary scheme was proposed 'for making a

---

[1] Pomfret, 'Cruelty and Lust', *Poems*, p. 164. This poem is based on an incident during Monmouth's rebellion.
[2] *Two Treatises of Government*, p. 291.
[3] *Works*, p. 103. The phrase 'our blessed Constitution' occurs in the first section of the *Character* (*Works*, p. 62), which also includes a parallel between 'our Government' and 'our Climate' (p. 63).
[4] Addison, *Spectator* no. 219.

sharp and permanent division between classes such as prevailed in France. The nobles were to be raised higher above the masses; the commons confined to trade; the clergy entrusted with jurisdiction; and so on.'[1] Regimentation on this scale would have been intolerable to all true-born Englishmen. Yet the project was simply a straight-forward and crude attempt to reinstate the social hierarchy after the confusions produced by the levelling tendencies of the Civil War. It is reassuring to be able to divide humanity into one's superiors, one's equals, and one's inferiors, and thus to classify any member of society immediately and unerringly as 'a master, or a servant, or a friend.'[2]

At a personal level the main safeguard against disturbance and turmoil is the quality of Sense. At the beginning of the eighteenth century Sense was held in higher regard than at any time before or since: 'We live in an Age where Sense, good Sense, and Nothing but Sense, is required, and nothing else will be received.'[3] Sense is the soul of every art, the gentlemanly equivalent of the Puritan inner light:

> Good Sense, which only is the gift of Heav'n,
> And tho' no science, fairly worth the sev'n:
> A Light, which in yourself you must perceive;
> Jones and Le Nôtre have it not to give.
>
> (*To Burlington* 43–6)

Good Sense will avoid the blunders of imitating Fools and the inanities of Timon; theirs is the sort of tasteless conduct which 'shocks Reason, and the Rules of common Sense.'[4] Reason and Sense are commonly equated, as here by Oldham, and are commonly conceived as negative, curbing influences, much akin to prudence and circumspection. When Reason whispers in Pope's ear it advises caution and moderation:

---

[1] A. L. Smith, 'The Composition of Society', in *Social England*, ed. H. D. Traill (1893–7), vol. IV, p. 473.
[2] *Essay on Man* II 250.
[3] Matthew Concanen, *The Speculatist* (1730), p. 41.
[4] Oldham, 'Horace his Art of Poetry, Imitated in English', line 21, in his *Poems and Translations* (1684).

"Friend Pope! be prudent, let your Muse take breath,
"And never gallop Pegasus to death. . . ."[1]

Thus Reason, in the accents of common sense, warns the poet against literary enthusiasm. Even wit, so dear to the Augustans, may tempt men into immoderate extremes. Its operations, as Edward Young argues, may be mischievous:

> Nature has shewn by making it so rare,
> That *Wit*'s a Jewel which we need not wear;
> Of plain sound *Sense* life's current Coin is made,
> With that we drive the most substantial Trade. . . .
>   Prudence protects and guides us, Wit betrays,
> A splendid source of ill ten thousand ways;
> A certain snare to miseries immense;
> A gay Prerogative from common sense. . . .[2]

To say that a man has good sense is to give him the highest praise. For Sense is the foundation of all that is valuable. Edward Young, a little earlier in this same 'Epistle to Mr Pope' asks rhetorically: 'What is Virtue but superior Sense?'; and Halifax is certain that 'where Sense is wanting, every thing is wanting.'[3]

Sense makes for equilibrium and continuity because it can be readily identified as the common factor in all that is meritorious in human society, past and present; beneath the differences of creeds and customs lies this firm basis. So Dryden can assert that 'good sense is the same in all or most ages',[4] and Pope can repeat Dryden's point in the Preface to the *Works* of 1717: 'For to say truth, whatever is very good sense must have been common sense in all times; and what we call Learning, is but the knowledge of the sense of our predecessors.'[5] In this way, and because it is on the side of modera-

---

[1] *Epistle to Bolingbroke* (*Epistle I i*) 13–14. Cf. 'For Reason still is whispering in your Ear,/Where you are sure to fail, th'Attempt forbear': Dryden's translation of Persius, Satire v, lines 139–40.
[2] *Two Epistles to Mr Pope, Concerning the Authors of the Age* (1730), pp. 31–2 (Epistle II, lines 95 ff.).
[3] 'Miscellaneous Thoughts and Reflections', *Works*, p. 248.
[4] 'Discourse concerning Satire', *Essays*, vol. II, p. 80.
[5] Twickenham Edition, vol. I, p. 7.

tion and discretion, Sense helps to satisfy the emotional craving for stability. The age was very ready to believe that 'all things in the World reduce themselves to a certain kind of Balance.'[1] The vagaries of human behaviour may temporarily upset this balance, but equilibrium is the proper condition of the universe, the condition to which it constantly seeks to revert.

> Hear then the truth: " 'Tis Heav'n each Passion sends,
> "And diff'rent men directs to diff'rent ends.
> "Extremes in Nature equal good produce,
> "Extremes in Man concur to gen'ral use."
>
> (*To Bathurst* 161–4)

In the *Epistle to Bathurst* human extremes are represented by the miser and the prodigal. 'Pale Mammon', 'a backward steward for the Poor', fills a whole reservoir of wealth; his spendthrift heir releases the hoarded riches 'in lavish streams to quench a Country's thirst' (lines 173 ff.). Lord Bathurst carefully moves between these extremes, and the poet hopes that others may follow his illustrious example; God alone can reconcile the extremes, making them concur to general use.[2] Not that the poem offers us any clear instance of this concurrence. For when it passes on to consider the particular cases of Cotta and his son we find that extremes in man are merely detrimental to other men. If Cotta refuses hospitality and charity to the needy, his lavish son is no more charitable, for his unthinking bonhomie serves only to fill 'the capacious Squire, and deep Divine'. The most that can be said for their composite usefulness is that it keeps money in circulation, which safeguards the nation's economy, which in turn helps to assure a yearly income for the charitable Man of Ross. Only in this very tenuous way can the miser be regarded as a backward steward for the poor. When Pope comes to apply the doctrine of concurring extremes to actual cases he is too much of a realist to deceive himself and his reader into thinking that the miser's

---

[1] Pierre Nicole, *Moral Essays* (1677–80), vol. II, p. 119. For Pope's knowledge of these *Essays* see his letter of May 1720 to John Caryll, *Correspondence*, vol. II, p. 43.
[2] See Wasserman, *Pope's 'Epistle to Bathurst'*, pp. 33–40, where the subtlety and originality of Pope's thought in this part of the *Epistle* are very persuasively argued.

money finds its way, through the channel of prodigality, into the
pockets of the needy. In fact Pope scarcely allows us time to ponder
the application of his doctrine to human affairs. Between the senten-
tiousness of

> "Extremes in Nature equal good produce,
> "Extremes in Man concur to gen'ral use"

and the witty imagery of reservoir and fountain, comes a dignified
passage which absorbs Man in Nature, and draws all extremes to a
common centre:

> Ask we what makes one keep, and one bestow?
> That POW'R who bids the Ocean ebb and flow,
> Bids seed-time, harvest, equal course maintain,
> Thro' reconcil'd extremes of drought and rain,
> Builds Life on Death, on Change Duration founds,
> And gives th'eternal wheels to know their rounds.

The human extremes here are not miserliness and prodigality, but
'keeping' and 'bestowing'; and since 'bestow' suggests charitable
giving, we are the more willing to see the hand of Providence behind
these activities. Seed-time and harvest, drought and rain, the Ocean's
ebb and flow, are analogues of economic and financial cycles, so that
the circulation of money is dignified both by its association with
natural process and by the Biblical verse that moulds Pope's expression of that process: 'While the earth remaineth, seed-time and
harvest, and cold and heat, and summer and winter, and day and
night shall not cease.'[1] Pope conceives stability as a condition far
removed from mere stasis. He has inherited the Elizabethan insight
that permanence can be founded on mutability because the entire
cycle of change is controlled by God's law, which 'gives th'eternal
wheels to know their rounds'.

Pope also preserves something of the Elizabethan conception of
Degree, an awareness that Order is not a rigid and mechanical
structure (as some of his contemporaries seem to have regarded it),
but a flexible and dynamic state, a matter of ordered activity and co-

---

[1] Genesis viii 22.

operation. The closing lines of the *Epistle to Burlington* display this sense of Order. So too does a passage towards the end of the third Epistle of the *Essay on Man*:

> 'Twas then, the studious head or gen'rous mind,
> Follow'r of God or friend of human-kind,
> Poet or Patriot, rose but to restore
> The Faith and Moral, Nature gave before;
> Re-lum'd her ancient light, not kindled new;
> If not God's image, yet his shadow drew:
> Taught Pow'r's due use to People and to Kings,
> Taught nor to slack, nor strain its tender strings,
> The less, or greater, set so justly true,
> That touching one must strike the other too;
> 'Till jarring int'rests of themselves create
> Th'according music of a well-mix'd State.
> Such is the World's great harmony, that springs
> From Order, Union, full Consent of things!
> Where small and great, where weak and mighty, made
> To serve, not suffer, strengthen, not invade,
> More pow'rful each as needful to the rest,
> And, in proportion as it blesses, blest,
> Draw to one point, and to one centre bring
> Beast, Man, or Angel, Servant, Lord, or King.

The emphasis here falls not on rigidity and system but on co-operation and interdependence, on serving and strengthening, on the 'full Consent of things'. Part of Pope's effect derives from his use of traditional images of musical harmony to describe the perfection of social harmony. More important, the passage is infused with the life of its verbs, with a sense of artistic creativity ('re-lum'd', 'drew', 'create', 'springs'), a sense of active becoming rather than of static being. The hierarchies are in motion; the cosmic categories of Beast, Man and Angel, repeated in the human classes of Servant, Lord and King, are all being drawn to one point. Order is not incompatible with energy.

It is not surprising that Pope responded to the appeal of Sense, Moderation, and Order. It would have been more surprising if he had not. He felt the attractiveness of the available defences against troubled times, the charms of ease and politeness, and the pleasures of a retired life which promised immunity from conflict within and without. Nor did he disregard the teachings of Stoicism:

> Let Lands and Houses have what Lords they will,
> Let Us be fix'd, and our own Masters still.[1]

What distinguishes his response is that it is the response of a poet and a satirist. Pope is more searchingly critical of the defences than most of his contemporaries. He is also more subtle in his understanding of Order and Balance, partly because he has preserved continuity with his Elizabethan predecessors. Above all, his reaction to the standards and values which his contemporaries cherished is, like his reaction to the crimes and follies of the age, vital and passionate. One reason for this vitality would seem to be that the satirist, by virtue of his office, enjoys an intimate and ambivalent relationship, almost a parasitic relationship, with the forces of folly and misrule. The simplest way to urge moderation is to describe and repudiate the extremes of human conduct, but the better the description, the more the extremes are brought to vigorous life. In courtesy-books the most energetic writing goes into the sketches of pedants, dogmatists, fops and country squires, so that in spite of the tributes dutifully paid to sense and moderation there is a tacit acknowledgement of the appeal of eccentricity, an unspoken admission that it takes all sorts of behaviour to make a world that is worth living in. Similarly, Edward Young views with contempt, but also with amused fascination, the epidemic Love of Fame that rages among his fellowmen. Pope's imagination is caught by the multiple blunders of the 'Imitating Fools' who travesty Burlington's architectural designs, and by the delicious absurdities of Grubstreet verse:

> Here gay Description Ægypt glads with show'rs,
> Or gives to Zembla fruits, to Barca flow'rs;
> Glitt'ring with ice here hoary hills are seen,
> There painted vallies of eternal green,
> In cold December fragrant chaplets blow,
> And heavy harvests nod beneath the snow.
>
> (*Dunciad* I 73–8)

---

[1] *To Bethel* 179–80.

The satirists take a barely concealed delight in some of the forces of disorder and irresponsibility that society is officially committed to bringing under control. For these dunces and fools are at least active, even creative, though their activity is hopelessly misguided and their creations grotesque. They are silly rather than culpable, and they are far from possessing the stature of Timon, or Peter Walter, or the goddess of Dulness. Dulness, indeed, has less in common with her more frivolous sons than with the immaculate Cloe, who reposes in a state of emotional and moral inertia:

> "With ev'ry pleasing, ev'ry prudent part,
> "Say, what can Cloe want?" – she wants a Heart.
> She speaks, behaves, and acts just as she ought;
> But never, never, reach'd one gen'rous Thought.
> Virtue she finds too painful an endeavour,
> Content to dwell in Decencies for ever.
> So very reasonable, so unmov'd,
> As never yet to love, or to be lov'd.
> She, while her Lover pants upon her breast,
> Can mark the figures on an Indian chest;
> And when she sees her Friend in deep despair,
> Observes how much a Chintz exceeds Mohair.
>
> (*To a Lady* 159–70)

Cloe is nothing more than an efficient machine. Ungenerous and unmoved, her feelings petrified, she is appropriately locked in the most rigid of couplets. She exemplifies Stoic 'apathy' and 'indolence', terms which had for Pope much of their modern pejorative sense:

> In lazy Apathy let Stoics boast
> Their Virtue fix'd; 'tis fix'd as in a frost,
> Contracted all, retiring to the breast;
> But strength of mind is Exercise, not Rest:
> The rising tempest puts in act the soul,
> Parts it may ravage, but preserves the whole.
> On life's vast ocean diversely we sail,
> Reason the card, but Passion is the gale.
>
> (*Essay on Man* II 101–8)

Opponents of Stoicism always insist that the passions supply the impetus to human action, and that they support and invigorate the

[ 199 ]

intellectual faculties. Plutarch observes that 'if all the Passions, if that were possible, were clean rooted out, Reason in most Men would grow sensibly more dull and unactive than the Pilot of a Ship in a Calm'; and he reproves those 'who would take away all Love, that they may destroy mad and wanton Passions',[1] a course of action which Pope pretends to approve in the *Epistle to Bolingbroke*. Plutarch's line of argument is pursued by Montaigne: 'it is very well known, that the greatest and most noble Actions of the Soul proceed from, and stand in need of, this Impulse of Passions.'[2] Such also is Swift's attitude. And it is shared by the anonymous author (traditionally identified as Pope himself) of a letter published in the *Spectator* on 18 June 1712.[3] This writer holds that the passions preserve the understanding from stagnation and corruption, and are 'necessary to the Health of the Mind'. He concludes with a political analogy which is something of a commonplace: 'Since therefore the Passions are the Principles of humane Actions, we must endeavour to manage them so as to retain their Vigour, yet keep them under strict Command; we must govern them rather like free Subjects than Slaves.' Pope, whether he is the author of this paper or not, certainly believes that the 'Passions are the elements of Life';[4] but when he makes his fullest statement of this doctrine he employs an original, and brilliantly apt, analogy (by 'this Passion' he intends the Ruling Passion in man):

> Th'Eternal Art educing good from ill,
> Grafts on this Passion our best principle. . . .
> As fruits ungrateful to the planter's care
> On savage stocks inserted learn to bear;
> The surest Virtues thus from Passions shoot,
> Wild Nature's vigor working at the root. . . .

---

[1] Plutarch, 'Of Moral Virtue', *Morals*, vol. III, pp. 513 f.
[2] Montaigne, 'Apology for Raimond de Sebonde', *Essays*, trans. Charles Cotton, 3rd ed. (1700), vol. II, p. 389.
[3] *Spectator* no. 408. This letter was first claimed for Pope by John Nichols, but there is no good evidence for his authorship: see Donald F. Bond, 'Pope's Contributions to the *Spectator*', *Modern Language Quarterly*, vol. V (1944), pp. 69–78.
[4] *Essay on Man* I 170.

> Lust, thro' some certain strainers well refin'd,
> Is gentle love, and charms all womankind:
> Envy, to which th'ignoble mind's a slave,
> Is emulation in the learn'd or brave:
> Nor Virtue, male or female, can we name,
> But what will grow on Pride, or grow on Shame.[1]

By means of the finely sustained horticultural metaphor Pope creates a sense of vitality and energy, of active collaboration between Virtues and Passions. Moreover, the advantages are all on the side of the Virtues, which might otherwise have withered as exotics, but are now healthy and 'sure'.

'Strength of mind', Pope declares, 'is Exercise not Rest'. Without the benefit of animating passion a man will sink into the condition of those souls who

> but peep out once an age,
> Dull sullen pris'ners in the body's cage:
> Dim lights of life that burn a length of years,
> Useless, unseen, as lamps in sepulchres;
> Like Eastern Kings a lazy state they keep,
> And close confin'd to their own palace sleep.[2]

It is the 'confinement', the contractedness of such lives which renders them 'useless'; they find a suitably inanimate parallel in the selfish futility of Timon's stately home. This passage from the 'Elegy' is echoed at the end of Pope's poetical career, when Dulness recommends lethargy to her slaves:

> The common Soul, of Heav'n's more frugal make,
> Serves but to keep fools pert, and knaves awake:
> A drowzy Watchman, that just gives a knock,
> And breaks our rest, to tell us what's a clock.

> (*Dunciad* IV 441–4)

Throughout his life Pope attacked the self-centred and the somnolent, in verse whose power and packed density is itself an indictment of dulness. His lines vibrate with the 'spirit' which he considers an

---

[1] *Essay on Man* II 175 ff.    [2] 'Elegy to the Memory of an Unfortunate Lady' 17–22.

essential quality both of good writers and of good critics, who 'read each Work of Wit/With the same Spirit that its Author *writ*'.[1] 'Spirit' is also, because it is synonymous with energy and passion, a necessary constituent of good men; Sir John Barnard 'in spirit, sense, and truth abounds'.[2]

For the Horatian satirist of social follies the eccentric behaviour which he condemns may have a covert attraction. Its wild vigour may be working at the root of his censure. For the moral satirist the passionate impulse behind his verse must spring from indignant repulsion, from the strong antipathy of good to bad. He is one who hates the evil and loves the good. In his energetic singlemindedness he will scorn the compromises and half-measures which the majority of men are willing to settle for. Pope increasingly comes to feel that the defences and refuges of the age are convenient excuses for cowardice and inaction. It is easier to turn one's back on the potentially dangerous half of man's nature than to come to terms with it. In the end moderation and balance, however highly the satirist may esteem them, must give way before the satirical 'spirit' which impels him to speak out, to enter his protest. He is the incarnation of the hypothetical orator whom Aristotle represents as declaring with passion that he cannot endorse the maxim 'Nothing in excess', because wicked men deserve to be hated to excess.[3] The satirist, if he is to be worthy of the sacred weapon entrusted to him, must be an extremist: 'no Degree of Love, or Hatred, or Desire, or Fear, or Anger, or Grief, or any other simple Passion, can be too intense, when placed upon worthy Objects, and directed to worthy Ends'.[4] As the portrait of Sporus proceeds, the historical identity of Lord Hervey is submerged in the image of Satan, a proper object of intense and immoderate hatred. Similarly, in the fourth Book of the *Dunciad* Dulness is no longer the comically vulgar 'Mighty Mother' of the poem's opening line:

---

[1] *Essay on Criticism* 233–4. In the *Epistle to Dr Arbuthnot* bad critics are accused of lacking 'spirit, taste, and sense': line 160.
[2] *Epistle to Bolingbroke* 85.
[3] *Rhetoric* II xii 14.
[4] Stanhope, Preface to *Epictetus*, sig. A5ᵛ.

The rose the Seed of Chaos, and of Night,
To blot out Order, and extinguish Light,
Of dull and venal a new World to mold,
And bring Saturnian days of Lead and Gold.

(IV 13-16)

The whole action of the *Dunciad* is suspended between the mock-
Creation in Book I (where a 'warm Third day' brings forth poetic
maggots, where 'Ocean turns to land', and presiding Dulness 'with
self-applause her wild creation views'), and the Second Coming at
the end of Book IV, which exploits the conventional diction of
contemporary Odes on the Day of Judgment. The progress of Dulness is a grotesque parody, not simply of the progress of Western
European civilization, but of the whole history of mankind. The sons
of Dulness threaten to extinguish the human spirit. The carnation-
grower and butterfly-collector of Book IV, considered as individuals,
are unbalanced, immature, and innocuous. But collectively these
virtuosi have the devastating force of a plague of locusts,[1] and the
reader is warned not to rest too secure in his contempt for the '*weak
Instruments*' who may accomplish 'so great a Revolution in Learning':
'Remember what the Dutch stories somewhere relate, that a great
part of their Provinces was once overflow'd, by a small opening made
in one of their dykes by a single *Water-Rat*.'[2] Hence the need for
unceasing vigilance, for a vehemence which may sometimes appear
disproportionate to the stature of its immediate victim, and for a
strength of purpose and moral conviction that is a kind of righteous
pride:

Yes, I am proud; I must be proud to see
Men not afraid of God, afraid of me:
Safe from the Bar, the Pulpit, and the Throne,
Yet touch'd and sham'd by *Ridicule* alone.
  O sacred Weapon! left for Truth's defence,
Sole Dread of Folly, Vice, and Insolence!
To all but Heav'n-directed hands deny'd,
The Muse may give thee, but the Gods must guide.[3]

---

[1] Book IV 397, and note.    [2] Book III, note to line 333.    [3] *Dialogue II* 208-15.

In 1717 Pope declared that 'the life of a Wit is a warfare upon earth'.[1] With these words he issued a direct challenge to those who demanded moral and social peace at any price. More important, he was already looking towards the passionate satires that were to crown his career, and in which battle was to be joined with the forces of evil. The place of the satirist, as Pope conceived and filled that role, is in the forefront of the battle.

---

[1] Preface to *Works* (1717), Twickenham Edition, vol. I, p. 6.

# Additional Notes and References

CHAPTER I · 'ALEXANDER POPE OF TWICKENHAM'

The discussion of the satirical *persona* in this introductory chapter, and of *To Fortescue* and *To Bethel* in Chapter II, has been influenced by three stimulating essays: Maynard Mack, 'The Muse of Satire', *Yale Review*, vol. XLI (1951–2), pp. 80–92; Irvin Ehrenpreis, 'Personae', in *Restoration and Eighteenth-Century Literature. Essays in Honor of Alan Dugald McKillop*, ed. Carroll Camden (Chicago, 1963), pp. 25–37; and Donald J. Greene, ' "Dramatic Texture" in Pope', in *From Sensibility to Romanticism: Essays Presented to Frederick A. Pottle*, ed. Frederick W. Hilles and Harold Bloom (New York, 1965), pp. 31–53.

PAGE 8. Harold F. Brooks's important study of 'The "Imitation" in English Poetry, Especially in Formal Satire, before the Age of Pope', *Review of English Studies*, vol. XXV (1949), pp. 124–40, examines the intricate literary relationships among Restoration satirists, and their links with their predecessors; it also specifically considers Pope's debt to Oldham. See too Rachel Trickett, *The Honest Muse* (Oxford, 1967), ch. iv.

CHAPTER II · 'TALKING UPON PAPER'

PAGE 23. Relevant aspects of Horace's Satires and Epistles, in particular their subtle modulations of tone, are discussed by Eduard Fraenkel in his *Horace* (Oxford, 1957), especially pp. 94, 310 ff. and 323–7; and by Reuben A. Brower in *Alexander Pope: the Poetry of Allusion* (Oxford, 1959), pp. 168 ff.

The 'confusion and interaction' between the terms *railing* and *raillery* are fully treated in Norman Knox, *The Word 'Irony' and its Context, 1500–1755* (Durham, North Carolina, 1961), pp. 189–208. An account of the fluctuating fortunes of these concepts in the satire of the Restoration period will be found in Ruth Nevo, *The Dial of Virtue: A Study of Poems on Affairs of State in the Seventeenth Century* (Princeton, 1963), ch. viii.

## CHAPTER III · THE COMPLETE GENTLEMAN

PAGE 48. Pope's skilful handling of tone in the *Epistles* and *Imitations of Horace* has been thoroughly demonstrated by R. A. Brower, *Alexander Pope: the Poetry of Allusion*, chs. viii and ix.

PAGE 52 f. This summary of post-Renaissance attitudes towards gentlemanly behaviour draws on W. Lee Ustick's article, 'Changing Ideals of Aristocratic Character and Conduct in Seventeenth-Century England', *Modern Philology*, vol. XXX (1932–3), pp. 147–66.

PAGE 61. I am indebted to James Lees-Milne's *Earls of Creation: Five Great Patrons of Eighteenth-Century Art* (1962), for some details of Burlington's career.

PAGE 62. On the London building boom during the 1720s see Summerson, *Georgian London*, ch. vii, and T. S. Ashton, *Economic Fluctuations in England 1700–1800* (Oxford, 1959), pp. 93–4.

## CHAPTER IV · RURAL VIRTUE

PAGES 64 ff. The impact of Continental formalism on English garden design after the Restoration is discussed in Edward Malins, *English Landscaping and Literature, 1660–1840* (1966), pp. 4–16; on p. 29 he refers to the tentative steps away from symmetry taken by French gardeners. For important anticipations of Addison's arguments against excessive formality, and for other factors affecting the evolution of landscape-gardening, see Maren-Sofie Røstvig, *The Happy Man: Studies in the Metamorphoses of a Classical Ideal*, vol. II (Oslo, 1958), ch. ii.

PAGES 68 ff. A full account of Pope's taste in gardening will be found in A. L. Altenbernd, 'On Pope's "Horticultural Romanticism",' *J E G P*, vol. LIV (1955), pp. 470–7 (reprinted in Mack, *Essential Articles*, pp. 136–45); see also Spence, vol. I, pp. 249–57. Kent's garden at Rousham is described, and the theory behind it elucidated, in Christopher Hussey's 'A Georgian Arcady', *Country Life*, vol. XCIX (1946), pp. 1084–7 and 1130–3. For a lucid history of the ha-ha, and of Lord Cobham's gardens at Stowe, see Laurence Whistler, *The Imagination of Vanbrugh and his Fellow-Artists* (1954), pp. 166–9 and 178 ff.

PAGE 75. The way in which the country house focused the life of a landed family is discussed in H. J. Habakkuk's chapter on the English aristocracy in A. Goodwin (ed.), *The European Nobility in the Eighteenth Century* (1953), pp. 1–21; and by G. E. Mingay, *English Landed Society in the Eighteenth Century* (1963), chs. vii and ix.

PAGE 77. This brief account of the gentleman's role in the village economy draws mainly on the diaries and papers of the Stapley family, of Hickstead Place, Sussex, published by Edward Turner in *Sussex Archaeological Collections*, vol. II (1849), pp. 102–28, and vol. XXIII (1871), pp. 36–72.

PAGE 78. Complaints that Italian influence on architectural design was helping to drive out traditional English hospitality are cited in B. Sprague Allen's *Tides in English Taste* (Cambridge, Mass., 1937), vol. I, pp. 97–103.

PAGE 84 f. In addition to Trevelyan's *England under the Stuarts* my paragraph on the administration of the Poor Law is indebted to Mingay, *English Landed Society*, p. 276, and to Max Beloff, *Public Order and Popular Disturbances, 1660–1714* (1938), pp. 13–14 and 23.

## CHAPTER V · COURTLY VICE

PAGE 90 f. I have discussed the satirical aspects of Pope's editorial taste more fully in 'Pope's Shakespeare', *J E G P*, vol. LXIII (1964), pp. 191–203.

PAGE 98. On relations between Pope and Addison see the detailed account in Norman Ault's *New Light on Pope* (1949), pp. 101–27; reprinted in Mack, *Essential Articles*, pp. 463–94.

## CHAPTER VI · 'NO FOLLOWER, BUT A FRIEND'

PAGE 109. I am indebted for these points about Pope's self-characterisation to Elder Olson's 'Rhetoric and the Appreciation of Pope', *Modern Philology*, vol. XXXVII (1939–40), pp. 13–35, in which the rhetorical strategy of the *Epistle to Arbuthnot*, and the way in which the poem establishes Pope's moral character are clearly demonstrated; and to pp. 373–6 of Alwyn Berland's 'Some Techniques of Fiction in Poetry', *Essays in Criticism*, vol. IV (1954), pp. 372–85.

On the 'Atticus' lines see Robert W. Rogers, *The Major Satires of Alexander Pope*, Illinois Studies in Language and Literature, vol. XL (Urbana, 1955), pp. 87–8, and Benjamin Boyce, *The Character-Sketches in Pope's Poems* (Durham, North Carolina, 1962), pp. 59–62.

By etymology the Devil is first and foremost a traducer and false accuser (Greek *diabolos*). This makes even more meaningful the identification of Sporus, the type of the malicious slanderer, with Satan. The spiteful enemy of the noble satirical poet is seen to be yet another role adopted by the Enemy of Mankind.

## CHAPTER VII · MAMMON

PAGE 132. On the line 'An honest Man's the noblest work of God' see Twickenham Edition, vol. III (i), p. 151, where Maynard Mack adduces examples of the 'wide' meaning of *honest* from the works of George Herbert, Walter Charleton, Sir William Temple and Richard Cumberland. See also William Empson, *The Structure of Complex Words* (1951), p. 196.

PAGE 133. The manner in which Pope's political attitude diverges from that expressed in the *Craftsman* has been examined by Hugo M. Reichard in 'The Independence of Pope as a Political Satirist', *J E G P*, vol. LIV (1955), pp. 309–17.

PAGES 147 ff. Earl R. Wasserman has drawn attention to a steady tradition of Biblical commentary and exegesis which identified Balaam as 'a type of the avaricious man who employs dishonest means': *Pope's 'Epistle to Bathurst'*: *A Critical Reading, With an Edition of the Manuscripts* (Baltimore, 1960), pp. 46 ff. On pp. 40 ff. Professor Wasserman assesses the contribution made by the portrait of the Man of Ross to the total structure of the *Epistle*.

## CHAPTER VIII · 'THE STOIC'S PRIDE'

PAGE 166. Correspondences between the *Essay on Man* and the writings of Marcus Aurelius and Seneca are noted in the Twickenham Edition of the poem, and in Bonamy Dobrée, *The Broken Cistern* (1954), pp. 30–3.

## CHAPTER IX · DISCORDS AND HARMONIES

PAGES 168 ff. See Beloff, *Public Order and Popular Disturbances*, pp. 19–20, for examples of the ease with which tempers could be lost, even in church; and ch. vi for an account of the constant friction between the civilian population and the military, exemplified here by the report of Stedman's trial.

REFERENCES

PAGE 172. On the political prejudice displayed in *Windsor-Forest* see J. R. Moore, '*Windsor Forest* and William III', *Modern Language Notes*, vol. LXVI (1951), pp. 451–4; reprinted in Mack, *Essential Articles*, pp. 232–6.

PAGE 178. For a full account of the concept and development of the English villa see Summerson, 'Classical Country House', *Journal of the Royal Society of Arts*, vol. CVII (1959), pp. 551–2 and 570–87. Mrs Howard's villa at Marble Hill, Twickenham, is discussed by James Lees-Milne in *Earls of Creation*, pp. 86–90.

PAGE 180, note 3. Professor Maresca's article on *To Fortescue* has now been incorporated in his *Pope's Horatian Poems* (Ohio State University Press, 1966). I regret that this book came to hand too late for me to profit from its author's insights and to readjust my argument in order to avoid repeating some of the points he has already made. Nor has it been possible to take full account of the most recent of Professor Mack's three valuable essays on the retirement motif in Pope's poetry: ' "The Shadowy Cave" : Some Speculations on a Twickenham Grotto', in *Restoration and Eighteenth-Century Literature*, ed. Camden, pp. 69–88; 'A Poet in his Landscape: Pope at Twickenham', in *From Sensibility to Romanticism*, ed. Hilles and Bloom, pp. 3–29; and '*Secretum Iter*: Some Uses of Retirement Literature in the Poetry of Pope', in *Aspects of the Eighteenth Century*, ed. Earl R. Wasserman (Baltimore and London, 1965), pp. 207–43.

PAGE 181. Detailed information about Prior's activity as an art collector is given by H. Bunker Wright and Henry C. Montgomery, 'The Art Collection of a Virtuoso in Eighteenth-Century England', *The Art Bulletin*, vol. XXVII (1945), pp. 195–204; an abridged version of this article is printed in *Studies in the Literature of the Augustan Age*, ed. Richard C. Boys (Ann Arbor, 1952), pp. 321–41.

PAGE 185. The decay of economic morality during the seventeenth and early eighteenth centuries is traced in R. H. Tawney, *Religion and the Rise of Capitalism*, 2nd ed. (1936), ch. III, section iii.

PAGE 191. The evolution of Pope's plans for his ethical *Opus Magnum* is clearly revealed in Spence's *Anecdotes*, ed. Osborn, vol. I, pp. 128–34; the influence of this ambitious project on the *Epistles to Several Persons* is discussed by F. W. Bateson in the Twickenham Edition, vol. III (ii), pp. xvi ff., and by R. W. Rogers, *Major Satires of Pope*, pp. 32–44.

PAGE 193. Two further instances of the eighteenth-century equation of

[ 209 ]

human reason with common sense may be cited: 'I am a good deal inclin'd to beleive Mr Hobbs that the State of Nature is a State of War, but
thence I conclude Humane Nature not rational, if the word reason means
common sense, as I suppose it does': *The Complete Letters of Lady Mary
Wortley Montagu*, ed. Robert Halsband (Oxford, 1965–7), vol. I, p. 305
(letter to Pope, 12 February 1717). 'But as common sense is every where
the same, and what is reason in *English*, will be reason in *Latin* too. . . .':
John Constable, *Reflections upon Accuracy of Style* (1731), p. 9. To act
according to Reason is simply to act reasonably. At the same time, but more
abstractly, Reason is the name for the Divine Power which orders the
whole universe: 'As Nature is Order and Rule, and Harmony in the visible
World, so Reason is the very same throughout the invisible Creation. For
Reason is Order, and the Result of Order. . . . Whatever God created, he
designed it Regular': John Dennis, *Critical Works*, ed. E. N. Hooker
(Baltimore, 1939 and 1943), vol. I, p. 202.

PAGE 200. Swift's attitude towards the human passions has been thoroughly investigated by Charles Peake in 'Swift and the Passions', *Modern
Language Review*, vol. LV (1960), pp. 169–80.

# 1 Pope

This is divided into five sections: I satirical targets; II values; III characteristics of Pope's satire; IV literary relationships; V works cited and discussed. Main entries are in bold type.

I SATIRICAL TARGETS
Admiration, 164–6, 174–5; the Court, 90–107, 122; covetousness, 137–8, 145–7, 156; Dunces, 51–2, 156, 198–9, 203; logic, 42; metaphysics, 181; moneyed men, 136–41; 'Patriots', 87–8; pride, 156, 188; property, 142–5; sensuality, 154–5; Stoicism, 161–7, 199–201; trade, 128–33

II VALUES
Charity, 148–52; decorum, 45–6; friendship, 108–15, 119; gardening, 63, 66–8, 70, 72–3, 109, 181, 206; good humour, 166–7; honesty, 131–3; hospitality, 71–2, **79–83**; a 'mixt life', 179–80; moderation, 190–1; Nature, 56–7, 67, 144; order, 61, 195–7; passions, 157–61, 198–9, 201–4; self-knowledge, 188–90; Sense, 56–7, 193–4; Stoicism, 198, 208; taste, 55, 56–8; 'Use', 66, 73–4, 141–2, 144

III CHARACTERISTICS OF POPE'S SATIRE
Character of the satirist, 9, 13, 109–10, 118–21, 207; as country gentleman, 77–8, 88–9; as friend, 115–16, 119; humble, 188; independent, 9, 12, 116; his moral fervour, 202–4; plain-spoken, 100–3, 105–7; as polite gentleman, 5, 38–9, 41, 48, 51–2, 108; his self-restraint, 168–9;
Irony, 3, 24;
*Persona*, 6–7, 10, 34, 205;
Raillery and delicacy, 6, 26–7, 32–8, 100–4;
Tone, 5, 48; conversational, 18, **20–2**, 38; modulations of, 81–2, 206; public and oratorical, 9–10;
Verse-epistle, technique of, 4, 110; types of, 23

IV LITERARY RELATIONSHIPS (allusions and imitations)
Barrow, 148
Bible, 96, 104, 140, 145, 146, 151, 196
Boileau, 58, 116
Crashaw, 133

V WORKS CITED AND DISCUSSED

A Poems and translations:

# 11 General

[ 217 ]